"KEEP A-INCHIN' ALONG"

Carl Van Vechten, Fania Marinoff, and Taylor Gordon, caricature
by Miguel Covarrubias, 1929 *(Courtesy University of Washington Press
[from* Born to Be *by Taylor Gordon])*

"KEEP A-INCHIN' ALONG"

Selected Writings of Carl Van Vechten about Black Art and Letters

Edited by Bruce Kellner

Contributions in Afro-American and African Studies, No. 45

Greenwood Press,   Westport, Connecticut • London, England

Library of Congress Cataloging in Publication Data

Van Vechten, Carl, 1880-1964.
    "Keep A-Inchin' Along"

    (Contributions in Afro-American and African studies ;
no. 45 ISSN 0069-9624)
Includes bibliographical references and index.
    1. Arts, Afro-American. I. Kellner, Bruce.
II. Title. III. Series.
NX512.3.A35V36   1979   700'.973   78-67912
ISBN: 0-313-21091-8

Library of Congress Catalog Card Number: 78-67912
ISBN: 0-313-21091-8
ISSN: 0069-9624

First published in 1979

Greenwood Press, Inc.
51 Riverside Avenue, Westport, Connecticut 06880

Printed in the United States of America

10 9 8 7 6 5 4 3 2 1

To the memory
of Fania Marinoff Van Vechten
1887–1971

Keep a' inchin' along,
Keep a' inchin' along,
Massa Jesus is comin' by an' by.
Keep a' inchin' along
Like a po' inch worm,
Massa Jesus is comin' by an' by.
                    —*Negro Spiritual*

Go inspectin'
With Van Vechten!
                    —*Andy Razaf*

Contents

Illustrations

Acknowledgments

Selections from *In the Garret, Excavations, Nigger Heaven,* the introduction to *The Weary Blues* by Langston Hughes, the introduction to *The Autobiography of an Ex-Coloured Man* by James Weldon Johnson, *Parties, Sacred and Profane Memories,* and the advertisement for *Nigger Heaven* by Aaron Douglas, reprinted by permission of Alfred A. Knopf, Inc. Selections from *Opportunity* reprinted by permission of the National Urban League, courtesy of James D. Williams. Selections from the *New York Herald Tribune Books* reprinted by permission of I.H.T. Corporation. Selections from *Crisis* and the *NAACP 1929 Benefit Program* reproduced with permission of Crisis Publishing Company, Inc., courtesy of Warren Marr II. Quotation from "Go Harlem!" by Andy Razaf, copyright © 1930 & 1937 by Mayfair Music Corp. Copyrights renewed, assigned to Edwin H. Morris & Co., used by permission. "My Friend: James Weldon Johnson" reprinted by permission of Fisk University, courtesy of Walter J. Leonard. Selections from "How the Theatre is Represented in the Negro Collection at Yale" reprinted by permission of The Theatre Library Association as original copyright holder, courtesy of Richard M. Buck. "A Note by the Author of Nigger Heaven" reprinted from *Nigger Heaven,* New York: Avon Books, Inc., courtesy of Robert B. Wyatt. "Memories of Bessie Smith" reprinted from *Jazz Record,* courtesy of Rudi Blesh. "In the Heart of Harlem" and "Simple Speaks His Mind," © 1950/53 by the New York Times Company, reprinted by permission. Selection from *Fragments from an unwritten autobiography* reprinted courtesy of Yale University Library. "Soft Voice of Feeling" reprinted by permission, © Saturday Review, 1956. All rights reserved. Selection from "Terpsichorean Souvenirs" reprinted courtesy of *Dance Magazine* (January 1957) and William Como. Selections from "Portraits of the Artists" from *Esquire* (December 1962). Copyright © 1962 by Esquire, Inc. Reprinted courtesy of *Esquire* magazine and Anne Putnam. Selections from an obituary for Carl Van Vechten and from unpublished verses by Langston Hughes reprinted by permission

of Harold Ober Associated Incorporated, copyright © 1965. The introduction to *Born to Be* by Taylor Gordon and the illustration by Miguel
Covarrubias reprinted by permission of the University of Washington
Press, copyright © 1975. "Eloquent Alvin Ailey," copyright 1963 by Dance
Perspectives Foundation, reprinted by permission of Dance Perspectives,
courtesy of Selma Jeanne Cohen. Photographs, pp. 67 and 70 reproduced by
permission of the New York Public Library; pp. 16, 68, 69, 193, 197, and
202 reproduced courtesy of Yale University Library; pp. 196 and 199 reproduced courtesy of Paul Padgette; other illustrations and photographs
are in the collection of the editor. Carl Van Vechten's photographs may
not be reproduced without written permission of the Estate of Carl Van
Vechten. Carl Van Vechten's manuscripts for *Nigger Heaven* are in the
manuscript and Archives Division of the New York Public Library, with
attendant correspondence; additional manuscripts, and his letters to
Arna Bontemps, Langston Hughes, Chester Himes, Harold Jackman, Grace
Nail and James Weldon Johnson, Claude McKay, and Henry Van Dyke,
which are published for the first time in this anthology, are in the Collection of American Literature at Yale University in the Beinecke Rare Book
and Manuscript Library; his letters to Walter White are in the NAACP
Archive of the Library of Congress.

Introduction

Many of the readers who made *Nigger Heaven* a best-selling novel during the Harlem Renaissance of the Twenties had never heard of Carl Van Vechten, and those who had were for the most part unaware that his interest in the arts and letters of black Americans had begun twenty-five years before. If much of his own roaring during the Twenties occurred in Harlem cabarets, he had been writing essays, reviewing plays and books, evaluating dramas, or producing program notes and dust-jacket blurbs about Negroes and for Negroes for over a decade. When the Harlem Renaissance ended, and everyone, black and white alike, went "rolling down the hill toward the Works Progress Administration," as Langston Hughes put it,[1] Van Vechten kept right on working to start a second renaissance. He did not live far enough into the Sixties to witness its flowering, but his thirty-year photographic record—of nearly every black writer, musician, painter, composer, entertainer, sports figure, politician, actor, singer, and humanitarian—charts the course. This hobby—for he photographed for his own pleasure and then gave the pictures to their subjects and to friends—became at least one of the cornerstones of the James Weldon Johnson Memorial Collection of Negro Arts and Letters. He founded it at Yale University, on the basis of the material he had amassed during the first half of the century. What had begun with theater programs and pictures during his student days in Chicago had grown, by the time of his death at the age of eighty-four in 1964, into one of the most significant collections of its kind. With the present interest in black studies, students and scholars will find themselves increasingly grateful to Carl Van Vechten for this legacy. I believe they may also come to recognize that his own contributions to the collection are of considerable importance.

Carl Van Vechten left Cedar Rapids, Iowa, at the turn of the century, to enroll at the University of Chicago and, later, to work as a reporter on the *Chicago American* and other local newspapers. Bored with his classes as well as with college life, he began investigating the city's theatrical haunts almost immediately. Perhaps it was inevitable that he would discover the Negro entertainments of the period as well. He had already had an excellent introduction in Cedar Rapids, the stopover spot for one-night-stand companies on their way from Chicago to the West. In addition to Richard Mansfield and Otis Skinner and other well-known white performers, he had seen Sissieretta Jones, the "Black Patti," as she was advertised after the opera singer, Adelina Patti, and her troupe of black entertainers. Rather than a conventional minstrel show, she and her fifty troubadours offered "a revelation of comedy, burlesque, vaudeville and opera, embodying 'coon songs,' 'cake walks,' 'back dances' and inspiring grand and comic opera melodies by the most talented and versatile singers, dancers and comedians of the Sunny South, headed by The Greatest Singer of Her Race," an advertisement of the period declared.[2] Sissieretta Jones was as well known as any other singer in the country, Van Vechten averred half a century later, recalling "her dress of black sequins, her long white gloves, and her stately dignified appearance when she was singing" with "America's Premier Rag-time Entertainers."[3]

Within a few weeks of his arrival at college, Van Vechten had been introduced to Chicago ragtime as well, by a fraternity brother. Instead of studying, they hied themselves regularly to the Old Pekin Theatre at Twenty-seventh and State streets, where Robert T. Motts ran more or less continuous entertainments. James "Slaprags" White played the piano, standing up and with his back to the keyboard; Ernest Hogan sang his enormously popular "All Coons Look Alike to Me," wearing blackface makeup on his own black face; dancers strutted through elegant cake-walks. When Carita Day, who was "very beautiful and sang like an angel," opened in Hogan's Georgia Minstrels, Van Vechten attended performances as regularly as if he were getting academic credit, he later told me. At one point he even escorted the singer and her accompanist-husband to his fraternity house and probably shocked — this was 1902 — the brothers of Psi Omega. Further, he was shortly familiar with what he called the "supreme unction" of George Walker's dancing and Bert Williams's pantomimes and monologues. Bob Cole, another black entertainer Van Vechten saw frequently, pointed out what was not yet apparent to white audiences, however: "The drama is that the Negro is in your midst, the comedy is that he survives, the tragedy is that he is black."[4]

Although Van Vechten's initial exposure came through the only available sources — black performers often catering to the demands of white audiences — his private associations were more deeply rooted. If his chores for the Chicago American gave him little opportunity to write about the black entertainments, he had already used black acquaintances for subject matter in an undergraduate writing course taught by white authors William Vaughn Moody and Robert Morss Lovett at the University of Chicago. For his first assignment, preserved among Van Vechten's papers in the Manuscript Division of the New York Public LIbrary, he wrote about "Biondina," the precocious daughter of his fraternity's cook-housekeeper; another, entitled "The Inky Ones," as much autobiography as story, was based on his relationship with the mother herself: Aurelia Veta Clement, called variously Desdemonia Sublett or Sidonia Manchester.

Van Vechten frequently skipped fraternity parties and dances to accompany Mrs. Clement to "colohed affahs" at the Quinn Chapel in Chicago's Darktown or Darkytown, as the area was called without derision.

For three of Van Vechten's four years at the University of Chicago, Mrs. Clement served as his excuse for avoiding the college rowdies with whom he had little in common. He seems, however, to have genuinely enjoyed himself in her company, just as he had always enjoyed the company of older people during his childhood. Indeed, a black washerwoman and a black yardman were the first adults he knew outside his immediate family; moreover, he had been reared to address them as "Mrs. Sercey" and "Mr. Oliphant," with the same respect due any other adult. The elder Van Vechten also addressed them formally, not a surprising habit for him: Charles Duane Van Vechten cofounded the Piney Woods School for Negro Children in Mississippi, when a young black educator, Laurence Jones from Marshalltown, Iowa, wanted to start a school there.

By the time Carl Van Vechten met Mrs. Clement in Chicago, he had been innoculated against race prejudice. She was a generous, rambunctious woman, apparently, except during church meetings when she wore a "proper ecclesiastical expression." As for Van Vechten, he wrote that he was "invariably taken for a coon," and found there were so many "light-skinned Negroes" that anyone "with a proper escort is sure of not being identified as white." Through meeting Mrs. Clement's friends, he concluded that black people had an "over-estimated idea of a white man's importance which is bred into them, I suppose. . . . They will confide in any white man in much the same way . . . a white man would confide in an angel." At Quinn Chapel Van Vechten played the piano for their entertainment and then stayed on to accompany the singing. The songs, of course, were more often Baptist hymns than the Spirituals he strove to popularize in later years. In 1903, he saw these new acquaintances as "an intensely uncultured and uneducated race but just as intensely good hearted, humorous, interesting and even clever." They were, he concluded, "colored members of the human family." In 1979, such observations may suggest condescension or patronage; in 1903, from a twenty-three-year-old, they do not, although the innocence of ignorance is invariably difficult to approximate once we have escaped it. Of far greater significance—given Van Vechten's extraordinary contributions to an aesthetic race consciousness—is the period of time during which his devotion to black arts and letters developed. It refutes his critics' charges, particularly during the Twenties at the time of the great popularity of his novel, *Nigger Heaven*, that his knowledge of and interest in the race were necessarily superficial because they were so new.

Aside from an encomiastic review of J. Leubrie Hill's Darktown Follies, in 1913, and some friendly press-agentry for the revue in his Sunday editorials when Van Vechten was drama critic for the *New York Press*, his first professional writing devoted exclusively to the Negro appeared in his sixth volume of essays, *In the Garret*, in 1920. By that time he had become a critic of some reputation.

After being fired from the *Chicago American* for "lowering the tone of the Hearst syndicate," according to his editor—Van Vechten had written satirically about Chicago's society matrons—he was hired as a cub reporter by the *New York Times*. Almost immediately he was appointed assistant music critic, and by 1912 when he left the *Times* he had become America's first dance critic—the greatest ballet critic, Edwin Denby, himself a contender, called Van Vechten—having covered with serious attention and affection the initial performances of Isadora Duncan, Anna Pavlova, Maud Allan, Loie Fuller, and other early dancers. Moreover, he was a formidably successful interviewer of the opera luminaries of the period: Mary Garden, Olive Fremstad, Feodor Chaliapin, Giacomo Puccini, Geraldine Farrar, and Oscar Hammerstein, for example. He reviewed early performances of Rachmaninoff and Mahler. He served a term as Paris correspondent. More pertinent to an account of Van Vechten's activities involving the Negro, he reviewed a recital by Kitty Cheatham and the black composer, Henry Thatcher Burleigh, on 18 April 1911.

Miss Kitty Cheatham—Van Vechten once described her to me as a cross between Ethelbert Nevin in drag and Shirley Temple—gave semi-annual recitals, at Christmas and Easter, designed for families. She sang flower songs, prayers set to music, and songs about little girls; she recited poems and told stories; she shared jokes about puppies falling into the lemonade. She performed on stages laden with bouquets of flowers and populated with chickens, kittens, rabbits, puppies. At her 1910 Christmas recital, Engelbert Humperdinck, the composer of *Hansel und Gretel*, surprised the audience by accompanying her in one of his songs; at her subsequent Easter recital, Van Vechten wrote, "Miss Cheatham had reserved a surprise which carried with it still more pleasure":

H.T. Burleigh, the Negro composer, who has arranged so many of the old Negro plantation songs and harmonized them so that they could become better known in the concert room, appeared with Miss Cheatham and played her accompaniments in his own arrangements of these songs. He also joined in and sang with her, in thirds, in the Negro fashion, to the great delight of the auditors. The part of Miss Cheatham's programme devoted to the old Negro songs is always attractive, but yesterday, for this reason, it was doubly so. The effect on the audience was spontaneous, and the two were recalled many times to add many numbers to the one song with which they commenced.

Lillian Nordica, the Metropolitan Opera soprano, sat in an upper box, Van Vechten's review concluded, and at the end of the performance "threw a fluffy Easter chicken over" to join the menagerie onstage.[5]

Two years later, when Van Vechten left the *New York Times* for the *New York Press*, he turned his attention to theater, and by the time he reviewed a show put on by the Darktown Follies the range of his experience was sufficiently broad to encourage six subsequent volumes of essays. *Music After the Great War, Music and Bad Manners, Interpreters and Interpretations, The Merry-Go-Round, The Music of Spain,* and *In the Garret* included the first writings in America on the music of Igor Stravinsky and Erik Satie, on coordinated musical scores for motion pictures, on the Russian Ballet and Nijinsky, on Spanish music, and, inevitably, on "The Negro Theatre" in the last of the series, in 1919. That essay just preceded the sudden craze which had begun with an all-black musical revue called *Shuffle Along,* bringing in the Jazz Age. As Nathan Huggins observed, "The Postwar hangover that encouraged a generation of Americans to lose themselves in cabarets, rhythms, dances, and exotica could not help but approve this lively Negro musical.... *Shuffle Along* ushered in a vogue of Negro singing and dancing that lasted until the Great Depression."[6]

During the first half of that same decade, Carl Van Vechten had become a popular novelist; his first, *Peter Whiffle,* was published in 1922. Three more followed in quick succession: two, *The Blind Bow-Boy* and *Firecrackers,* were about "the Splendid Drunken Twenties" in New York, as he often called the period. Then, in 1926, his controversial, best-selling *Nigger Heaven* appeared. By that time he was a self-proclaimed, unpaid press agent for black poets and black singers, for Spirituals and for Blues, for Harlem's intelligentsia and for its cabarets. "Sullen-mouthed, silky-haired author Van Vechten has been playing with Negroes lately," *Time* reported, "writing prefaces for their poems, having them around the house, going to Harlem."[7] His interest, however, was hardly as superficial as the magazine's gossip might suggest. Van Vechten had become "violently interested in Negroes," he declared in his Oral History for Columbia University in 1960 — "violently because it was almost an addiction."

His first black literary acquaintance was Walter White, whom he met through their mutual publisher, Alfred A. Knopf. They "got on like a house afire" in the beginning, although in time each came to realize they were useful rather than intimate friends, one working as liaison for the other. His friendship with James Weldon Johnson, however, was of lasting affection and unreserved admiration. Through White and Johnson, Van Vechten came to know Langston Hughes, Countée Cullen, and Zora Neale Hurston, and, through them, Eric Walrond, Wallace Thurman, and many other young black writers. Van Vechten soon had arranged for some poems of Cullen and Hughes to appear in *Vanity Fair,* the popular, fashion-setting magazine, and through his instigation Knopf published Hughes's first collection of verse, *The Weary Blues,* as well as books by black novelists Nella Larsen and Rudolph Fisher. For *Vanity Fair* he wrote several articles about black singers and music, and for the black publication,

Crisis, he contributed another. Concurrently, *Vanity Fair* declared Van Vechten was getting a heavy tan and, as he only appeared in public after dark, he had to be acquiring it in a taxi, bound for the nightclubs in Harlem. He became, in Nathan Huggins's apt phrase, "the undisputed downtown authority on uptown night life."[8] A Van Vechten tour of Harlem became de rigueur for white foreigners, visiting white writers, and white flappers and philosophers out of F. Scott Fitzgerald's books.

If Van Vechten devoted an inordinate amount of time to shabby pursuits — getting drunk in speakeasies, collecting handsome Harlem sycophants about him, unconsciously propagating stereotypes through his own delight in primitive and exotic elements — his respect and admiration for blacks were genuine. His response to black writing and music was firmly grounded in nearly a quarter of a century of musical and literary criticism. Moreover, his desire to share his discoveries resulted in a cultural interchange unique at the time. In their extravagant apartment on West Fifty-fifth Street in Manhattan, Carl Van Vechten and his actress-wife, Fania Marinoff, entertained frequently and lavishly, and always with fully integrated guest lists. Their parties were eventually reported as a matter of course in some of the black newspapers in the city. "I don't think I've given any parties since 1923," Van Vechten said in his Columbia Oral History, "without asking several Negroes." Walter White often called the address "the mid-town office of the NAACP."

However, when in 1926 Van Vechten's novel, *Nigger Heaven*, attempted to reflect his enthusiasm, not even the support of several influential black writers overcame the widespread feeling that he had used his Harlem acquaintances badly. The title of the book was inflammatory to begin with, destined to offend any unwary reader; further, Van Vechten's long reputation as a dandy, as a dilettante, as a writer of resolutely frivolous novels, did not help. For many readers of *Nigger Heaven*, the black slang word for a white person — "ofay," pig latin for "foe" — renewed its double meaning. For blacks familiar only with the book's title, that reaction is not surprising, for Harlem knew him as a regular customer in the cabarets, as a white judge for the black transvestite balls at the Savoy or the Rockland Palace Casino, as someone whose name turned up in the society columns of black newspapers, as a guest in Harlem homes and salons. In Rudolph Fisher's novel, *The Walls of Jericho*, a black says to Conrad White, a character patterned after Van Vechten, " 'you're the only fay I know that draws the color line on other fays.' 'It's natural,' " White replies fatuously. " 'Downtown I'm only passing. These,' he waved grandiloquently, 'are my people.' "[9] It is not difficult to see here a Van Vechten uncomfortably close to the posturing Van Vleeck in Thomas Wolfe's *The Web and the Rock*, author of "books about tattooed duchesses, post-impressionist moving picture actresses, and negro prize-fighters who read Greek,"[10] or even to Ishmael Reed's viciously funny Schuyler Von Vampton in his recent *Mumbo Jumbo*, exaggerated, perhaps, but inevitable.

Whatever its limitations, *Nigger Heaven* strengthened Van Vechten's ties with the race—certainly he lost no friends because of it—and increased his loyalty. Through the rest of his long career, he devoted his energies to a wide recognition of black achievement, primarily through photography, recording nearly every celebrated black, missing only those such as Sidney Poitier and Ralph Ellison who chose to snub him. (Ralph Bunche did not.) If the endeavor suggests sycophancy, it was nevertheless as sincere as his "addiction," as he called it, was unflagging. Van Vechten easily admitted he was quite star-struck all his life, at least from the time he met Bert Williams, the greatly beloved black comic, in 1906, until the last summer of his life when he wrote to me, "I am in my usual state of gaping enthusiasm. (Will it never end? Probably NOT.) I heard André Watts at the [Lewisohn] Stadium and sans doute he is the greatest living pianist. He has everything, including good taste and he will end in glory, as he has begun." Bert Williams, of course, did not live long enough to be photographed by Van Vechten, and Van Vechten died before he could get to André Watts, but hundreds of other subjects—white as well as black—came in between. The list of black subjects is staggering, not only in quantity but in quality, especially the number of people photographed before their talents were generally recognized: Leontyne Price at twenty-three; Lena Horne at twenty-two; Diahann Carroll at eighteen; and James Baldwin, Alvin Ailey, LeRoi Jones, and Harry Belafonte more than twenty years ago. Any longer catalog only further indulges in name-dropping. Whatever payment Van Vechten ever received for reprint rights of his photographs or for various book reviews or other essays about blacks he donated to the endowment fund of the James Weldon Johnson Memorial Collection of Negro Arts and Letters, which he established in 1941.

In 1942, the James Weldon Johnson Literary Guild gave a dinner in Van Vechten's honor, for which Langston Hughes rhymed a tribute in cheerful doggerel, delivered by the actor, Canada Lee, in a carefree manner. A brief passage may express what Hughes declared for everyone there; it has not been previously published:

> You always wish all gamblers would throw a lucky seven
> And you've done your best to bring my people
> Out of their—peanut gallery.
> You know what I mean, that old segregated heaven,
> Away from it all,

That you and I know
Ain't no heaven at all.[11]

The Yale Collection opened officially in 1950, but it had been growing for the preceding decade to include the work of nearly every American black artist and writer, as well as some from other countries. Charles S. Johnson, then president of Fisk University in Tennessee, delivered the Bergen address at the opening ceremonies for the collection. Of Van Vechten, Johnson said, in part:

In his portrayals of the modern American Negro under metropolitan conditions, he was neither sentimental nor macaronic. With a realism, fired by the novelty of his own discovery of racial differentiation into personalities good and bad, beautiful and sordid, glamorous and dull, wise and stupid, he created an interest in voyages far beyond sophisticated literary circles. In the process . . . he became a captive of his own skill, and even today, twenty-five years after his first book in this field, he continues to be a master medium for the interpretation of the many and interesting new social structures and personalities emerging from the shadows of our racial system into the full brilliance of American life.[12]

Five years later—by which time Van Vechten had established a valuable collection of music and musical literature at Fisk University—Charles S. Johnson delivered the peroration, written by Arna Bontemps, when Fisk awarded Van Vechten an honorary doctorate. Another friend, black musician Nora Holt, echoed privately the public sentiments:

It will be decades before America and the Negro in general realizes that you have done more to engender social equality and human rights between the races than any other individual or organization in the country. . . . The social equation of an individual stems from first-hand contact and unbiased evaluations. And you proved that the much debated and untouchable order of social equality could be achieved, not by force, but by the fundamental means of intercourse, interchange of ideas, and respect for human dignity.[13]

James Weldon Johnson had anticipated Nora Holt by a quarter of a century, in his inscription in Van Vechten's catalog of photographic subjects:

Dear Carl, Has anyone ever written it down—in black and white—that you have been one of the most vital factors in bringing about the artistic emergence of the Negro in America? Well, I am glad to bear witness to the fact. . . .[14]

Langston Hughes shall have the last of these words: In 1961, when Van Vechten was still hard at work on his photography, on his collections, on

continuing to call attention to black achievements, and just one month
away from his eighty-first birthday, Hughes sent him this telegram:

> I SEE IN THE PRESS YOU AND I ARE TO REPRESENT THE RACE IN THE
> NATIONAL INSTITUTE OF ARTS AND LETTERS WHICH DELIGHTS ME
> HAVING SUCH GENIAL COMPANY THEREIN SO I SALUTE YOU WITH
> SOMERSAULTS AND HANDSPRINGS[15]

With the passing of time, however, Carl Van Vechten's significance has
diminished, on occasion, it may be, by design. In *Harlem Renaissance
Remembered*, a selection of essays edited by his friend, Arna Bontemps,
Van Vechten is referred to only as "an adviser with Alfred A. Knopf" and
as Langston Hughes's "friend and editor with Knopf." Several of his
photographs are included in the book, but without any credit to the
photographer. Van Vechten's famous photograph of Bessie Smith—as
well known and as often reproduced as his celebrated profile of Gertrude
Stein—turned up a few years ago as a pop culture poster, not only uncredited but foully reproduced. *Black Magic*, a plush anthology devoted
to black musicians and entertainers, used fifteen Van Vechten photographs,
crediting them only to "Author's Collection." In a public forum dealing
with the significance of the Harlem Renaissance in relation to the "New
Negro," Charles S. Johnson identified Van Vechten only as one of several
white judges for literary contests in *Opportunity*, the magazine of the
National Urban League. Even half a dozen years before his death in 1964,
Van Vechten was no more than another white liberal of the Twenties, in
J. Saunders Redding's view, "invited to parties given by the Negro elite."
One recent writer has even quoted Langston Hughes out of context in an
unsuccessful effort to prove, in the pages of a black periodical, that his
long affection for Van Vechten was actually false. Robert Hemenway,
biographer of Taylor Gordon and Zora Neale Hurston, continues to have
difficulty accepting Van Vechten's sincerity, even though he has never
mustered evidence to support his suspicions.

The most serious recent attention to Van Vechten's role in the Harlem
Renaissance came from Nathan Huggins in his excellent book on the
movement. His conclusions do not underestimate Van Vechten's contributions, but he contends "it is open to question how well, or in what
way, Van Vechten served Harlem and the Negro" and equally important
to question how they "served him."[16] By the time Van Vechten became
"violently interested" as he put it, however, he was already well established as a music and dance critic of considerable perception and, on the
strength of his highly popular novels, as a successful writer, hardly in
need of being "served." Van Vechten simply discovered early on that
"black is beautiful," and he did so with the same enthusiasm he had

brought to the avant-garde on previous occasions: Gertrude Stein, Stravinsky, popular music as an art form by way of George Gershwin, overlooked American literature by way of Herman Melville, film scores, ballet. Still, Van Vechten's literary biographer, Edward Lueders, anticipated Nathan Huggins's reservations by several years: "His importance to the rise of the American Negro is difficult to assess, chiefly because his contributions have been made outside the usual focus of the press and simply as a matter of personal interest."[17]

It is not difficult to understand why critics might misinterpret Van Vechten's motives, assuming on the basis of his reputation as a dilettante that he was not only self-serving but slumming. Leon Duncan Coleman, former professor of Afro-American Studies at the University of Maryland, has offered the best defense against such subjective opinion:

By making racial tolerance and understanding fashionable and "smart," Van Vechten hoped to extend the knowledge of whites about Negroes. He believed that prejudice was the result of ignorance; if ignorance could be overcome, prejudice would disappear on all social levels. Unfortunately, this solution was too simple for the complexity of the problem; but Van Vechten was not alone in believing in the efficacy of this line of attack on racial injustice. During the Twenties and even later, the theory was current that the Negro of exceptional ability represented the best means for securing the acceptance of his race. The fallacy of this approach to the betterment of race relations is now obvious, although the racial problem still remains unsolved. One of Van Vechten's major contributions to the Negro Renaissance was that, through his own efforts, he was successful in breaching the wall of prejudice to bring Negro and white intellectuals into contact, even though he failed to achieve his primary goal.[18]

An examination of the selections in this anthology can only reinforce Leon Coleman's further assertion:

Almost all of the artists of the Negro Renaissance were personally indebted in some measure to Van Vechten for his contributions to their artistic careers. And all of them benefitted from his general concern with the furthering of the cause of Negroes in the arts.[19]

George Schuyler, editor of the black newspaper, the *Pittsburgh Courier*, "that irascible, Menckenesque journalist," in Nathan Huggins's phrase, should be permitted the final word in this refutation for his old friend: "Carl Van Vechten . . . has done more than any single person in this country to create the atmosphere of acceptance of the Negro."[20]

This anthology does not presume to undermine the zeal for an independent black consciousness; it does, nevertheless, purport to establish Carl Van Vechten's assistance during the painful journey of the American black artist. I have included virtually all of Carl Van Vechten's writings about black arts and letters. There are exceptions: his college themes and other juvenilia, which he did not wish to have published under any circumstances; a few minor newspaper items about Negroes, written as routine assignments during the years 1903-1913, which are of neither historical nor literary interest; some book reviews and articles which repeat substantially the same information better utilized elsewhere. Further, I have not included his review or his editorial in the *New York Press* or his longer essay in the magazine, *Trend*, all concerned with Ridgely Torrence's *Granny Maumee*, a play about blacks written by a white author and featuring white actors. Certainly its production fired Van Vechten's imagination for establishing a black theater with black playwrights and black actors as early as 1914, but that aspect is fully covered in his essay, "The Negro Theatre," which, of course, is included. On occasion I have combined two or three similar pieces into a single essay, indicating such editing in headnotes; on occasion, I have deleted titles and names too often repeated; elsewhere, I have joined two or three pieces consecutively to make a single memoir, again indicating such editing in headnotes. The selections are not always arranged in chronological order, nor always grouped according to type, since Van Vechten was as often acting as a publicity agent as he was as a critic.

Beginning in 1921, while he was writing his first novel, Van Vechten gave up italics and quotation marks entirely and began to affect English spellings more readily than he had in the past, although not always consistently. Alfred A. Knopf indulged him in these idiosyncrasies—sending the typescripts of Van Vechten's subsequent books directly to the printer without benefit of editorial assistance—but magazine editors invariably altered some of these stylistic touches to conform with their own policies. To facilitate reading, I have followed conventional mechanics, italicizing titles, placing quoted material inside quotation marks, and I have silently altered some spellings (color, for example, from colour because of its wide range of use in these papers) and corrected punctuation whether they were Van Vechten's responsibility or the errors of a typesetter. There are exceptions: the "Prologue" to *Nigger Heaven* is printed from galley proofs as Knopf set them; the composite essay, "Nassau Out of Season," is arranged from selections in two other Knopf volumes, which Van Vechten had revised to conform with his later manner; the excerpt from his last novel, *Parties*, here called "The Lindy Hop," is similarly reproduced.

In Chapter 1 I have grouped some early pieces anterior to Van Vechten's major work on behalf of black arts and letters, followed by a series of essays and book reviews, most of which appeared during the Harlem Renaissance. The next chapter is devoted to *Nigger Heaven*. James Weldon Johnson and the collection Van Vechten established in his memory comprise Chapter 3. Chapter 4 is a verbal portrait gallery of singers, writers, and personalities, most of whom are illustrated with examples of Van Vechten's photography. Chapter 5 is devoted to the Nassau and Lindy Hop pieces. Chapter 6 is composed of various ephemeral but never trivial materials. Finally, Chapter 7 is a selection of Van Vechten's correspondence with a number of celebrated black writers.

During Van Vechten's life, particularly at the time of their composition, most of this work—always excepting *Nigger Heaven*—probably had only a minor impact: those who most needed to be informed of such riches awaiting discovery would not have been readily exposed to the sources in which the various papers appeared. Perhaps this "excavation"—to borrow the title of one of Van Vechten's books—will awaken interest in the present generation of readers, black readers especially, in his contributions to the advancement of Negro arts and letters in America.

The phrase *as a matter of fact* occurs probably more often than any other in the selections which follow. But Van Vechten, I think, did not simply repeat it by accident, nor use it as a cliché. If he said, over and again, "as a matter of fact" in reference to the voice of a singer or the artistry of a dancer or a novelist's prose or a poet's verses, he meant it wholeheartedly: "as a matter of fact" because such matters were, indeed, facts requiring recognition and acceptance as facts.

Shortly before her death in 1971, Carl Van Vechten's widow, Fania Marinoff, asked me to undertake this anthology, for she shared her husband's passion for racial equality and recognition of black artists and writers. I am grateful for her encouragement and I dedicate the task to her memory. I am most deeply grateful to Donald Gallup, Carl Van Vechten's literary trustee and curator of the American Literature Collection in the Beinecke Rare Book and Manuscript Library at Yale University, for his assistance and support, and for his permission to print unpublished manuscripts and correspondence as well as previously published work. Further, I am indebted to William Koshland, of Alfred A. Knopf, Inc., for his cooperation, and to Joseph Solomon, representing the Van Vechten Estate, for his cooperation and permission to publish the writings and photographs of Carl Van Vechten in this anthology.

I welcome the opportunity to acknowledge several libraries: the Manuscript and Archives Division of the New York Public Library, for the Carl Van Vechten Collection, with special thanks to the Annex Archivist, Michael Nash; the Beinecke Library at Yale University, for the James Weldon Johnson Memorial Collection of Negro Arts and Letters, with special thanks to its librarian, Joan Hofmann; the Library of Congress, for the National Association for the Advancement of Colored People Archive, with special thanks to Charles Cooney; and the Ganser Library of Millersville State College, where I teach, for expert detective work.

Finally, I am glad to be able to publicly thank Grace Nail Johnson (represented by Ollie Jewel Okala), Chester Himes, and Henry Van Dyke, for permission to print selections from Carl Van Vechten's correspondence with them; to thank my friend, Paul Padgette, himself the compiler of a Van Vechten anthology, *The Dance Writings of Carl Van Vechten* (Brooklyn: Dance Horizons, 1975), for his sound advice and unflagging interest; to thank my friend, Bruce Parker, of the Hannibal Goodwin Photographic Laboratory and Gallery in Westwood, New Jersey, for his careful attention in preparing illustrations; to thank my wife, Margaret Wilcox Kellner, for her usual, careful proofreading; and to thank my son, Hans Carl Kellner, at fourteen a patient filer, an expert indexer.

23 August 1978

NOTES

1. Langston Hughes, *The Big Sea* (New York: Alfred A. Knopf, Inc., 1940), p. 223.

2. Quoted from an illustration in Ann Charters, *Nobody: The Story of Bert Williams* (New York: The Macmillan Company, 1970), p. 43.

3. Carl Van Vechten, "Unsung Americans Sung," *Responsibility* (fall 1944), p. 2.

4. Quoted in Charters, *Nobody*, p. 6.

5. Carl Van Vechten, "Kitty Cheatham's Recital," *New York Times*, 18 April 1911.

6. Nathan Huggins, *Harlem Renaissance* (New York: Oxford University Press, 1971), p. 289.

7. Carl Van Vechten Collection, Manuscript Division, New York Public Library, an undated newspaper clipping, circa 1925, from his scrapbooks.

8. Huggins, *Harlem Renaissance*, p. 100.

9. Rudolph Fisher, *The Walls of Jericho* (New York: Arno Press and the New York Times, 1975), p. 117.

10. Thomas Wolfe, *The Web and the Rock* (New York: Charles Scribner's Sons, 1938), p. 481.

11. Langston Hughes [untitled], Collection of American Literature, Beinecke Rare Book and Manuscript Library, Yale University.

12. Charles S. Johnson, "Literature and the Practice of Living," *Exercises marking the opening of the James Weldon Johnson Memorial Collection of Negro Arts and Letters* (New Haven: Yale University Library, 1950), pp. 9-10.

13. Nora Holt, quoted in a letter from Van Vechten to Bruce Kellner, 8 July 1955.

14. James Weldon Johnson, quoted in *80 Writers whose books and letters have been given over the past twenty years to the Yale University Library by Carl Van Vechten, compiled in honor of his 80th birthday, 17 June 1960,* Donald Gallup, ed. (New Haven: Yale University Library, 1960), p. [12].

15. Carl Van Vechten Collection, Yale University, Beinecke Library of Rare Books and Manuscripts.

16. Huggins, *Harlem Renaissance*, p. 93.

17. Edward Lueders, *Carl Van Vechten* (New York: Twayne Publishers, Inc., 1965), p. 95.

18. Leon Duncan Coleman, "The Contribution of Carl Van Vechten to the Negro Renaissance: 1920-1930," University of Minnesota, Ph.D. dissertation, 1969, pp. 237-38.

19. Ibid., p. 240.

20. Quoted in Lueders, *Carl Van Vechten*, p. 95.

Carita Day, circa 1900 *(Courtesy James Weldon Johnson Memorial Collection of Negro Arts and Letters, Yale University)*

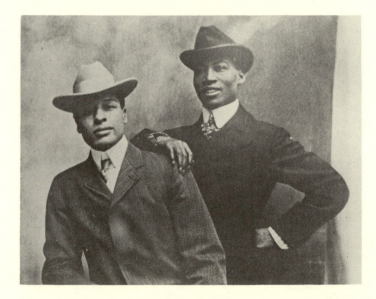

Bert Williams and George Walker, circa 1900

1

Anteriors and Advocacies

In the late summer of 1913, Carl Van Vechten became the drama critic for the *New York Press* and, on December 14 of that year, reviewed J. Leubrie Hill's *My Friend From Kentucky* as one of his regular Sunday editorials. The newspaper editor titled it "New York's 'Darktown' Would Do Well on Broadway," referring to the Lafayette Theatre's general bill, the Darktown Follies. This article, and a 1914 review of *Granny Maumee*, a play by white writer Ridgely Torrence, based on black characters but performed by white actors, motivated Van Vechten's first extended writing about black entertainment. "The Negro Theatre" first appeared in his *In the Garret* (New York: Alfred A. Knopf, Inc., 1920) as one of several "Theatres of the Purlieus," the others being considerations of Spanish, Yiddish, and Italian. Van Vechten revised at least one section of the Darktown Follies editorial to insert in the later essay; I have, therefore, deleted the earlier version. He also included what was relevant from his *Granny Maumee* review; it is worth noting that as early as 1914 Van Vechten was calling for the formation of a Negro theater organization, with black actors and black playwrights.

In spite of himself, Van Vechten perpetuated some invidious racial stereotypes in these early pieces, but in 1913 and even in 1919, his experience was limited. The white world—Van Vechten included—was largely unaware of racial pride; certainly there was evidence to suggest that blacks wanted to "broaden out into an imitation of white life" in the plays and entertainments available at the time. As Paul Padgette cogently observed, however, in his note on a passage from "The Negro Theatre" in *The Dance Writings of Carl Van Vechten* (Brooklyn: Dance Horizons, 1975):

Readers born since 1925 should bear in mind that at the time Van Vechten wrote the following article on the Negro theatre in 1919, the words "coon," "nigger," and certain references to the Negro dance which may seem crude and disrespectful to us, at the time of his writing were socially acceptable in Harlem as well as elsewhere. Carl Van Vechten, as much as any white writer, was sympathetic to and worked for the social improvement of the Black man's life in America. Any cursory investigation of his works and career supports this view. (p. 34)

Five years after "The Negro Theatre" was published, Van Vechten told several black friends that he thought it was "out of date," but black writer Eric Walrond wrote to Van Vechten that he thought its ideas and points of view would still be pertinent a decade later. Moreover, he avowed that had he not known Van Vechten he would have thought the essay written by a black because of its racial bias. James Weldon Johnson was motivated by "The Negro Theatre" to urge Van Vechten to write further about blacks out of his "larger knowledge and more intimate experience."

"A Note on American Letters" was published in a Yiddish translation by Nathan Belkin in *Die Zeit*, 11 September 1921. Van Vechten wrote this survey of literature, art, music, and criticism, with an emphasis on Jewish contributions, at the request of his brother-in-law, Jacob Marinoff, editor of *Der Grosse Kundes*, who occasionally wrote for *Die Zeit*. Van Vechten's essay included a brief passage about black music.

THE DARKTOWN FOLLIES

New York at last has a Negro theatre devoted to entertainments given by Negroes and for Negroes. It is significant that the Williams and Walker company, aside from the efforts of the two stars, never gave New York so interesting a performance of exclusively colored people.

The Lafayette Theatre is on Seventh Avenue, between 131st and 132d streets. It is a modern playhouse with a façade that strangely resembles that of the Folies Bergère in Paris. This façade is elaborately lighted. The situation of the theatre, it scarcely seems necessary to state, is in the midst of the black belt.

The interior is neither flamboyant nor dully colored. It is comfortable and there is a good line of vision from all the seats to the stage. There also is room for a goodly number of spectators, and performances are given twice a day to crowded houses.

The night I attended the house was crowded to its utmost capacity. One or two of the boxes were stretched a bit to make way for some Broadway theatrical managers and some detectives from Commissioner Waldo's office— for even detectives occasionally like to see good theatricals. But most of the audience was black.

The entertainment on view was J. Leubrie Hill and the Darktown Follies in a three-act musical comedy entitled *My Friend from Kentucky*. It is my impression that this entertainment is still to be seen. It should be able to draw packed and delighted houses for months to come. Remembering how gratefully white audiences attended performances given by the Williams and Walker company,[1] it is not beyond reason to suppose that if it were moved farther downtown it would do a large business.

One thing is certain. There are few musical entertainments on Broadway that compare with this one. *My Friend from Kentucky*, says its sponsor, does for the Negro what *Bunty Pulls the Strings* did for the Scots and *General John Regan* does for the Irish.[2]

This is not an exact description, but it is suggestive of Mr. Hill's purpose (for J. Leubrie Hill not only enacts the principal character, but he wrote the words and music and staged the piece). *My Friend from Kentucky*, as a matter of fact, is the only Negro musical comedy I remember to have seen in which there is some attempt made to present the Negro as he is—and not as he wants to be on stage.

The result is that of a sort of spontaneity and effectiveness in the performance which should be the envy of producers, who tear all the hair out of their heads trying to get a lot of chorus men and women to do what is wanted of them. These chorus men and women LIKE what they are doing, and as a result they do it well. They enjoy themselves.

The feeling, of course, is communicative, and the spectators soon reach that semi-hysterical state of enjoyment which a camp meeting of the better sort is able to bring about.

They rock back and forth with low croons; they scream with delight; they giggle intermittently; they wave their hands; they shriek, and at the pauses they pound their palms vigorously together in an attempt to get more out of the entertainers, and more always follows.

Of course a certain sophistication, of which so much is seen on our stage, is lacking in this representation and in the audience. Neither audience nor players are blasé. That helps the spirit. Still, to prove that that is not all that makes the performance spontaneous, it is only necessary to listen to the conventional bits of Broadway which drift in. . . .

I have mentioned the chorus, but it is almost necessary to dwell on this adjunct of the piece. All the boys and girls are exceptionally good singers and dancers. There is a number in the first act in which the dancing of the chorus is so splendidly rhythmical, so aesthetically satisfying in its "thrill," that it is caused to be repeated for a great length of time. In fact, the repetitions of many of the numbers were so numerous that the curtain fell on the second act, with another long act still to come, shortly before 11 o'clock.

The piece has been staged with a due regard for its atmosphere, and here unconventionality has generally been observed until, as has been suggested, Mr. Hill's spirit yearns for Broadway. But there are numerous examples of "business" for the chorus which are novel and which give the spectator, who is used to the conventions of musical comedy, something of a surprise.

There is a quartet, for instance, a newsboys' quartet, which is handled in such a manner that it does not obtrude itself as an interrupting musical number. The boys who are heard in it continue to "shoot" craps and polish shoes while they sing.

There are no waits in the performance. It moves on from one event to another with deft clarity, and there are few dull spots. These few are caused by the aforesaid interruptions from Broadway.

The first act in Virginia is almost unalloyed joy with its plantation niggers and its general atmosphere of pleasure. The second act in Washington contains many of the less spontaneous numbers, to which allusion has already been made.

It is the chorus, after all, that one chiefly remembers in coming away from this entertainment, but there is reason to mention a few members of the cast. Mr. Hill, himself, for instance, whose picture of a Negro mammy is both humorous and full of artistic reserve. It is the sort of performance that might consort well with Bert Williams's method. Praise for this sort of thing can go no further.

Julius Glenn as Jim Jackson Lee, who deserts his wife to go to Washington as Mr. Booker Tee, is a generally amusing figure, and his offspring are represented by side-splitting little colored girls.

The most memorable song of the evening is undoubtedly "Rock Me in the Cradle of Love," but perhaps a lot of its haunting possibilities are summed up in the personality of the singer, Alice Ramsey, who seems to possess qualities for doing this sort of thing that have been lacking from the stage since the temporary disappearance of Ada Overton Walker.[3]

The music as a whole has snap and languor and is well orchestrated and played. F[lorenz] Ziegfeld, Jr., has become so excited over its possibilities, it is said, that he has bought chunks of it for use in his new *Follies of 1914*. Why not import the entire Darktown Follies downtown? I think it would keep any Broadway theatre out of the clutches of the "movies" for an indefinite period.

1. Bert Williams and George Walker were popular entertainers at the turn of the century, about whom Van Vechten wrote extensively in "The Negro Theatre" (q.v.).

2. These plays by G. Moffat and Canon Hannay, respectively, had stimulated some recent popular interest in Scotland and Ireland, according to Van Vechten's own editorials in the *New York Press* at the time.

3. Ada Overton, or Aida Overton as she later called herself, was responsible for popularizing the cakewalk with her husband, George Walker.

THE NEGRO THEATRE

When I was twenty-one the wonderful Williams and Walker Company was in full blast and bloom. The two comedians headed a large troupe of blacks and offered musical entertainment in a sense sophisticated but which did not dilute the essential charm, the primitive appeal of the Negro. There were reminiscences of the plantation, reminiscences of the old minstrel days, and capital portraits of the new coon, who was in those days a real figure and not a myth like the new woman, who, as Agnes Repplier has pointed out in an amusing paper, has been in existence since the days of Eve.[1] This organization must have travelled extensively, though I saw it only in Chicago, for I remember the posters which covered the South Side fencings and boardings, picturing Williams and Walker appearing at Windsor, *by royal command*, and Williams and Walker meeting Queen Victoria and the Prince of Wales. I am almost certain that one picture showed us the pair taking tea with royalty, but to this I cannot swear. These were the days of *Sons of Ham* and *Abyssinia*. . . . Bert Williams shuffled along in his hopeless way; always penniless, always the butt of fortune, and always human. He reblackened his face, enlarged his mouth, wore shoes which extended beyond the limits of even extraordinary feet, but he never transcended the precise lines of characterization. He was as definite as Mansfield, as subtle as Coquelin. Duse saw him on one of her American tours and promptly decided he was America's finest actor.[2] His pantomimic powers were great and for their exploitation he relied almost entirely on his eyes and his hands, with the occasional aid of a bracing smile. In his poker game, for example, he developed a scene, without speaking a single word, which was enjoyable even to those spectators who did not play cards. To have heard him sing "I May Be Crazy but I Ain't No Fool," "The Phrenologist Coon," "All Goin' Out and Nothin' Comin' In," or the inimitable "Nobody" was to have heard and seen something as fine in its way as the contemporary theatre had to offer. Tobias Wormwood, Jasmine Jenkins, whatever character he assumed, left us trembling between hysterical laughter and sudden tears. . . . George Walker, on the other hand, the Rastus Johnson, the Harty Laffer, was the spick and span Negro, the last word in tailoring, the highest stepper in the smart coon world. How the fellow did prance in the cakewalk, throwing his chest and his buttocks out in opposite directions, until he resembled a pouter pigeon more than a human being! And we all shrieked applause until he had varied his walk nineteen times and repeated all the variations. As an Abyssinian monarch, breast, back, arms, and legs bare, a live bronze statue, Walker was a more barbaric figure, but even here his inclusive smile, which disclosed several glittering gold teeth, created a bond between Africa and Broadway. And his unction in "Bon Bon Buddy, the Chocolate Drop"! Supreme unction, I call it! . . . There were other features of these entertainments, Ada Overton Walker, for instance, who later became Aida, who danced as few white women have danced (the cry went, "Ain't she loose?") and who sang "Miss Hannah of Savannah" and "I Want to Be a Leading Lady." I can't recall these memories without crying. I feel very much the way William Winter must have felt when he thought of Edwin Booth.[3] For George Walker is dead and so is his wife. Bert Williams drifted into the *Follies*, via vaudeville, but either the *Follies* or vaudeville killed him, for the Bert Williams of the *Follies* today is no more the Bert Williams of the Williams and Walker days than I am the Carl Van Vechten of 1898.

In December 1913 there was a renaissance of the Negro theatre. I do not mean to say that between 1908 and 1913 no Negro companies appeared in our theatres: I do not mean to say that no Negro company attracted my attention and my patronage. But in December 1913 I learned (didn't everybody?) that a certain J. Leubrie Hill was appearing in a piece of his own concoction called *My Friend from Kentucky* with his organization known as the Darktown Follies at the Jefferson Theatre in the New York black belt.[4]

This entertainment shared a fault common to all such enterprises, imitation of the white man's theatre. Mr. Hill evidently believed it necessary to add a dash of tenor, a sprinkling of girls in long satin gowns to his otherwise entirely fresh Negro salad. In due course these ingredients were stirred in. Then the actors on the stage singing conventional hymns to the moon, with accompanying action which Ned Wayburn[5] might have devised, lost interest and the audience became listless and restless. But the greater part of the show was distinctly coon and the manner in which both entertainers and public entered into its spirit was again a great demonstration of a truth which is becoming more and more evident to those who work in the theatre that there must be complete cooperation between public and actor, that the audience indeed must become an integral part of any successful theatrical performance. The spectators at the Darktown Follies appeared to be enjoying themselves after the semi-hysterical fashion of a good camp meeting . . . in an effort, which was availing, to make the entertainers work hard.

And the entertainers worked. They certainly did work. In *My Friend from Kentucky* some attempt was made to present the Negro as he really is and not as he wants to be on the stage. The first act on a Virginia plantation diffused a general atmosphere of black joy. How the darkies danced, sang, and cavorted. Real nigger stuff, this, done with spontaneity and joy in the doing. A ballet in ebony and ivory and rose. Nine out of ten, nay ten out of ten, of those delighted niggers, those inexhaustible Ethiopians, those husky lanky blacks, those bronze bucks and yellow girls would have liked to have danced and sung like that every night of their lives, and they showed it. How they stepped about and clapped their hands and "grew mad with their bodies," and grinned and shouted. *Then I saw the Congo*:

> . . . cake-walk princes in their long red coats,
> Canes with a brilliant lacquer shine,
> And tall silk hats that were red as wine.
> And they pranced with their butterfly partners there,
> Coal-black maidens with pearls in their hair,
> Knee-skirts trimmed with the jassamine sweet,
> And bells on their ankles and little black feet.[6]

Passion and pleasure, pleasure and passion, a wholesome and tantalizing confusion, not at all like Spanish dancing but somehow suggestive at times of the primitive spirit of Spanish dancing.

In good Negro entertainment of this kind there is an inexorable rhythm, like the rhythm of a camp-meeting. Once under way it spreads from side to side of the stage. The separate figures become part of this great rhythm; the scenery and the stage boards take it up; the footlights flicker to it. J. Leubrie Hill reserved his great effort in this direction for the final scene of the piece in a number called "At the Ball" in which each entity of the company turned his body into that of a serpent, and then together they became one enormous serpent that coiled and recoiled all along its boneless and intolerable length. After the fiftieth repetition of this number the rhythm dominated me so completely that for days afterwards I subconsciously adapted whatever I was doing to its demands.

Night after night Florenz Ziegfeld sat admiringly in a box at this show, drinking in the details of the admirable stage direction, the spontaneity of the performers, their characteristic lax ease, and the delightfully abandoned tunes. Several of these he bought, together with their accompanying action, and transplanted them into his *Follies of 1914*, but the effect was not the same. The tunes remained pretty; the *Follies* girls undoubtedly were pretty, but the rhythm was gone, the thrill was lacking, the boom was inaudible, the Congo had disappeared.

On the evening of March 30, 1914, the now defunct Stage Society of New York, which had puttered and prowled about among minor masterpieces for a couple of seasons, produced a great play, Mr. Ridgely Torrence's *Granny Maumee*. So far as I know this play was the first serious attempt to depict the Negro, from his own point of view. The theme of this piece is set to the chords of Voodoo worship and sympathetic magic. It shows the proud Negro grandmother disdaining an alliance with white blood. By burning in effigy the white man who has seduced her granddaughter and lynched her son she hopes to expiate the crime of the one and revenge the other. But out of the flames, as the Lord presented himself to Moses in the burning bush, the image of her boy appears to her and she dies forgiving. The sweep of this drama is great; it is a satisfactory presentation of a big theme. Both play and Dorothy Donnelly's superb interpretation of the title part impressed me so deeply, indeed, that I attended the second and final performance the next afternoon. And immediately I was seized with the idea of founding a real Negro theatre, in which Negroes should act in real Negro plays, as the Irish of the Abbey Theatre had produced charactristic Irish plays.

The difficulty, of course, was to secure the plays. The Irish, it would seem, are a playwriting race. The Negroes, it would seem, are not. During my visits to the Jefferson Theatre I had come in touch with a young man, whose name I have forgotten, who had taken a course in the drama with Professor [George Pierce] Baker of Harvard. I now bethought myself of this fellow and wrote him to send me some plays. They came, five-act tragedies with Hannibal and Trajan as heroes, three-act comedies about modern life in Boston and its environs. They did not seem to be about Negroes at all! The young man, when questioned, said he doubted if I could find what I wanted. Events proved that he was right. The educated Negro dramatist has no desire to remind himself or his prospective audiences of the dark days and unpleasant traditions, which he thinks best forgotten. Negroes have written plays, but so far as I can discover these plays have no racial significance; they are, always excepting certain scenes in the Williams and Walker and J. Leubrie Hill entertainments, imitations of the theatre of the white man, and consequently quite worthless. So I was forced to abandon my scheme. It was easy enough to find Negro actors; most Negroes have a talent for acting, but you cannot open a theatre without plays.

But Ridgely Torrence as a playwright had the advantage. Already he had produced *Granny Maumee*. He wrote two more plays, engaged a Negro company, and at the Garden Theatre in April 1917 he opened the first Negro theatre of the kind, I think, that had been attempted in this country. One of these plays, *Simon the Cyrenian*, is based on the presumption, which has an ironic modern significance, that the cross-bearer for Jesus was a black man. The other new piece, *The Rider of Dreams*, even excels *Granny Maumee* as the ideal of the type of play suitable for Negroes to perform in a playhouse of their own. This play has the true folk spirit. The subject is somewhat similar to that of [John Millington] Synge's *Playboy* [*of the Western World*] but the treatment is entirely different. The lazy good-for-nothing, dishonest, delightful dreamer, Madison Sparrow, is not only a distinct addition to the meagre gallery of portraits offered us by the contemporary theatre, it is also an essentially Negro character. As played by Opal Cooper it was easily one of the theatrical delights of the season of which it formed a part. These three plays produced, however, there was nothing to go on with and in due time the enterprise came to a halt. Mr. Torrence has published these plays as *Three Plays for a Negro Theatre* but even the title does not seem to have stimulated other playwrights to work in the same field. Three plays for a Negro Theatre there are, and, so far as I know, there are no more.[7] J. Leubrie Hill is dead; George Walker is dead; Aida Overton Walker is dead, but something of the spirit of these, something of the dancing and singing life of the Negroes can be seen and heard in the Negro cabarets where, indeed, at times you may prevail on the musicians to give you a "spirtule," incongruously set, to be sure, but wonderfully sung. But the manner of singing Negro songs correctly is nearly forgotten so far as the respectable Negro is concerned. The dancing is becoming Broadwayized and sophisticated; the singing is fast losing its essential style. The Negro, who has suffered so much, wants to forget the old environment of slavery and broaden out into an imitation of white life. One evidence of this is that the richest woman in the Negro colony in New

York is the inventor of a lotion which straightens kinky hair.[8] The Negro race has given this country its only valuable folk music, for the folk music of the Indians is more or less negligible musically although probably some of it has an ethnological value. This folk music has been pretty well collected, but the art of singing it is passing. A few years ago I heard the Tuskegee singers sing Spirituals as if they were Bach cantatas; their tone, attack, and phrasing were impeccable and the authentic Negro manner forty thousand leagues away. At the Negro Music School Settlement in Harlem I once heard a young colored girl sing "Nobody Knows de Trouble I'se Seen" just about as Mme. Melba might have sung "John Anderson, My Joe."[9] She even corrected characteristic grammatical errors in the traditional text! She undoubtedly would have sung "Nobody knows how much trouble I have seen" if the music had permitted it.

The last time I visited the Jefferson Theatre it had become the home of a stock company. I heard two acts of *Madame X* there, given in imitation of all the worst conventions of Broadway, with pauses and "crosses," etc. The acting was no worse and no better than conventional Broadway acting. The next week *The Yellow Ticket* was to be the bill but, while the prospect of seeing a black girl impersonate a Jewish prostitute excited my mirth, it did not draw me to the theatre. Nor did I go to see *Othello*. Actors have to act what there is to act. They cannot appear in Negro plays if there is none. But it is doubtful if Negro audiences would go in large numbers to see a characteristic Negro play, the musical play excepted. Negroes as a whole are astonishingly lacking in race pride. Many of them have succumbed to the effect of white domination: they are ashamed of their race. To be sure Negroes who marry whites are seldom well spoken of by their compatriots but the rich burning race pride of Granny Maumee would be hard to duplicate, in New York at least. Unless Mr. Torrence writes more plays, and other white men follow his example, I am afraid there will never be a Negro theatre, and if there is one I am sure it will appeal more to whites than to blacks. The Negro will always prefer Mary Pickford to Bert Williams.[10]

1. Agnes Repplier, American writer, 1858-1945.

2. Richard Mansfield, international actor, 1857-1907; Coquelin, French pantomimist, circa 1900; Eleanora Duse, Italian actress, 1859-1924.

3. Edwin Booth, American actor, 1833-93; William Winter, drama critic, 1836-1917, whose *Shakespeare on Stage* examined various actors in various roles.

4. Van Vechten places the Darktown Follies in the Lafayette in his 1914 review. The theater changed its name during the interim, although Van Vechten refers to the Lafayette as a contemporary theater in 1926, in *Nigger Heaven*.

5. Ned Wayburn, Broadway producer of the period.

6. Vachel Lindsay, *The Congo*, 1913.

7. Laurence Eyre's play, *Sazus Matazus*, was about Negroes, but seems to have been conceived from the white point of view. It was produced and played for at least a week, but it never reached New York. I do not know that Mary Burrill's interesting one-act play, *Aftermath*, which deals with a Negro problem from a Negro point of view, has been performed. It may, however, be added to the short list of plays for a Negro theatre [note by C.V.V.].

8. Madame C.J. Walker, about whose daughter A'Lelia Van Vechten later wrote (q.v.).

9. Nellie Melba, Australian opera singer, 1861-1931, who corrected the Scots dialect in Robert Burns's lyric.

10. Mary Pickford, a popular white actress, and Bert Williams (q.v.), a popular black performer.

FROM A NOTE ON AMERICAN LETTERS

A reason for the lack of tradition in American letters lies primarily in the vast extent of the country. Each section has its own scenery, its own dialect, its own customs. Another lies in the unhomogeneous character of the nation. The Southwest was settled by the Spaniard, the Northeast by the Englishman; French, Bohemian, Irish, Jew, Pole, and Italian, German, and Swede have settled somewhere. Each of us has foreign ancestors. Some of us, indeed, were born in this country within an hour of our mother's landing here. There is the Indian, too, who certainly belongs here if anybody does, and the Negro, who in his folklore, a combination of shrieking Methodism or total-immersion Baptism and the horrid, nocuous, voodoo rites of the African savage, has become a very different sort of person from the African Negro.

To the Negroes, indeed, we are indebted for the rhythm of our best music, the only American music, aside from that of the Indian, which has a folk quality, the music which such a man as Irving Berlin writes. Now the music of Irving Berlin, to particularize, such a melody as "Alexander's Ragtime Band," is worth more than all the scores of such professional mediocrities as Henry Hadley, Frederick Converse, and Professor Horatio Parker put together. It is essentially folk music and, in spite of the Negro influence, it is essentially American, because it is certainly not the kind of music that the Negroes sing in Africa.

"Prescription for the Negro Theatre," "Folksongs of the American Negro," and "The Black Blues" originally appeared in *Vanity Fair* in October, July, and August 1925, respectively. These papers, and Van Vechten's simultaneous reviews of books about black music, were among the first efforts to call attention to Spirituals and Blues as serious artistic endeavors. *"Vanity Fair,"* Van Vechten later wrote to me, "was the *first* of the better magazines to publish Negro material repeatedly (something that occurs frequently now) and this was largely due to my influence with Frank Crowninshield." Van Vechten had been an irregular contributor to *Vanity Fair* for nearly a decade, which might explain in part why Crowninshield "just published a number of articles about the race by me and then called upon Negro authors to contribute material, notably Countée Cullen & Langston Hughes. He was the first, I think, to publish photographs of racial favorites such as Paul Robeson & Florence Mills, made by great photographers such as Steichen & Hoyinguen-Heune."

At the time he wrote these articles, Van Vechten's acquaintance with Harlem was substantially broader, although his material was largely public and not yet entirely free of the racial climate of the Twenties, especially in his suggestions for black theatrical entertainments. Still, James Weldon Johnson in his *Book of American Negro Spirituals* (Viking Press, 1926), and W.C. Handy and Abbe Niles in their anthology, *Blues* (Boni, 1926), quoted at length from Van Vechten's evaluations of black music in the pages of *Vanity Fair*. Not of least interest is the extended quotation from a letter of Langston Hughes to Van Vechten in the third of these essays, perhaps the earliest published evaluation of the Blues by a black writer.

To "Folksongs of the American Negro" I have appended a selection of Van Vechten's reviews of several collections of music and folklore: "Religious Folksongs of the American Negro," a review of *The Book of American Negro Spirituals*, appeared in *Opportunity*, November 1925; "The Songs of the Negro," including a review of *The Negro and His Songs*, appeared in *New York Herald Tribune Books*, 25 October 1925; "Don't Let Dis Harves' Pass," including reviews of *Negro Workaday Songs* and *Folk Beliefs of the Southern Negro*, appeared in *New York Herald Tribune Books*, 31 October 1926, the latter concluding with a plea for serious attention to the Blues.

To "The Black Blues" I have appended two reviews: the first, also from "The Songs of the Negro," *On the Trail of Negro Folksongs*, appeared in *New York Herald Tribune Books*, 25 October 1925; the second, "Mean Ole Miss Blues Becomes Respectable," a review of *Blues*, appeared in *New York Herald Tribune Books*, 6 June 1926.

PRESCRIPTION FOR THE NEGRO THEATRE

Since that summer, four years ago, when *Shuffle Along* aroused so much enthusiasm among paying theatregoers, producers have made a consistent effort to repeat the success of that Negro revue. *Put and Take, Oh Joy, Strut Miss Lizzie, How Come, Runnin' Wild, Liza, Dixie to Broadway, The Chocolate Dandies*, and *7-11* are the titles of the most conspicuous of these pieces, not one of which won the popularity of its celebrated forerunner, although a few attracted an ephemeral attention.

Latterly, the lack of public interest in these African frolics has become so pronounced that it has come to be believed along the upper stretches of Seventh Avenue and in the dusky section of Tin Pan Alley that any Negro musical show is now foredoomed to certain failure and faces are long and features are glum as a result. It might be well, therefore, to study some of the causes contributing to the apathy of the admirers of this exotic form of entertainment, an apathy which has been the direct occasion for this false psychological reaction among the entrepreneurs.

In the first place it is an error to take it for granted, as so many of those recently initiated into the titillations of these agreeable buffooneries are prone to do, that *Shuffle Along* was the first notable Negro revue. A little inquiry by those born too young to be privy to the facts would easily elicit the information that Bert Williams and George Walker, for many seasons in many vehicles, were greeted with applause on both sides of the Atlantic and showered with dollars and sovereigns. The name of Ernest Hogan may be forgotten, but in his day he was a comedian of parts who starred at the head of his own company. Bob Cole is dead, but Rosamond Johnson is very much alive to remind us that the popular team of Cole and Johnson once existed. In 1913, J. Leubrie Hill produced his Darktown Follies at the Lafayette Theatre and rewon an audience which had been captivated thirteen years earlier by Williams and Walker, but which, through Walker's death and Williams's subsequent abandonment of his troupe in favor of vaudeville, had been deprived of a suitable opportunity to express its approval of these Ethiopian carnivals. The Darktown Follies, if I remember rightly, continued its run in the heart of Harlem and was not delivered over to a Broadway house, but Broadway flocked to the Lafayette and Florenz Ziegfeld bought three songs from this revue for the coeval edition of his own Follies.

Moreover, apparently it has also been forgotten that the musical shows of Williams and Walker, Ernest Hogan, and J. Leubrie Hill had their own imitations which soon faded into that obscurity which has gathered in the majority of the successors of *Shuffle Along*. As a sympathetic witness who has attended these Negro diversions for twenty-five years, I may state that the reason for the occasional public apathy is perfectly clear to me: these entertainments are built upon a formula which varies so little in its details that only once in five years or so, after the customers have forgotten the last one, is it possible to awaken interest in a new example, and only then when there is an exceptional cast or especially tuneful music. It is well to keep in mind that Bert Williams was a comedian almost of the first rank, a perfect artist within his limitations, who would have made a name for himself anywhere; he might have enjoyed a considerable career had he relied solely on his pantomimic gifts. For a decade, after the demise of his troupe, he was a leading figure in the music halls and in the Follies. George Walker, too, was inimitable in his own line, that of portraying the smartly dressed, Negro swell, prancing with heaved chest, while his wife, Ada Overton Walker (later, I believe, she became Aida, perhaps responding to the urge of some insistent numerologist), was a singer and dancer of personal magnetism and far from negative talent. If J. Leubrie Hill's company included no such stars, his show boasted three or four good tunes and he exhibited a plethora of ingenuity in his staging of the intricate dancing numbers. *Shuffle Along* possessed not only a score which set the town to whistling and the phonographs to whirling, but also a cast which included [Noble] Sissle and [Eubie] Blake, [Flournoy] Miller and [Aubrey] Lyles, and Gertrude Saunders, the latter eventually supplanted by Florence Mills. These performers have since separated to head their own respective companies.

Aside, however, from the music of *Shuffle Along* and the talent of certain of the principals, no new element was introduced to give a kick to the connoisseur of such shows. The dancing of the chorus was a delight, but the dancing in any Negro revue is always *hors de concours*. All the old stuff was strutted, together with the fulsome imitation of white revues which has come to be such a discouraging feature of these entertainments. One of the hits of this piece was a tune in the moth-eaten, sentimental ballad form, "Love Will Find a Way." The innumerable encores allotted at every performance to "I'm Just Wild about Harry" were occasioned by a strutter who maneuvered his chest and buttocks after the manner made famous by George Walker. Any one who had ever enjoyed the privilege of observing George Walker negotiating the cakewalk would not have been very much excited over the modest prowess of his successor. The customary cavortings in overalls and bandannas, clog dancing on the levee, also were in evidence. All Negro revues open either the first or second act with a levee or a plantation scene.

Further, the comedians blacked their faces and carmined and enlarged their lips. This is a minstrel tradition that seems to die hard, even with colored minstrels. Bert Williams, who had a very light complexion, may have had some excuse for following this tradition, although, personally, I do not believe that he had. For it to be followed blindly, unthinkingly, by practically every comedian in the Negro theatre is worse than an absurdity. In the end it will amount to suicide.

This is not the only unworthy tradition perpetuated by *Shuffle Along* and its less vital successors. The tendency which is likely to have the ultimate effect of destroying the last remnants of general public interest in these revues is the persistent demand, on the part of the producers, for light chorus and dancing girls. The girls latterly on exhibition are so nearly white that what with the injudicious application of whitening and the employment of amber illumination (together with the added fact that all of them have straight, and many of them red or blonde hair), there is nothing to distinguish them from their sisters in the *Scandals* or *Artists and Models* save their superior proficiency in the Charleston.

In professional agility and vitality these girls must be the envious despair of many a Ned Wayburn. Nor can it be said that the Negro stage is lacking in more highly skilled talent. I could name fifty exceptionally clever colored actors, singers, and dancers, some of them as yet undiscovered save by cabaret habitués. . . . But these performers do not write the revues, much less produce them, and it is in these two departments that weakness is betrayed, for as yet no Negro has written or produced a revue which indicates that any original thought has been expended on the job.

Awaiting the appearance of a dusky Charlot or a chocolate Ziegfeld, permit me to offer a few hints to prospective purveyors of Negro revues. First and last: advertise for a dark chorus. I don't think it will be necessary to look for "chocolate to the bone" cuties. Indeed, a fascinating effect might be achieved by engaging a rainbow chorus: six black girls, six "seal-browns," six "high Yellas," and six pale creams. With the proper costumes, and a director capable of contriving appropriate evolutions and groupings, it is impossible to set a limit to what might be done with this human palette of color. In case, for some reason, this scheme is found impracticable, as many dark girls as possible should be engaged. There are certainly many Negroes who prefer dark girls; white people who go to Negro shows expect to see them and are disappointed when they don't. Seek beauties who can dance and sing, and see that the lightest is about the shade of strong coffee before the cream is poured in, and I guarantee that your show will be a success even if you throw in all the old stuff, the cemetery scene with the ghost, the moon song rendered by the tenor who doesn't know what to do with his hands, and the "I want to be in Dixie," or the Mammy, or the cotton-bale song. It might be well, however, to eliminate these stale features also, together with the repulsive liver-lips and cork complexions of the comedians. I believe, if I were a Negro and it were my profession to make people laugh, that I could parade my material as successfully without these childish adjuncts as with them. At any rate it would be a welcome relief to see somebody make the attempt.

Let me offer a few more suggestions as substitutes for the discarded features. Why doesn't some sapient manager engage Bessie Smith, "the empress of the Blues," or Clara Smith, "the world's greatest moaner," to sing the Blues, not Blues written by Sissle and Blake or Irving Berlin, but honest-to-God Blues, full of trouble and pain and misery and heartache and tribulation, Blues like "Any Woman's Blues," "If You Only Knowed," or "Nobody Knows the Way I Feel Dis Mornin' ":

> I feel like I could scream an' cry dis mornin',
> I feel like I could scream an' cry dis mornin',

I feel like I could scream an' cry,
But I'm too downhearted an' I'd rather die;
Nobody knows the way I feel dis mornin'.
I even hate to hear yore name dis mornin',
I even hate to hear yore name;
I could kill you quicker than an express train:
Nobody knows the way I feel dis mornin'.

To hear Clara Smith sing this song is an experience that no one, who has had the privilege, will soon forget. Her voice, choking with moaning quarter tones, clutches the heart. Her expressive and economic gestures are full of meaning. What an artist! Yet I do not think she has ever appeared in one of the first-class revues, although her phonograph records are famous wherever disks of Blues are bought.

On the streets of Harlem this summer, or even on Broadway during the theatre hour, you may have encountered a crowd of pickaninny ragamuffins dancing the Charleston for baksheesh. These gamins are so proficient and skilful in varying their steps, their appearance is so picturesque, that no sooner do they begin their exhibition of terpsichorean virtuosity than a large crowd collects. Has it occurred to any Negro producer that this scene on the stage would create a riot of enthusiasm in his auditorium? It has not. Nor has he arrived at the conclusion that an hysterical camp-meeting number with a chorus singing evangelical Spirituals would probably cause so great a gathering to assemble before his box office that it would be necessary to call out the police reserves.

The reproduction of a scene in an authentic Negro cabaret, such as Small's (if it could be reproduced), would be another excellent plan. Naturally it would not bear the slightest resemblance to the cabaret scene ordinarily exhibited on the stage. The difficulty would not be to match the ebullient entertainers, or the dancing waiters, or the eccentric jazz band, with its mad drummer, who might all be transplanted successfully in person, but to recapture the spirit of the frequenters of the resort as they go through the paces of the Black Bottom, the Hey Hey, the Scronch, and the gestures of the Itch and Picking Cherries, and all the other gestures and paces that accompany the insane tappings of the drum, the moans of the hatted trumpet, and the harmonious thumping of the piano. And if the comedian of the troupe could not get a laugh occasionally by admonishing certain couples in the crowd to "get off that dime," he would do less than the saturnine floor managers of the real cabarets.

For the culmination of my spectacle—which might include a scene in Strivers' Row, as the block of yellow brick houses designed by Sanford White on 139th Street between Seventh and Eighth Avenues is so reasonably dubbed by the Negroes who do not live there, and a scene in a typical Harlem beauty parlor, the humor of which would not have to be exaggerated—I offer a wild pantomimic drama set in an African forest with the men and women as nearly nude as the law allows. There, in front of a background of orange-tinted banana fronds and amethyst palm leaves, silhouetted against a tropical blue sky divided by a silver moon, the bucks, their assegais stabbing the sky like the spears of the infantry in Velásquez's *Las Landas*, and their lithe-limbed, brown doxies, meagerly tricked out in multihued feathers, would enact a fantastic, choreographic comedy of passion.

The scenes in this ideal revue should riotously contrast one with the other, now relying on a picturesque realism for their effect, now on a chromatic, colorful arrangement of rhythm and form. It is unfortunate that Léon Bakst was never invited to stage such a revue, but there are other designers— Miguel Covarrubias for one—who would seize such an opportunity gratefully.

I have spoken above about the regrettable imitation of white revues in the Negro musical shows already staged. To be perfectly fair, I should state that practically all the dancing and a good share of the musical rhythms now to be seen and felt on the white stage have been raped from the Negro. The white producer, however, quite intelligently steals the best features of the Negro stage, while the Negro producer is content to take over the stalest features of the white stage. No white dancers, however, can hope to rival the Negro in those special dances which are peculiarly his own and which make even his poorest shows exciting whenever they occur, just as no Negro can ever hope to make a favorable impression with such a number as "Apple-Blossom Time in Normandy." If the Negro will stick to his own, embellishing it and displaying some originality in his treatment of it, I predict that he will be able to evolve with the talent at his disposal—where in the world else are there two dancers to compare in their specialties with Eddie Rector and Bill Robinson?—a type of entertainment which will be world-famous instead of the fad of a few people for a few moments. The ideal director will not harbor an exclusive taste for yellow gals and it will be easy for him to sacrifice liverlips, burnt cork, sentimental ballads warbled by anemic tenors, bandannas, basses who sing "Old Black Joe" and "Georgia Rose," in fact all the tiresome clichés that at present prevent the Negro revues from raising the roof.

FOLKSONGS OF THE AMERICAN NEGRO

Writing an introduction to Samuel Coleridge-Taylor's *Transcriptions of Twenty-Four Negro Melodies*, published by Oliver Ditson in 1904, Booker T. Washington was moved to lament: "It is a cause for special gratitude that the foremost musician of his race, a man in the zenith of his powers, should seek to chronicle, and thus perpetuate, the old melodies that are so rapidly passing away." Twenty years ago, indeed, despite the fact that they were sung constantly at the Negro colleges and institutes, Hampton, Tuskegee, and Fisk, there was cause for fear that, aside from such examples as had already been collected and set down, the Negro Spirituals, surely the traditional manner of their performance, would soon be forgotten. The Negroes themselves were ashamed of these songs, reminiscent as they were of slave days. Except in the smaller communities, where they were still to be heard in the churches, they were regarded with disfavor.

To be sure the Fisk Jubilee Singers, as early as 1871, had undertaken a tour of America, to be followed by a triumphal tour of Europe which included among its notable incidents a breakfast party given by Gladstone and performances before Queen Victoria and the royalty of other nations, occasions glowingly described in two books by G.D. Pike in which many of the Spirituals, hitherto unpublished, were set down in arrangements for four voices by Theodore F. Seward. Aside from *Slave Songs of the United States*, a collection issued in 1867, and now almost unobtainable, this was the first attempt made to capture these spontaneous musical outpourings of the Negro on paper. Hampton Institute, however, soon issued a rival collection and set out on a tour.

Dvořák's utilization of "Swing Low, Sweet Chariot"; his employment of the pentatonic scale (lacking the fourth and seventh of the diatonic scale of the typical "Scotch snap," in which a short note on the accented part of a measure is followed by a long note on the unaccented part); and [his use] of the flatted seventh—all peculiarities of African music, imported to Afro-America by the slaves—in his symphony, *From the New World*, composed in New York and orchestrated in Iowa, might have indicated to serious composers a possible manner in which to develop this music. Save in isolated instances it did not.

In 1914, H.E. Krehbiel's *Afro-American Folksongs* was published, but this book, written largely for the technical musician and containing long discussions of African and Spanish forerunners, could not serve to popularize the songs. In 1917, H.T. Burleigh's arrangements of the Spirituals began to appear. J. Rosamond Johnson, David Guion, William Arms Fisher, R. Nathaniel Dett, and others made arrangements of their own. Natalie Curtis-Burlin went to Hampton and with the aid of a phonograph set down scientifically (or as scientifically as one can set down such music by the Procrustean method of adapting its quarter tones to the tempered scale) the singing of a Negro quartet. Suddenly—perhaps the date coincides with Roland Hayes's return to this country, for it is certain that he has placed a group of Spirituals on his every program—they were not only appreciated, they achieved popularity, a popularity attested to by the flood of transcriptions issued by the music publishers, culminating recently in a book of the most frequently sung examples, arranged by Hugh Frey, and in the success of the All-Negro programs given by Paul Robeson and Lawrence Brown. Such a joyous number as "All God's Chillun Got Wings" is even sung in vaudeville, occasionally with an added infectious but impious verse to the effect that "all God's chillun got a Ford"! The time has come, indeed, a time that Booker T. Washington never dreamed would come, when the intelligent members of the race are doing more to perpetuate these melodies, the most important contribution America has yet made to the literature of music, than anyone else. At the moment, indeed, James Weldon Johnson has undertaken the colossal task of editing a series of volumes which it is promised will include practically all the available examples.

Musicians and musical people have long recognized the rare beauty of these songs which originated on the southern plantations during slave days. Other origins have been attributed to them, including that of the old "Aunty" who explained: "When Massa Jesus He walked de earth, when He feel tired He set a'restin' on Jacob's well an' make up dese yer spirchuls for His people." It is as good an explanation as any. However they came into being, the unpretentious sincerity that inspires them makes them the peer or the superior of any folk music the world has yet known. So much has been written in regard to the music that the poetic quality, however crude, of the words is sometimes overlooked. Observe, for example, the poignant symbolism of

> When Israel was in Egypt's land, —
> Let my people go!
> Oppressed so hard they could not stand,
> Let my people go!
> Go down, Moses!
> Way down in Egypt's land!
> Tell ole Pharaoh
> Let my people go!

In decided contrast is the scherzo-like

> Little David, play on your harp,
> Hallelu! Hallelu!
> Little David, play on your harp,
> Hallelu!
> He killed Goliath with a stone
> Then clapped his hands and ran back home.
> Little David, play on your harp,
> Hallelu!

or the austere dignity of "Weepin' Mary":

If there's anybody here like weepin' Mary,
Call upon your Jesus, an' He'll draw nigh.
If there's anybody here like weepin' Mary,
Call upon your Jesus, an' He'll draw nigh.
O, glory, glory, hallelujah!
Glory be to my God, who rules on high!

It is not novel to state that the Spirituals are the source of our modern popular music. They contain, indeed, every element of modern jazz save the instrumentation. Such songs as "The Gospel Train (Get on Board, Little Children)," "All God's Chillun Got Wings," "I Don't Feel Noways Tired," and "I'm a-Trav'lin' to the Grave," set to secular words might almost be mistaken for compositions by George Gershwin, a statement I feel sure, which the composer of "I'll Build a Stairway to Paradise" would be very glad to corroborate. An extremely popular song of a season or two ago, "Dear Old Southland," is almost a literal transcription of two Negro Spirituals, "Deep River" and "Sometimes I Feel like a Motherless Child," although the Negro musician whose name appears on the cover made no acknowledgment of his indebtedness.

It is less generally known that there are quite as many work songs, convict songs, as religious songs, although as yet hardly any of these have been collected. A few, however, such as the ubiquitous "Water Boy" in Avery Robinson's arrangement, Mr. Burleigh's version of "Scandalize My Name," and the cotton pickin', corn huskin', and hammer songs assembled by Natalie Curtis Burlin, are more or less familiar. Another class of Negro folksong, the Blues, has evolved in the less respectable quarters of Memphis. Many of these spontaneous inventions of nondescript pianists and cabaret singers have been published (necessarily with new verses!) with no word of credit as to the impudicity of their origin. In his preface to *The Book of American Negro Poetry*, James Weldon Johnson asserts that the first piece of ragtime to achieve wide popularity was "The Bully," sung by May Irwin. He further avers that this is an arrangement of a roustabout song, long familiar on the Mississippi. It is not necessary, however, to go out of the range of the Spirituals themselves to discover variety. These religious songs are created in every mood, from the tender and wistful pathos of "By an' By" and "Steal Away," the heartbreaking resignation of "Nobody Knows de Trouble I Seen," the grandeur of "You May Bury Me in de Eas'," the broad, flowing, melodic poignancy of "Deep River" and "Swing Low, Sweet Chariot," to the abandoned evangelical joy of "Every Time I Feel de Spirit," "I Know de Lord Laid His Hands on Me," "Joshua Fit de Battle of Jericho," and "I'll Be a Witness for My Lord."

Negro folksongs differ from the folksongs of most other races through the fact that they are sung in harmony, and as Negroes harmonize instinctively, each performance differs in some particular from every other performance, although the melody retains its general integrity. It is the custom, indeed, for Negro singers in choruses to sing tenor or bass at will, according to their mood. It is, therefore, not a work of supererogation to harmonize these songs for piano and voice, as the piano, to a certain extent, fills in the harmony properly supplied by the other singers, although, as its scale lacks quarter tones, occasionally a flat seventh is substituted for the more esoteric note.

The progress of these Spirituals into the repertory of most public singers is due, perhaps, more than to any other one man, to the indefatigable efforts of H.T. Burleigh. For nearly a decade, Mr. Burleigh, who is still occupied with the task, has been issuing his concert arrangements of these masterpieces of homely music. Nevertheless, I cannot look upon all of Mr. Burleigh's arrangements with favor, principally because they have been instrumental in bringing these songs to the attention of white singers and I do not think white singers can sing Spirituals. Women, with few exceptions, should not attempt to sing them at all. White singers have been attracted to Mr. Burleigh's arrangements, because they include many of the "tricks" which make any song successful, while the accompaniments are often highly sophisticated. This is not true of all of Mr. Burleigh's arrangements and I think it may safely be stated that it is only true of any of them insofar as he failed to express the real love for this music that he indubitably feels.

In his foreword to his transcriptions, however, Mr. Burleigh has warned performers against making an attempt "to imitate the manner of the Negro in singing them, by swaying the body, clapping the hands, or striving to make the peculiar inflections of voice that are natural with the colored people." As a piece of advice directed to white singers this may be all very well, but I have already stated my conviction that white singers had better leave them alone. The trouble with this advice is that it is being heeded by too many colored singers, who not only avoid the natural Negro inflections, but are inclined to avoid the dialect as well. That is the reason that many people will prefer the traditional, evangelical renderings of Paul Robeson to the more refined performances of Roland Hayes. It is to be remembered that when Caruso sang Neapolitan folksongs he sang them in dialect, as much as possible in the manner of the authentic interpretation. The fact that the Spirituals are religious in their nature does not alter my point of view. I am merely arguing for a maintenance of the *original* manner in which they were sung.

To date, too many of the concert arrangements—and I do not refer alone to Mr. Burleigh's—have apparently been made from the four-part versions to be found in the Fisk and Hampton collections. What is needed at present is more original research. A trained Negro musician—to no other than a Negro would the material be available—should scour the South, not only for new songs, but to make accurate records of harmonized performances of the old ones before it is too late. Any such seeker, it is evident, will find a mine of hitherto unearthed material in the work and convict songs, and in the underworld of the southern cities.

Messrs. Guinzberg and Oppenheimer hit upon a happy idea when they decided to inaugurate their new publishing house, the Viking Press, with a volume devoted to Negro Spirituals [*The Book of American Negro Spirituals*, edited with an introduction by James Weldon Johnson (New York: Viking Press, 1925)]. There has existed, for some time, a demand for a book of this character, in which the more celebrated of the religious folksongs of the American Negro are set down in an arrangement for solo voice and piano, with an informative introduction. Some Negro should have compiled it ten years ago. In the circumstances, it is cause for congratulation that these publishers should have turned to the very best Negro talent available.

As a matter of fact, it is the Negro himself, in the face of determined opposition on the part of the majority of his race, who has kept these songs alive. Fisk University, Hampton Normal and Agricultural Institute, and Calhoun School have not only sent out singers to tour this country and Europe, disseminating the sorrow songs, but also they have published a number of volumes preserving them. The limitation of these collections is that they record only the melodies or an arrangement for four voices and therefore are not practical for home or concert use. Several of these collections, too, are out of print and available only in libraries. To be sure, H.T. Burleigh, William Arms Fisher, David W. Guion, Nathaniel Dett, W.C. Handy, Carl Diton, N. Clark Smith, Lawrence Brown, and J. Rosamond Johnson, among others, have all made arrangements of the Spirituals for solo voice and piano, but these have been issued in sheet-music form and are only purchasable separately. Moreover, in too many instances, these arrangements give a false impression of the original Negro spirit of these songs. Too often they have been adulterated with sophisticated modern French harmonies or disfigured by effective "concert endings."

J. Rosamond Johnson and Lawrence Brown have not fallen into these errors. Their arrangements have reproduced, insofar as it is possible for a piano to do so, the harmonies that might be employed by a Negro chorus in the actual performance of the Spirituals under the conditions incident to their creation. They have done more than this; certain figures and arpeggios actually suggest the moans and groans, the startled, "Oh yesses!" of a congregation of mourners.

The selection of Spirituals, from more than three hundred recorded examples, is exceedingly happy. Most of the songs in the repertory of the Fisk Jubilee Singers, the Sabbath Glee Club of Richmond—an organization about which too little is known—Roland Hayes, Paul Robeson, Julius Bledsoe,

and Marian Anderson are to be found herein: "Joshua Fit de Battle ob Jericho," "Deep River," "Go Down, Moses," "Swing Low, Sweet Chariot,"
"My Way's Cloudy," etc. In addition, Mr. Johnson has made versions of
certain rare songs. Of these, "Somebody's Knockin' at Yo' Do'," "Stan' Still,
Jordan," and "Singin' Wid a Sword in Ma Han'," are bound to achieve popularity, now that concert arrangements are available.

I have long complained about the effort made by certain colored arrangers
and singers of Spirituals to disregard the dialect, which is an integral part of
the charm of these naïve songs. Thus one sometimes hears "nobody knows
the trouble I've seen," clear grammatical English, as far away as possible
from the true spirit of the original. I believe the retention of the dialect to be
essentially important to the successful rendering of these numbers and I am
delighted to discover that the editor under discussion, Mr. James Weldon
Johnson, agrees with me on this point. Without being pedantic—thus he
writes "sword" although it is pronounced "soad," realizing that the latter
form would be unintelligible to many readers—he has tried to restore the
dialect in all the songs, more than that, to make it as consistent as possible.
This is a nice problem, inasmuch as false readings have crept into the text
from time to time; further, because Negro dialect differs according to locality.
I think, however, that he has arrived at a very happy solution of this difficult
question. I have examined a number of songs in this collection with this
point in mind and generally found the results exceedingly felicitous.

James Weldon Johnson has also supplied a preface to the volume, which
not only pays full homage to the beauty of the Spirituals, but also is somewhat in the nature of an analytical and historical survey. I do not very well
see how the subject could have been presented in a more clear, logical, and
readable fashion. The book is bound so that it will open easily on the music
rack and it is of a convenient size to peruse at ease in the library. The songs
it assembles are the richest heritage of the Negro race. They are known and
admired by cultivated people of every race.

Of an entirely different character is *The Negro and His Songs*, the work
of two white men, Professors Howard W. Odum and Guy B. Johnson, of
the University of North Carolina. In this [1925] volume, a great many of the
more modern religious, social, and work songs of the Negro are brought
together and an attempt is made—the conclusions arrived at generally appear
to be reasonably sound—to estimate something of Negro character and life
from the evidence they present. The music, unfortunately, is lacking, but so
little emphasis has hitherto been laid on the poetic value of the words, flash-
ing with imagery and descriptive phraseology, crude though they may be,
that it is a relief to pick up a book in which this theme is fully developed, a
theme generally dealt with, by the way, in James Weldon Johnson's preface
to *The Book of American Negro Spirituals*. In *The Negro and His Songs*

an entire chapter is devoted to it and scarcely a page lacks some reference to it.

Another feature of this study which has not previously received the requisite amount of attention is the discussion of the influences of white ballads and popular songs on Negro secular song. This process of transmutation is working both ways, as a matter of fact. Many of the songs in this book . . . are obviously related to published songs. In some cases the Negro has twisted the words and music of such songs to his own purposes, recreating something essentially his own. In other cases, the published song has emanated from the folksong. It will soon be too late to clarify these distinctions. The matter of the traditional ballads has been fully dealt with by Messrs. Odum and Johnson in this book, but the matter of popular songs remains still in abeyance for research on the part of some industrious Negro scholar.

The professors' book would benefit by the inclusion of more footnotes. Certain characters mentioned in the songs deserve extended explanation and comment; occasionally, the very meaning of words is left in doubt. Further, the professors assure us that, owing to its obscene nature, they have been obliged to reject a great part of the material they have assembled. I have long contended that some of the finest imagery of these unknown Negro bards—the phrase is James Weldon Johnson's—is to be found in the songs deriving from the so-called hours of pleasure. Certainly, these poems of dusky Aretinos are worthy of preservation, if only for the peeps they offer into ebony amorous life.

When we come to *Negro Workaday Songs* [1926] we are dealing with another kind of material. It is the business of Professors Odum and Johnson, of the University of North Carolina, to collect songs rather than arrange them, and they have gone into that business with a great deal of enthusiasm and considerable expertness. The volume containing the first results of their labors, *The Negro and His Songs*, was published last year. . . . This second volume is even better. In the first place the melodies of a considerable number of examples are given. Then several pages are devoted to phono-photographic plates of Negro singing, which demonstrate clearly that it is impossible to take down Negro melodies correctly in current musical notation. It is only on the phonograph that the exact effect may be approximated.

The authors go into this matter of phonograph records extensively in their chapter on the Blues. They prove conclusively not only that the commercial Blues are derived from folksongs, but also that these phonograph records form the nuclei for further folksongs. Aparently the circle is endless. In this connection it is interesting to note that it is the opinion of James Weldon Johnson, as expressed in his preface to *The Second Book of Negro Spirituals*, that the Blues will be the final contribution of the American Negro to folklore.

Messrs. Odum and Johnson assert that no future study of these songs can be made without reference to the phonograph records. It behooves students, therefore, to lay in a complete set of the records of Bessie and Clara Smith. The investor will find them as "educational" as anything Lorelei Lee did in Europe.

An entire chapter is devoted to the epic of John Henry, the Negro Paul Bunyan, and several variations are given of the song celebrating the career of this famous (if legendary) "steel-drivin' man." The most fascinating chapter in the book is awarded to Left Wing Gordon, an itinerant Negro workman to whom the authors are indebted for a great number of their songs. His adventures at work and in love are recorded in some detail. It seems to me that both John Henry and Left Wing Gordon almost scream aloud to have novels written around them. I hope some of the younger of the colored literati will take this suggestion seriously. If I knew a little more about his background I'd be tempted to tackle Left Wing Gordon myself.

Newell Niles Puckett's *Folk Beliefs of the Southern Negro* is another volume in this valuable series issued by the University of North Carolina Press. Dr. Puckett has gone into his subject thoroughly, even to the extent of practicing as a voodoo doctor in New Orleans in order to gain the confidence of other voodoo men. He not only succeeded in his mission, he also effected some extraordinary cures. Let him tell you about them. Burial customs, ghosts and witches, positive control signs, minor charms and cures and taboos are all discussed and tabulated in detail. These superstitions have been collected from no less than 407 informants and each folk belief is followed by a reference to the person who reported it. There is also a useful bibliography and a complete index. A scholarly piece of work and a fascinating one. No one at all interested in such matters can afford to be without it. It supplements Frazer's erudite volumes. Indeed Dr. Puckett might have called his book *The Ebony Bough.*

It is interesting to discover that Dr. Puckett traces the origin of the majority of these superstitions to southern whites, going back in many instances to European sources. I may say, indeed, that the author indulges in unusual frankness in his preface, unusual frankness, that is, for a southern Nordic. I quote:

After twenty years or more of close association with the Negro, an honorary membership in "de Mount Zion Missionary Baptist Church" and several years' experience as an amateur "hoo-doo-doctor," I am convinced that "de signs an' wonders" disclosed here are but outward manifestations of a well-nigh inscrutable Negro soul. My peep behind the curtains has destroyed for me the fable that "the Southern white man thoroughly understands the Negro," and has opened my eyes to the importance of objective study as a means of establishing more cordial relationships.

In a general sort of way the Southerner does understand the Negro, but this under-standing is limited almost completely to the practical affairs of life and consists chiefly in knowing how to make the Negro work. Regarding the feelings, emotions and the spiritual life of the Negro the average white man knows little. Should some weird, archaic Negro doctrine be brought to his attention he almost invariably considers it "a relic of African heathenism," though in four cases out of five it is a European dogma from which only centuries of patient education could wean even his own ancestors.

If any race boasts a more interesting folklore than the American Negro I do not know what that race is. There is, therefore, matter for congratulation in the fact that this folklore is being so assiduously collected and appraised. Authoritative volumes now exist on the folksong, religious and secular, on folk tales (Uncle Remus), and on the superstitions. Nevertheless, a good part of the field yet remains unexplored. When, I wonder, are we to have a selection of the ballads of the chocolate troubadours of the underworld?

THE BLACK BLUES

The Negro, always prone to express his deepest feeling in song, naturally experiences other more secular emotions than those sensations of religions published in the Spirituals. Perhaps the most poignant of all his feelings are those related to his disappointments in love, out of which have sprung the songs known as the Blues. These mournful plaints occasioned by the prema-ture departure of "papa," these nostalgic longings to join the loved one in a climate of sunlight and color—although in at least one instance the singer indicates a desire to go back to Michigan—are more tragic to me than the Spirituals, for the Spirituals are often informed with resignation, or even a joyous evangelism, while the Blues are consistently imbued with a pas-sionate despair.

Like the Spirituals, the Blues are folksongs and are conceived in the same pentatonic scale, omitting the fourth and seventh tones—although those that achieved publication or performance under sophisticated auspices have generally passed through a process of transmutation—and at present they are looked down upon, as the Spirituals once were, especially by the Negroes themselves. The humbleness of their origin and occasionally the frank obscenity of their sentiment are probably responsible for this condition. In this connection it may be recalled that it has taken over fifty years for the Negroes to recover from their repugnance to the Spirituals, because of the fact that they were born during slave days. Now, however, the Negroes are proud of the Spirituals, regarding them as one of the race's greatest gifts to the musical pleasure of mankind. I predict that it will not be long before the Blues will enjoy a similar resurrection which will make them as respectable, at least in the artistic sense, as the religious songs.

The music of the Blues has a peculiar language of its own, wreathed in melancholy ornament. It wails, this music, and limps languidly; the rhythm is angular, like the sporadic skidding of an automobile on a wet asphalt pavement. The conclusion is abrupt, as if the singer suddenly had become too choked for further utterance. Part of this effect is indubitably achieved through the fact that the typical Blues is created in three-line stanzas. As W.C. Handy, the artistic father of the Blues, has pointed out to me, the melodic strain can thereby be set down in twelve bars instead of the regulation sixteen. Not only are the breaks between verses and stanzas frequent, but also there are tantalizing and fascinatingly unaccountable—to any one familiar with other types of music—gaps between words, even between syllables. These effects are more or less characteristic of other Negro music, but in the case of the Blues they are carried several degrees further. When these songs are performed with accompaniment, the players fill in these waits by improvising the weirdest and most heart-rending groans and sobs, whimpers and sighs, emphasizing, at the same time, the stumbling rhythm. Extraordinary combinations of instruments serve to provide these accompaniments: organ and cornet, mouth organ and guitar, saxophone and piano; sometimes a typical Negro jazz band—and by this I do not mean the Negro jazz band of the white cabaret—is utilized by a phonograph company to make a record. Many of these men do not read music at all. Many of these songs have never been written down.

Notwithstanding the fact that the musical interest, the melodic content of these songs is often of an extremely high quality, I would say that in this respect the Blues seldom quite equal the Spirituals. The words, however, in beauty and imaginative significance, far transcend in their crude poetic importance the words of the religious songs. They are eloquent with rich idioms, metaphoric phrases, and striking word combinations. The Blues, for the most part, are the disconsolate wails of deceived lovers and cast-off mistresses, whose desertion arouses the desolate one to tell his sad story in flowery language. Another cause has contributed to the inspiration of symbolic poetry in these numbers. Negroes, especially in the South, indulge in a great deal of what they themselves call "window dressing," in order to mislead their white employers. This is the reason for the prevalent belief in the South that Negroes are always happy, for they usually make it a point to meet a white man with a smile and often with a joke. It is through this habit of window dressing that the Negroes have grown accustomed to expressing their most commonplace thoughts in a special tongue of their own. For example, a Negro boy who intends to quit his job surreptitiously sings to his colored companions: "If you don't believe I'm leavin', count the days

I'm gone." A favorite phrase to express complete freedom has it: "I've got the world in a jug, the stopper's in my hand."

The Blues bulge with such happy phrases: "The blacker the berry, the sweeter the juice," referring to the preference yellow girls frequently bestow on extremely black men, or the contrasting refrain, which recurs in a score of these songs, "I don't want no high yella." Other picturesque locutions are: "I've put ashes in my papa's bed so that he can't slip out," "Hurry sundown, let tomorrow come," "Blacker than midnight, teeth like flags o'truce."

Certain refrains, for a perfectly logical reason, recur again and again in these songs. For instance, "I went down to the river":

> I went down to the river, underneath the willow tree.
> A dew dropped from the willow leaf, and rolled right down on me.
> An' that's the reason I got those weepin' willow blues.

or

> Goin' to the river, take my rockin' chair.
> Goin' to the river, take my rockin' chair.
> If the blues overcome me, I'll rock on away from here.

or

> Goin' to the river, I mean to sit down.
> Goin' to the river, I mean to sit down.
> If the blue-blues push me, I'll jump over and drown.

So many of the papas and mamas depart on trains that the railroad figures frequently in the Blues:

> Got the railroad blues; ain't got no railroad fare.
> Got the railroad blues; ain't got no railroad fare.
> I'm gonna pack mah grip an' beat my way away from here.

or

> Goin' to the railroad, put mah head on the track.
> Goin' to the railroad, put mah head on the track.
> If I see a train a-comin', I'll jerk it back.

or

> I went up on the mountain, high as a gal can stan',
> An' looked down on the engine that took away mah lovin' man.
> An' that's the reason I got those weepin' willow blues.

There are many Blues which are interesting throughout as specimens of the naïve poetry, related in a way it would be difficult to define, but which it is not hard to sense, with oriental imagery of the type of "The Song of Songs." Such a one is that which begins:

A brown-skinned woman an' she's chocolate to the bone.
A brown-skinned woman an' she smells like toilet soap.

A typical example of this class of song is "The Gulf Coast Blues," which also happens to possess a high degree of musical interest which, unfortunately, I cannot reproduce here. However, as sung by Bessie Smith and played by Clarence Williams, it is perfectly possible to try it on your phonograph.

I been blue all day.
My man's gone away.
He went an' left his mama cold
For another girl, I'm told.
I tried to treat him fine,
I thought he would be mine,
That man I hate to lose,
That's why mama's got the blues.

The man I love he has done lef' this town.
The man I love he has done lef' this town.
An' if he keeps on goin', I will be Gulf Coast boun'.
The mailman passed but he didn't leave no news.
The mailman passed but he didn't leave no news.
I'll tell the world he lef' me with those Gulf Coast Blues.
Some o' yo' men sure do make me tired.
Some o' yo' men sure do make me tired.
You got a handful o' gimme an' a mouthful o' much oblige.

In connection with this depressing lament, Langston Hughes, the young Negro poet, has written me:

The Blues always impressed me as being very sad, sadder even than the Spirituals, because their sadness is not softened with tears, but hardened with laughter, the absurd, incongruous laughter of a sadness without even a god to appeal to. In "The Gulf Coast Blues" one can feel the cold northern snows, the memory of the melancholy mists of the Louisiana lowlands, the shack that is home, the worthless lovers with hands full o' gimme, mouths full o' much oblige, the eternal unsatisfied longings.

There seems to be a monotonous melancholy, an animal sadness, running through all Negro jazz that is almost terrible at times. I remember hearing a native jazz-band playing in the Kameroon in Africa while two black youths stamped and circled about a dance hall floor, their feet doing exactly the same figures over and over to the monotonous rhythm, their bodies turning and swaying like puppets on strings. While two black boys, half-grinning mouths never closed, went round the room, the horns cried and moaned in monotonous weariness— like the weariness of the world— moving always in the same circle, while the drums kept up a deep-voiced laughter

for the dancing feet. The performance put a damper on the evening's fun. It just
wasn't enjoyable. The sailors left . . .

Did you ever hear this verse of the Blues?

> I went to the gipsy's to get mah fortune tol'.
> I went to the gipsy's to get mah fortune tol'.
> Gispy done tol' me Goddam yore un-hard-lucky soul.

I first heard it from George, a Kentucky colored boy who shipped out to Africa
with me—a real vagabond if there ever was one. He came on board five minutes
before sailing with no clothes—nothing except the shirt and pants he had on and a
pair of silk socks carefully wrapped up in his shirt pocket. He didn't even know
where the ship was going. He used to make up his own Blues—verses as absurd as
Krazy Kat and as funny. But sometimes when he had to do more work than he
thought necessary for a happy living, or, when broke, he couldn't make the damsels
of the West Coast believe love worth more than money, he used to sing about the
gipsy who couldn't find words strong enough to tell about the troubles in his hard-
luck soul.

The first Blues to achieve wide popularity was "The Memphis Blues," by
W.C. Handy, who lived at that time in Memphis, and was well-acquainted
with life on the celebrated Beale Street. For this song—published in 1912, a
year after "Alexander's Ragtime Band"—Mr. Handy received a total of one
hundred dollars. Since then he has issued so many of these songs, "The St.
Louis Blues," "Hesitation Blues," "John Henry Blues," "Basement Blues,"
"Harlem Blues," "Sundown Blues," "Atlanta Blues," "Beale Street Blues,"
"Yellow Dog Blues," etc., that, taking also into account that he was the first
to publish a song of this character, he is generally known as the father of the
Blues. Nevertheless, Mr. Handy himself has informed me categorically that
the Blues are folksongs, a statement I have more than fully proved through
personal experience. To a greater degree than other folksongs, however,
they have gone through several stages of development. Originally, many of
these songs are made up by Negroes in the country to suitably commemorate
some catastrophe. As one of these improvised songs drifts from cabin to
cabin, verses are added, so that not infrequently as many as a hundred different stanzas exist of one song alone. Presently, these ditties are carried
into the Negro dives and cabarets of the southern cities, where they are served
up with improvised accompaniments and where a certain obscene piquancy
is added to the words. Many of the Blues, as a matter of fact, are casual
inventions, never committed to paper, of pianist and singer in some house
of pleasure. This does not mean that composers and lyric writers have not
occasionally created Blues of their own. For the most part, however, the
Blues that are sung by Negro artists in cabarets and for the phonograph are
transcribed versions of folksongs. Even with such Blues as are definitely
composed by recognized writers, it will be found that their success depends

upon a careful following of the folk formula both in regard to words and music.

So far as Mr. Handy's own Blues are concerned, he admits frankly that they are based almost without exception on folksongs which he had picked up in the South. Occasionally he has followed the idea of an old Blues; more frequently he has retained a title or a melody and altered the words to suit Broadway or Harlem's Lenox Avenue. For example, the tune of "Aunt Hagar's Blues"—Aunt Hagar's Children is the name the Negroes gave themselves during slave days—is founded on a melody he once heard a Negro woman sing in the South to the words, "I wonder whar's mah good ol' used to be." The "Joe Turner Blues" is based on the melody of an old Memphis song, "Joe Turner Come an' Got Mah Man an' Gone." Pete Turney at the time was governor of Tennessee. His brother, Joe, was delegated to take prisoners from Memphis to the penitentiary at Nashville, and the Negroes pronounced his name Turner. Mr. Handy has utilized the old melody and the title, but he has invented the harmonies and substituted words which would have more meaning to casual hearers.

Another of Handy's songs, "Loveless Love," is based on an old Blues called "Careless Love," invented by the Negroes to tell the story of the son of a governor of Kentucky, shot in a love affair. Handy's "Long Gone" is based on an old Negro song called "Long John, Long Gone." The story runs that with the arrival of some new bloodhounds on a plantation it was decided to experiment with them on Long John. Getting wind of this unpleasant prospect, the Negro supplied himself with a trap which he dragged behind himself in a barrel. Inveigling the bloodhounds into the trap, Long John escaped into the woods and was never caught. Hence the song, "Long John, Long Gone," which soon spread from shack to shack.

Long familiar with the words and tunes of such songs, the possibility of harmonizing them and treating them instrumentally came to Mr. Handy early in the present century. On tour with his band, he was playing for a white dance at Cleveland, Mississippi, when, during an intermission, three local Negroes appeared, and asked if they might perform a number. Permission was granted and the men, mandolin, guitar, and viola, began to play a mournful, wailing strain, the strain of the Blues. Nowadays such accompaniments to Blues are improvised in dimly lit cellars while you wait.

So far as I know there has been as yet no effort made—such as has been made with the Spirituals—to set down these songs, verses and music, as they are sung under primitive conditions. To me this is a source of the greatest amazement. Any Negro recently from the South knows at least half a dozen of them. I myself have heard as many as fifty in Lenox Avenue dives and elsewhere that have never been put down in any form. They are not only an essential part of Negro folklore but also they contain a wealth of eerie melody, borne along by a savage, recalcitrant rhythm. They deserve, therefore, from every point of view, the same serious attention that has tardily been awarded to the Spirituals.

Miss [Dorothy] Scarborough's book [*On the Trail of Negro Folksongs* (Cambridge: Harvard University Press, 1925)] in many respects covers the same ground as the Odum-Johnson volume [*The Negro and His Songs*]. In the circumstances, it is surprising that there is so little actual duplication of material. In one way, at least, this volume is superior to the other, that is, in its inclusion in numerous instances of the melodies of the songs reproduced, it would appear, from phonograph records. Miss Scarborough entirely neglects the Spirituals, feeling no doubt that they have received sufficient attention from other hands. In compensation she offers as songs under several more or less novel headings—lullabies, dance songs and reels, children's game songs (the latter mostly of white origin, although a great deal has been added by the juvenile Negro collaborators) and, more particularly, the Blues.

The Blues, a branch of folk music in which the Negro expresses his love emotions, as in the Spirituals he expresses his religious emotions, have hitherto been comparatively disregarded—unjustly, because they are often quite as interesting as the sorrow songs—by both music lovers and serious students of the folksong. I hope this neglect is temporary and artificial, as it will soon be too late to record them in anything like their original form. Miss Scarborough complains that the advance of the radio and the phonograph into unsophisticated territory is already working havoc with the folksongs. Negroes find it agreeable and simple to turn the latest popular ballads into songs of their own, which are tending to supplant the traditional music of the race. At the same time, composers are finding it convenient to transform the traditional Blues into popular songs.

Miss Scarborough's book . . . is immensely important in adding to our knowledge of the great variety of this material and of its aesthetic and ethnological value, but it seems to me that the final word on this subject must be spoken by a Negro. It is utterly impossible for any white man, even an educated Negro occasionally finds himself at a loss, consistently to comprehend the ignorant Negro's point of view, and it is to the ignorant Negro that we are indebted for these songs.

Mr. James Weldon Johnson, who has been a pioneer in several other fields, was the first, I think, to point out the fact that the Blues might just as reasonably as the Spirituals be called folksong. His argument is to be found in his preface to *The Book of American Negro Poetry*, issued in 1922, ten years after Mr. W.C. Handy had arranged his "Mr. Crump" for world consumption under the new title of "The Memphis Blues." Mr. Johnson's statement that a wealth of melody and folk verse might be discovered in the more vicious circles of Negro life was not permitted to pass unchallenged. The late H.E. Krehbiel, always the bitter opponent of ragtime and jazz, was stirred to furious invective by the spectacle of a Negro writer invoking the holy word *folksong* to describe tunes which had been taken down from the lips of harlots and the frequenters of low dives. He wrote nearly half a page in the *New York Tribune* to protest against what he considered the ultimate obscenity. Mr. Johnson replied to this jeremiad with a calm but curiously ironic letter, in which he refused to be moved one inch from his original position.

It might be of interest to note in passing that a correspondent has recently sent me an example of the Spiritual conceived in the Blues form. It is known as "The Gospel Blues":

Ef you wants to heah de ole Debbil howl,
Ef you wants to heah de ole Debbil howl,
Jes' wipe yo' teahs on duh Gospel towel.

If you wants to see de ole Debbil run,
Ef you wants to see de ole Debbil run,
Pull duh trigger o' duh Gospel gun.

Ef you wants to see duh Debbil shake in his shoes,
Ef you wants to see duh Debbil shake in his shoes,
Jes' sing a coupla verses o' duh Gospel Blues.

Come up, brethren, take mah han',
Come up, brethren, take mah han',
An' we'll march right into duh Gospel Lan'.

Lately ragtime and jazz have had many defenders—I believe that again Mr. Johnson was the first to point out the serious merits of this kind of music in his *The Autobiography of an Ex-Coloured Man* (1912), in which he predicted that popular music of this character would ultimately influence art music, thus foreseeing Mr. Gershwin's *Rhapsody in Blue* and Mr. Carpenter's *Krazy Kat*—and the social, work, and convict songs of the Negro have been awarded so much consideration that seemingly whole departments in certain universities are given over to collecting them and theorizing concerning them. The Blues, however, prior to the appearance of the book the Bonis [Albert and Charles] have just published [*Blues*, 1926], have had, aside from Mr. Johnson, but two serious advocates, Miss Dorothy Scarborough and myself. Nevertheless, the publication of the extremely attractive volume edited by Mr. Handy would seem to indicate that mean ole Miss Blues is fairly on her way to making an entrance into the company of the respectable family of collected folksong.

On several occasions I have stated in print my belief that these moans of primitive Negro lovers far transcend the Spirituals in their poetic values, while as music they are frequently of at least equal importance. There has been, however, so little effort made to study them in their natural habitat that any discussion of them remains even today largely in the realm of the conjectural. Certain facts, nevertheless, are at one's disposal. The form itself (three lines of verse, which limit the musician to twelve bars instead of the more conventional sixteen) and the name only grew up among Negroes early in the present century. The accompaniments which Mr. Handy has devised—lacking, of course, in pure folksong—were inspired by extemporary performances typical of a southern Negro band. American white composers have taken over the "Blues note," together with certain tricks of the musical form such as the "breaks," but they have so far been unanimous in their neglect of the twelve-bar formula, which is perhaps the most characteristic quality of true Blues. Although, like all of us, Mr. Abbe Niles, in his preface, has been obliged to resort to theory, nearly every statement he makes is plausible, although I might find fault with his clandestine and tortuous manner of saying it.

He places due emphasis on the matter of the folk Blues, but few musical examples are offered to the reader. For the most part the volume consists of reprints of arrangements made by W.C. Handy who, indubitably, gave the form and the name their currency. It may be noted, however, that Mr. Handy has very largely employed folk tunes, folk harmonies—originally improvised—and that his lines are usually elaborate mosaics of typical Negro imagery. Most of Mr. Handy's celebrated Blues—I miss the "Memphis Blues," to which, it is stated, its present publisher refused to relinquish his rights, and the "Basement Blues"—are included, and there are excellent examples by other Negroes, particularly effective numbers being those signed by Spencer Williams and N.E. Reed and Ethel Neal. Clarence Williams, inexplicably, is not represented.

I do not know what the average musician—untrained in this tradition—will make of these Blues. Mr. Niles suggests that the would-be performer study the phonograph records. This procedure, it seems to me, will only serve to confuse him, even though it tends to make him more appreciative of the rich and melancholy beauty of these moans. If, for example, he listens, score in hand, to Miss Clara Smith's extraordinary rendering of Mr. Handy's "Basement Blues," he will realize that Miss Smith sings more of her own notes than she does of Mr. Handy's, that she varies the accent to suit her mood, and that the accompaniment set down is hardly observed at all. Highly characteristic, all this, of the performance of this type of music, but scarcely calculated to give the amateur practical lessons in delivery. The fact of the

matter is that Blues are well-nigh unplayable save by instinctive Negro performers—it is worthy of note that Mr. Handy himself is a mediocre interpreter
of Blues—and that the names of their effective singers can almost be num-
bered on the fingers of one hand.

Mr. Niles asserts that they can best be rendered by Negro contraltos. I
would almost say that this is exclusively true, although an occasional Negro
tenor may satisfy the critical ear. I would go further and state that a Negro
contralto with Italian vocal traditions at her beck and call—Miss Marian
Anderson, for instance—would find herself at a complete loss. The Blues,
therefore, largely remain the property of the three great Smiths, Bessie,
Clara and Mamie, each of whom, by the way, has her own individual
method.

This volume of Blues, however, should have a decidedly stimulating effect.
It will, perhaps, encourage many who have not yet done so, to hear these
great singers who are as remarkable in their way as any other music hall
singers in the world, or, if that is found to be impracticable—the Smiths,
not sisters, by the way, appear exclusively in Negro theatres and in those,
for the most part, in the South; furthermore, they do not invariably sing
Blues—to listen to the remarkable records they have made. It would seem
incredible to me that anybody with any feeling—musical or otherwise—
could listen to Bessie Smith's recording of "The Weeping Willow Blues," or
Clara Smith's of "Nobody Knows duh Way Ah Feel dis Mornin'," without
becoming a convert. Further, the preface and the arrangement of the musical
numbers in the volume offer an excellent, although necessarily truncated,
survey of the subject, beginning with crude folksong and working up to an
excerpt from the middle movement of George Gershwin's *Concerto in F*,
avowedly founded on the Blues formula. Moreover, I think this volume
may inspire other Negro musicians to set down as many as possible of these
crude complaints in the form in which they were originally heard.

To the format of the book I can offer nothing but praise. The dustwrapper,
the cover, and the illustrations are by Miguel Covarrubias, an artist for
whose work I cherish the highest admiration and for whom, therefore, I
find it difficult to summon up more glowing superlatives than those I have
already employed. I may perhaps express my concrete opinion by stating
succinctly that in his drawings for this volume, Covarrubias has transcended
all his previous work. It may be said of him, indeed, that no other painter,
living or dead, has depicted the American Negro—it must be remembered
that up to date this Mexican's work has almost entirely concerned itself with
cabaret or Lenox Avenue types—with the imagination and fidelity to spirit
to be observed in his drawings. If, for example, you will examine the drawing of the trapdrummer, or that of the jazz band, which is employed as
frontispiece to this volume, or that of Miss Bessie Smith performing Blues
in a cabaret, you will find you can not only *see* these people, you can also
hear them.

Two similar pieces discussed the black artist's reluctance to either develop or exploit his unique racial qualities and the dangers inherent in making "a free gift" of them—Van Vechten used the phrase in both—to white artists. "Moanin' Wid a Sword in Mah Han'" appeared in *Vanity Fair* in February 1926, just at the time Van Vechten was completing his Harlem novel, *Nigger Heaven*. The following month, in his contribution to a *Crisis* symposium, he averred that such material would be exploited "until not a drop of vitality" remained. A few months later, when his novel was published, the irony of these observations must have struck readers as either apt or cruel, depending on their reactions to *Nigger Heaven*.

Between "Moanin' Wid a Sword in Mah Han'" and "The Negro in Art: How Shall He Be Portrayed?" I have placed Carl Van Vechten's "Uncle Tom's Mansion," an extended review of one of the most significant volumes of the Harlem Renaissance, *The New Negro*, edited by Alain Locke and containing contributions by virtually every black writer of the period. The review appeared in *New York Herald Tribune Books*, 20 December 1925. Locke had hoped to engage Van Vechten to write the introductory essay on "The Negro and American Art." At that time, however, Van Vechten was committed to his articles for *Vanity Fair*.

For *Crisis*, the publication of the National Association for the Advancement of Colored People, Carl Van Vechten prepared a questionnaire entitled "The Negro In Art: How Shall He Be Portrayed?" It was sent out to a number of "the artists of the world," both black and white, with a covering letter written by Van Vechten but signed by the black novelist Jessie Fauset, literary editor at *Crisis*.

Van Vechten's response was the first one printed, in the March 1926 issue, along with those of H.L. Mencken, white editor of *The American Mercury*, Du Bose Heyward, white author of *Porgy*, and Mary White Ovington, white humanitarian who was instrumental in establishing the NAACP. Subsequent issues of *Crisis*, through September 1926, included responses from black writers Langston Hughes, Walter White, Countée Cullen, Jessie Fauset, and Georgia Douglas Johnson, and white writers John Farrar, Vachel Lindsay, Sinclair Lewis, and Sherwood Anderson, among others.

Given the sensational aspects of *Nigger Heaven* and the controversy it aroused among black readers, Van Vechten's conclusion carries a not undisturbing irony. The novel was published less than six months later and, indeed, he had less than a week's work remaining on the final draft of his novel when the letter and questionnaire were distributed. The first two questions strongly suggest something of his own apprehension; the seventh anticipates the accusations of Nancy Cunard, Benjamin Brawley, and others, who felt Van Vechten's *Nigger Heaven* encouraged the worst rather than the best of efforts among young black writers who followed him.

"MOANIN' WID A SWORD IN MAH HAN'"

Recently I attended a song recital given by a Negro baritone. The program announced that he would sing songs in six languages, and I believe that he actually did so, but his enunciation was so imperfect that it was difficult enough to catch the words even when he sang in English. That he was the possessor of a beautiful voice and at least a superficial knowledge of the essential style of some of the music he delivered there was no gainsaying, although, ironically enough, this knowledge of style completely deserted him when he attempted a group of Negro Spirituals.

On the whole the concert left me cold, as, I am forced to conclude by their lack of enthusiasm, it left the remainder of the sparse audience cold. There was, to be sure, perfunctory applause, but we, who sat in the orchestra chairs, were not moved to make any excessive demonstration of spontaneous appreciation. The fact is, that the singer was no better and no worse than a dozen other singers who are patiently listened to by their friends and a few apathetic critics every month during the season.

After the concert I went home, drew on a dressing gown and a pair of comfortable slippers, and sat down to meditate. Theoretically, there appeared to be no reason why a Negro should refrain from offering a conventional recital program. Roland Hayes has made a successful specialty of such a program. But, reflection informed me, Roland Hayes is the exception. He is not only an unusually gifted artist, but he was the first Negro to attempt such a program before a wide audience. He is therefore something of a novelty.

To be frank, however, most of us are tired of song recitals. Several years ago, indeed, I wrote a paper called "Cordite for Concerts," in which I figuratively blew them up. Any impresario can tell you that 90 percent of the song recitals that are given in New York today are given at a loss to the performer before an audience of deadheads. No one, as a matter of fact, who proffers a conventional, classic program, save an exceptional genius, a Chaliapin, a Roland Hayes, can fill a hall today without punching holes in the tickets.

Curiously enough, did he but seize it, the opportunity lies in the hands of the Negro to wrest a conspicuous success out of this general apathy. It is sufficient cause for amazement, under the circumstances, that he has been so tardy in doing so. Within the past few years the fame of the Negro folk music, long relished by the few, has spread around the world. The Negro

Spirituals are admired everywhere they are known; book after book devoted to them has tumbled from the presses, culminating in that superb collection, *The Book of American Negro Spirituals*, arranged by J. Rosamond Johnson and James Weldon Johnson, with some assistance from Lawrence Brown. The world is aching to hear these Spirituals authoritatively sung, authentically performed, but with rare exceptions, the Negro himself is making comparatively little effort to satisfy this longing.

The Fisk Singers, to be sure, since 1871, have regarded the dissemination of these tunes almost in the light of a sacred obligation, but it was not until May 1925 that Paul Robeson, with the assistance of Lawrence Brown, gave what was probably the first song recital devoted entirely to Negro music, with a success that is a matter of record. Paul Robeson is a great artist. I say great advisedly, for to hear him sing Negro music is an experience allied to hearing Chaliapin sing Russian folk songs. In November, another pair of Spiritual singers gladdened the ears of New Yorkers: Taylor Gordon, whose evangelical performances of these rich and beautiful melodies, rendered in his brilliant tenor voice, with Rosamond Johnson playing his own versions of the harmonies at the piano, was received with a degree of enthusiasm that fell just short of rapture.

Two Negro couples then are giving concerts of Negro folksongs before audiences which pack the theatres to the doors whenever they appear, but the rest of the Negro world remains silent in this respect, at least in relation to the great public. As a matter of fact, no one but Negroes, as I have often before remarked in print, can give satisfactory renderings of these songs, but that will not deter white men, who have a nose that senses demand, from making the attempt. It is a foregone conclusion that with the craving to hear these songs that is known to exist on the part of the public, it will not be long before white singers have taken them over and made them enough their own so that the public will be surfeited sooner or later with opportunities to enjoy them, and—when the Negro tardily offers to sing them in public—it will perhaps be too late to stir the interest which now lies latent in the breast of every music lover.

This is the epitome of what has happened in the case of the Negro in other directions. It is generally regarded as an incontrovertible fact that ragtime and the later jazz grew out of Negro folk music. Many of the early songs were practically literal transcriptions of tunes and words popular on the Mississippi levees. But, as James Weldon Johnson has pointed out in his preface to *The Book of American Negro Poetry*, it was not long before the white man discovered that words dealing with white people might be fitted to these infectious rhythms, and soon Irving Berlin, and later George Gershwin—to name the two most conspicuous figures in a long list—were writing better jazz than the Negro composers.

The Negro is an original and highly gifted dancer. Every small community indulges in its folk dances which every child in the community knows. The Negro's most recent addition to the joy of living is the Charleston. Where the Charleston came from, apparently nobody knows; it is comparatively safe to state that it did not come from the city in South Carolina. Whatever its origin it quickly settled in the cabarets of Harlem, spread like wildfire through the streets of that quarter—there have been times when children might be observed performing it on nearly every corner—and finally, in *Runnin' Wild*, captured the town. All the purveyors of white revues borrowed it, and today you cannot go to any theatre where there is dancing without seeing it. Now, as any one knows who has sat through a Negro musical show, no one else can compete with a Negro in the intricate steps and loose-jointed movements of this dance, and yet the fact remains that if you were asked to mention one colored professional woman who was especially proficient in it, you would be unable to do so. Everybody knows that Ann Pennington and Adele Astaire can Charleston brilliantly, but not one woman of the Negro race has had the energy and foresight to achieve a great name for herself through a particularly telling performance, although at least two men, Eddie Rector and Bill Robinson, have added to their own glory and the glory of the Negro by their prowess in this direction.

Every professional white dancing teacher in New York is engaged in imparting this dance—or such a version of it as he has been able to acquire—but when several friends of mine asked me to find them a Negro teacher, it took me a week to dig one up, although I made assiduous inquiry.

A director of a prominent phonograph company informed me that he dared not permit his Blues singers to appear in white theatres or even to mingle with the more sophisticated members of their own race. "A few such contacts," he said, "and they won't sing Blues any more; they prefer white ballads. We've lost several excellent Blues singers this way."

Now the Negro has made no greater offering to the enjoyment of civilized mankind than the Blues. Yet I have never heard one of these songs—I am speaking of the real folk Blues—in a white theatre or even in a Negro revue intended for white audiences. It is almost impossible for a white man to persuade a real Blues singer to sing Blues even in a cabaret.

The Negro consistently freely delivers his best material to the white man in the matter of painting—Miguel Covarrubias and Weinold Reiss are the best known modern painters of the Negro, although I must admit that a young black man named Aaron Douglas will bear watching—and literature. There has been, in fact, a determined protest on the part of the Negro against the exploitation in fiction of his picturesque life. This distaste is largely based on the fact that white writers about the Negro have chosen to depict the squalor and vice of Negro life rather than its intellectual and cultural aspects. This proclivity is likely, however, to be permanent, for the low-life of Negroes offers a wealth of exotic and novel material while the life of the cultured Negro does not differ in essentials from the life of the cultured white man.

Until recently, in fact, the Negro writer has made a free gift of this exceptionally good copy—one should except Paul Laurence Dunbar and Charles W. Chesnutt from this indictment—to the white author. Lately, however, a new school of colored writers, of which the best known and the most gifted are probably Rudolph Fisher, Jean Toomer, and Langston Hughes—the talents of Countee Cullen, Walter White, and Jessie Fauset have been exercised in other directions—have perceived the advantage of writing about squalid Negro life from the inside. In the carrying out of this laudable ambition, it may be added, they have not met with much encouragement from the Negro public.

When the white author, who reasonably enough makes use of any good material he discovers, attempts to deal with this milieu, he is more than frowned upon. In a recent issue of the *Crisis*, one of the most influential of Negro periodicals, I read a criticism by Emmett J. Scott, Jr., of Haldane MacFall's novel, *The Wooings of Jezebel Pettifer*, in which the reviewer asserted, "A book less appealing to a coloured man would be hard to find." For purposes of disparagement Mr. Scott quotes my dictum to the effect that this is "probably the best book yet written about the Negro." It is quite true that I made this recommendation, but when I made it I was thinking of *Jezebel* as a work of art. It is certainly written with more skill and inspiration than any other novel about the Negro that I have read. Whether or not it presents an accurate picture of Negro life in the Barbadoes I have no means of knowing: I have never been in the Barbadoes. I do know, however, that it presents a credible picture, that the characters and scenes arouse my imagination.

There exists, it would appear, an explicable tendency on the part of the Negro to be sensitive concerning all that is written about him, particularly by a white man, to regard even the fiction in which he plays a role in the light of propaganda. Mr. Scott seems to be suffering from this prevalent sensitiveness. This will probably do no hurt to a work which has been as generally admired as *Jezebel*, but it is an attitude of mind which may be utterly destructive when it is applied to the writings of Negroes themselves. It is the kind of thing, indeed, which might be effective in preventing many excellent colored writers from speaking any truth which might be considered unpleasant. There are plenty of unpleasant truths to be spoken about any race. The true artist speaks out fearlessly. The critic judges the artistic result; nor should he be concerned with anything else.

I do not believe it was Mr. MacFall's intention to be unpleasant. Nevertheless, apparently because the author of *Jezebel* writes of "slipshod Negresses" and "slattern gossips"—the heroine of the novel is a prostitute—Mr. Scott conveniently dubs him a Negro hater, as if there were no "slipshod

Negresses." (Mr. MacFall was surely unaware of the unreasonable prejudice existing against the use of this feminine substantive. I myself, who can scarcely be called a "Negro hater," have often employed it, because all its synonyms are exceedingly clumsy.)

It would be quite as just, after reading that powerful novel, *The Fire in the Flint*, to call Mr. Walter White a white-man hater, but I am sure no good critic would think of doing so. Until novels about Negroes, by either white or colored writers, are regarded as dispassionately from the aesthetic stand-point as books about Chinese mandarins, I see little hope ahead for the new school of Negro authors. What, for example, will become of one of the most promising of the lot, Mr. Rudolph Fisher, if he be attacked from this angle? . . .

It will be recalled that Synge's poetic comedy, *The Playboy of the Western World*, was hissed in Dublin because the author, himself an Irishman, asked a character to refer to the heroine as appearing in her shift. This was con-strued as a direct insult to Irish womanhood. This attitude may always be expected from the uncultured mob. When it is detected in a book review in a serious magazine it may, however, be regarded with alarm. I am convinced, as a matter of fact, that such an attitude does more harm to a race in the eyes of its ready detractors than any amount of ridicule—and I persist hotly that *Jezebel* was never intended as ridicule—aimed from without.

The matter reduces itself to this, that the Negro is sensitive, justifiably so, regarding his past, and in facing the world wants to put on a new front. He is therefore inclined to conceal his beautiful Spirituals, his emotional Blues, to make too little of his original dances, to write, when he is an author, about an environment far removed from the sordid but fantastic existence of Lenox Avenue. Thus he readily delivers his great gifts to the exploitation of the white man without—save in rare instances—making any attempt, an attempt foredoomed to meet with success, to capitalize them himself. It is significant, however, that the great Negroes almost invariably climb to fame with material which is the heritage of their race. Perhaps even in the case of Roland Hayes it may be discovered that more people attend his concerts to hear him sing Spirituals than to hear him sing Schubert *lieder*.

UNCLE TOM'S MANSION

New York is celebrated for its transitory crazes. For whole seasons its mood is dominated by one popular figure or another, or by a racial influence. We have had Jeritza winters, Chaliapin winters, jazz winters, Russian winters, Spanish winters. During the current season, indubitably, the Negro is in the ascendency. Harlem cabarets are more popular than ever. Everybody is trying to dance the Charleston or to sing Spirituals, and volumes of arrangements of these folksongs drop from the press faster than one can keep count of them. At least four important white fiction writers have published novels dealing with the Negro this fall, while several novels and books of poems by colored writers are announced. Florence Mills, Bill Robinson, Taylor Gordon, Paul Robeson, Roland Hayes, and Ethel Waters are all successful on the stage or concert platform. *The New Negro* [Albert and Charles Boni, 1925] should serve as the most practical guidebook to those who are interested in this popular movement.

This is, indeed, a remarkable book. I am not certain but, so far as its effect on the general reader is concerned, it will prove to be the most remarkable book that has yet appeared on the Negro. Alain Locke, the editor, has done a superb job. Basing his material on the Negro number of the *Survey Graphic*, he has expanded here, cut down there, substituted in the third instance. He has put not merely the best foot of the new Negro forward; he has put *all* his feet forward. Herein is included, in fact, work by every young American Negro who has achieved distinction or fame in the literary world—Rudolph Fisher, Walter White, Jessie Fauset, Eric Walrond, Claude McKay, Counteé Cullen, Langston Hughes, Jean Toomer, and many others are represented. There are also contributions from the pens of a few of the older men, James Weldon Johnson, W.E.B. Du Bois, and William Stanley Braithwaite. Several excellent reasons might be adduced to justify the inclusion of James Weldon Johnson's poem, "The Creation." Not only is it a fine poem, but also it was the poem that broke the chains of dialect which bound Paul Laurence Dunbar and freed the younger generation from this dangerous restraint.

I think the fiction and poetry in this volume will amaze those who are cognizant only in a vague sort of way of what Negro youth is doing. Rudolph Fisher's "The City of Refuge," which appeared in the *Atlantic Monthly* for February 1925, is, I am convinced, the finest short story yet written by a man of Negro blood, except Pushkin, and Pushkin, save in one instance, did not write stories dealing with Negroes. It is, moreover, an ironical story, a fact perhaps worthy of note, considering that Dr. Fisher is the only American Negro storyteller I know who has employed this device save Charles W. Chesnutt, a writer only too little known, especially among Negroes, who has not published a book for twenty years. *The Wife of His Youth* is an extraordinary collection of short stories. I gape with astonishment when I recall that it was published in 1899. It is no wonder that it fell flat, especially among Negroes, for Negroes are no lovers of irony. They do not, for the most part, even comprehend it and are likely to read literalness where it is not intended.

Negro sensitiveness and fear of ridicule, justifiable enough, God knows, in the circumstances, have driven many a Negro writer into literary subterfuge. Mr. Locke's reference in his preface to "the gradual recovery from hyper-sensitiveness and 'touchy' nerves" is both a little optimistic and a little

premature. Dr. Fisher, however, has had the courage to treat his subject
with the same objectivity that he might if he were dealing with Australians
or Hindus. It is not likely that his work, for some time to come, at least, will
be widely popular among members of his own race. I hope that any internal
pressure brought to bear upon him will not cause him to deviate from his
present splendid artistic purpose. It is a pity that Mr. Locke saw fit to include
Dr. Fisher's "Vestiges." Inferior work, this, and an anticlimax after "The City
of Refuge."

Eric Walrond is an uneven writer. A good deal of his work is actually
bad; some of it is passable and a little of it brilliant. "The Palm Porch," in
this collection, is by far the best story of his that I have read. It appeared
originally in the *New Age* and it is worthy of appearance anywhere. It is
perhaps more of a picture than a short story, but it is a picture vividly observed and set down in a coruscant and exotic style. I do not think it will be
readily forgotten by anyone who reads it.

Of Jean Toomer's work it is unnecessary to speak at length. The character
studies included in this anthology were selected from *Cane*, and they are
well chosen. Mr. Braithwaite, justifiably, describes *Cane* as "a book of gold
and bronze, of dusk and flame, of ecstasy and pain." Zora Neale Hurston is
more or less of a newcomer. She has published comparatively little. The
story in this volume, "Spunk," won the second prize in the 1925 short story
contest instituted by *Opportunity* magazine. Miss Hurston may be highly
commended for her intimate knowledge of dialect and for her expert use of
free and natural dialogue, but her work is still somewhat diffuse in form. I
think, however, that "Spunk" is far superior to Mr. Matheus's "The Fog,"
which won the first prize in the same contest.

Countée Cullen and Langston Hughes are the youngest and the best of the
contemporary Negro poets. Both have sprung into prominence within the
last year. Both are already famous. *Harper's* recently issued Mr. Cullen's
Color, and Alfred A. Knopf will presently publish Mr. Hughes's *The Weary
Blues*. I do not think either of these young poets is here represented by his
best work, but the level is sufficiently high, in both instances, to offer a
taste of their fine talents.

If I were to attempt to discuss adequately the points raised in the various
articles in *The New Negro* I could fill an entire number of *"Books."* The
opportunities for controversy are endless. I must perforce content myself
with reference to a few of the more prominent papers. "The Negro in American
Literature," by William Stanley Braithwaite, presents in a few pages an able
survey of the range of American Negro literature from the time of Phillis
Wheatley to the contemporary hour. I agree with Mr. Braithwaite's judg-
ments in almost every respect; I would say that he lays exactly the proper
emphasis where it belongs. I am especially pleased that he deals so justly
with the work of Charles W. Chesnutt, a writer, I repeat, who, in spite of

his faults, cannot much longer be neglected, especially by those Negroes who pretend to an interest in the striking literary figures of the race. He came, as Mr. Braithwaite explains, at the wrong time, when the world, white or black, was quite unwilling to accept a realistic representation of the Negro, more especially an ironic realism. There was a demand for the conventional comic or sentimental darkey. It was the day of Paul Laurence Dunbar.

On one point, however, I would take decided issue with Mr. Braithwaite. He repeats the old cliché that Negro novels must be written by Negroes. Now I have said repeatedly that the Negro writer should deal with Negro subjects. In the first place, generally speaking, he knows more about them. In the second place, the Negro world, in spite of a popular misconception to the contrary, is largely unexplored, and if the Negro writers don't utilize the wealth of material at their fingertips, white writers, naturally, will be only too eager to exploit it.

And there is no reason why the white writer should not be successful in this experiment. The difference between the races, as a matter of fact, is largely a matter of an emotional psychology, created on either side by the social barrier. Nearly all the idiosyncratic reactions of the Negro are caused by an extreme sensitiveness, nearly all the reactions of the white man by an excessive self-consciousness, an almost pathetic attempt to do what is decent, so often construed by the alien race as condescension or patronage. Negroes among themselves, I am inclined to believe, behave and react very much as white people, *of the same class*, behave and react among themselves. In this connection it is well to remember that colored owners of human property in slavery days were among the most cruel masters.

If a white writer is cognizant of these facts I see no reason why he should not undertake to write a Negro novel. Charles W. Chesnutt wrote his novels from the white point of view, and if they are not wholly successful that is not the reason. He understood the point of view well enough. No one has informed the world that Lafcadio Hearn was impertinent when he wrote about the Japanese or Marmaduke Pickthall when he wrote about the Arabs.

I confess I was somewhat startled to discover that Mr. Locke had chosen Miss Jessie Fauset to write an article about the Negro theatre. If I had been the editor of *The New Negro* I am certain that she would have been about the last person I should have considered for the job. Not that Miss Fauset is lacking in literary talent, rather because I have never thought of her in connection with the theatre. My pleasure, perhaps, was doubled in reading her article by the realization that Mr. Locke had been wise in selecting her to write it. It is an extremely stimulating article; ideas spring out of every line. What she has to say is originally expressed and delightfully phrased. On the whole, I think it is the best discussion of the Negro in the theatre with which I am familiar.

With Miss Fauset, too, however, I must interpose a couple of objections. She states that Bert Williams became melancholy because he was constrained by the nature of his race to remain a clown. Here she overlooks a very general condition. All comedians are sad in private life. Is Miss Fauset familiar, I wonder, with the well-known anecdote concerning Grimaldi? Does she know anything about the personality of Charles Spencer Chaplin? It was not because of his color that Bert Williams was constrained to be funny; no such obstacle has beset the way of that fine actor, Paul Robeson. The fact is that so few authentic clowns are born into the world that when one comes along no manager will consent to his appearance in other than farcical situations.

Miss Fauset states truly, "There is an unwritten law in America that though white may imitate black, black, even when superlatively capable, must never imitate white," and suggestively, referring to the wide range of colors among Negroes, she pleads for a brown Othello, a yellow Butterfly, a near white Hamlet. There is certainly no cogent excuse to offer for the state of a theatre which makes this sort of thing difficult of accomplishment. On one or two occasions it has actually happened. I remember Evelyn Preer's Salome very vividly to this day. The Negro writer, however, has as yet been very feebly represented in the drama; most of the successful colored plays have been written by white men. I should hate to see Negro acting talent turned in this conventional direction, therefore, until the play-writing and histrionic talents of the race have been more fully exploited in actual racial fields. There will never be a true Negro theatre until it is founded on racial heritage. When we have that, by all means let Negroes play anything they please; before we have that I regard it as a mistaken aim to experiment with *The School for Scandal.*

Mr. Locke's paper on the Spirituals is rhapsodic and critical rather than historical. I think he is a little too condescending in his attitude toward the folk poetry of these songs. In this respect, indubitably, they are not on an equal plane with the Blues, themselves far inferior as music. Nevertheless, it would be hard to find folk poetry with deeper feeling or more imaginative imagery than that which exists in some of the Spirituals. He pleads for choral arrangements of the Spirituals after the manner of the arrangements Russian musicians have made of the Russian folksongs, forgetting that the Russian folksong is sung as melody, while the Spirituals, although probably created as melody, so soon fell into harmonic form that they are scarcely ever sung in any other fashion in that quarter of the country where they were born. I applaud his desire to hear these elaborate choral arrangements, but there will be time enough for that after a few of them are taken down in the authentic manner in which they are at present performed in the South. So far as I know, only quartet versions—and those usually after the singing of college men—have been set down. It is well to remember that a large Negro chorus sings in many more than four parts.

There is an unaccountable omission of the name of J. Rosamond Johnson. I suppose that *The Book of American Negro Spirituals* was not yet off the press when Mr. Locke wrote this article (it is listed in the bibliography), but this is not the first work that Mr. Johnson had accomplished in connection with the Spirituals. As for *The Book of American Negro Spirituals*, I should say that it has already done more to popularize these songs, not only with the great public, but also with musicians and critics, than the work of any other ten men. It is not technical books like H.E. Krehbiel's *Afro-American Folksongs* (a very faulty work, moreover, hastily thrown together from casual newspaper articles) or Ballanta-Taylor's pedantic *Saint Helena Island Spirituals* that interest the musician—unless he be actively engaged in arranging versions of the Spirituals—it is the real thing in practical form, just as the true musician is much more interested in the scores of Mozart's operas than he is in thematic guides to them. I have seen more copies of Mr. Johnson's book on the piano racks of my musical friends during the last two weeks than I have seen of Mr. Krehbiel's book in libraries since the day in 1914 when it first appeared.

Mr. Locke supplies three other interesting and provocative contributions. In his preface he paints a brilliant picture of the general intellectual attitude of the new literary figures, contradictory at that, for the New Negro does very little group thinking. "If it ever was warrantable," Mr. Locke very sensibly says, "to regard and treat the Negro *en masse*, it is becoming with every day less possible, more unjust and more ridiculous." In another paper Mr. Locke discusses at length the subject of African primitive sculpture.

But little space remains to devote to the many other excellent papers in this volume. I should like, however, to touch on a few. James Weldon Johnson offers a picture of the growth of the new Harlem, with its economic and cultural achievements and possibilities. Dr. Du Bois is represented by a scholarly account of the American Negro's point of view in regard to the French, German, Belgian, and English colonies in Africa. He points out bitterly that, while the slave trade has ended, these governments find it equally advantageous to exploit their natives in their own land. The condition remains. Elsie Johnson McDougald tells what it means to be a colored woman in the modern business and professional worlds. Walter White describes the psychology arising from race prejudice. He also goes beneath the surface and drags out the fact that this prejudice creates certain internal disagreements among the Negroes themselves. Charles S. Johnson explains why Negroes leave the South: "Enoch Scott was living in Hollywood, Miss., when the white physician and one of the Negro leaders disputed a small account. The Negro was shot three times in the back and his head battered— all this in front of the high sheriff's office. Enoch says he left because the doctor might some time take a dislike to him." He fills several pages with such incidents.

J.A. Rogers's article about jazz is disappointing and occasionally inaccurate.

He has comparatively little to say about the Harlem cabarets—surely among the most interesting features of the Negro's new Mecca—and there should be a great deal more to write about W. C. Handy, the "father of the Blues," Clarence Williams, and other popular composers, but I don't suppose it would be possible to do justice to all sides of the new Negro in one volume.

The bibliography, by no means complete, but certainly the most complete bibliography of the subject available, was compiled by Arthur B. Schomburg, Arthur H. Fauset, and Alain Locke. The volume is bountifully illustrated with reproductions of paintings, many in color, by Winold Reiss, Miguel Covarrubias, and Aaron Douglas, the last a Negro.

THE NEGRO IN ART: HOW SHALL HE BE PORTRAYED?: A QUESTIONNAIRE

We have asked the artists of the world these questions:
1. When the artist, black or white, portrays Negro characters is he under any obligations or limitations as to the sort of character he will portray?
2. Can any author be criticized for painting the worst or the best characters of a group?
3. Can publishers be criticized for refusing to handle novels that portray Negroes of education and accomplishment, on the ground that these characters are no different from white folk and therefore not interesting?
4. What are Negroes to do when they are continually painted at their worst and judged by the public as they are painted?
5. Does the situation of the educated Negro in America with its pathos, humiliation, and tragedy call for artistic treatment at least as sincere and sympathetic as *Porgy* received?
6. Is not the continual portrayal of the sordid, foolish, and criminal among Negroes convincing the world that this and this alone is really and essentially Negroid, and preventing white artists from knowing any other types and preventing black artists from daring to paint them?
7. Is there not a real danger that young colored writers will be tempted to follow the popular trend in portraying Negro characters in the underworld rather than seeking to paint the truth about themselves and their own social class?

THE NEGRO IN ART: HOW SHALL HE BE PORTRAYED?: A SYMPOSIUM

I am fully aware of the reasons why Negroes are sensitive in regard to fiction which attempts to picture the lower strata of the race. The point is that this is an attitude completely inimical to art. It has caused, sometimes quite unconsciously, more than one Negro of my acquaintance, to refrain from using valuable material. Thank God, it has not yet harmed Rudolph Fisher! But the other point I raise is just as important. Plenty of colored folk deplore the fact that Fisher has written stories like "Ringtail" and "High Yaller." If a white man had written them he would be called a Negro hater. Now these stories would be just as good if a white man had written them— but the sensitive Negro—and heaven knows he has reason enough to feel sensitive—would see propaganda therein.

You speak of "this side of the Negro's life having been overdone." That is quite true and will doubtless continue to be true for some time, for a very excellent reason. The squalor of Negro life, the vice of Negro life, offer a wealth of novel, exotic, picturesque material to the artist. On the other hand, there is very little difference if any between the life of a wealthy or cultured Negro and that of a white man of the same class. The question is: Are Negro writers going to write about this exotic material while it is fresh or will they continue to make a free gift of it to white authors who will exploit it until not a drop of vitality remains?

Advertisement for *Nigger Heaven*, designed by Aaron Douglas
(Courtesy Alfred A. Knopf, Inc.)

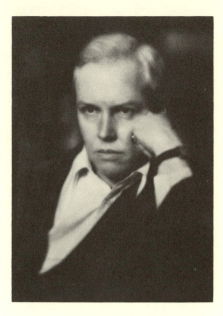

Carl Van Vechten during the
Harlem Renaissance,
photograph by E.O. Hoppé

Carl Van Vechten and James
Weldon Johnson, circa 1930
*(Courtesy Carl Van Vechten
Collection, Manuscript and
Archives Division, New York
Public Library)*

A'Lelia Walker, 1926 *(Courtesy James Weldon Johnson Memorial Collection of Negro Arts and Letters, Yale University)*

Clara Smith, circa 1925 *(Courtesy James Weldon Johnson Memorial Collection of Negro Arts and Letters, Yale University)*

Carl Van Vechten, caricature by Miguel Covarrubias,
1926 *(Courtesy James Weldon Johnson Memorial
Collection of Negro Arts and Letters, Yale University)*

Bookplate for the James Weldon
Johnson Memorial Collection of
Negro Arts and Letters founded by
Carl Van Vechten

Entrance to Harriet Beecher Stowe's house in Cincinnati, Ohio, 1896, from a cyanotype by Carl Van Vechten *(Courtesy Carl Van Vechten Collection, Manuscript and Archives Division, New York Public Library)*

2

Nigger Heaven

With *Nigger Heaven,* Van Vechten hoped to secure a sympathetic audience for Negroes, but he was aware of the difficulties, despite his own sincerity. He asked his publisher to announce the novel well in advance "to prepare the mind not only of my own public, but of the new public which this book may possibly reach, particularly that public which lies outside of New York..., so that the kind of life I am writing about will not come as an actual shock."

Alfred Knopf's announcement appeared in more than one early *Borzoi Broadside* in 1926:

Carl Van Vechten's novels have assured him of a leading position, as a social artist. He has abandoned that field, completely if perhaps temporarily, to write a novel whose materials are more realistic and whose approach is direct and serious. In NIGGER HEAVEN, he analyzes the fascinating and inscrutable drama that takes place in the gallery of the vast theatre of New York—from which the white world below can be seen, but which it cannot see.

For various reasons the book was a success. Certainly the subject matter was inflammatory; certainly it caused the kind of controversy among critics guaranteed to publicize it; certainly Van Vechten already had a large popular audience on the basis of four earlier successful novels. Moreover, he had included in *Nigger Heaven*—a title bound to attract attention in Harlem—several thinly disguised portraits of celebrated or at least recognizable blacks of the period, in Harlem, at least, even if twenty-five years later he still publicly disavowed having written a *roman à clef.* The heroine, Van Vechten told me, was patterned after Dorothy Peterson, the beautiful West Indian girl who worked in the Harlem branch of the New York Public Library, and his hero, Byron Kasson, was based physically at least on Harold Jackman, one of the handsome Harlem boys—in this case a schoolteacher—he collected about him during the period. Van Vechten's black social arbiter, Adora Boniface, was obviously A'Lelia Walker, the daughter of Madame C.J. Walker, "Queen of the De-Kink," as Osbert Sitwell described her, whose fortune had been made from a hair-straightening process. Nora Holt, one of Van Vechten's closest friends, correctly identified herself as Lasca Sartoris, the voluptuous courtesan whose attractions destroy the hero of the novel. Many other identifications were made in a letter to Van Vechten from another friend— and one about whom Van Vechten wrote extensively elsewhere—James Weldon Johnson: Van Vechten's pretentious Hester Albright cruelly suggested the novelist Jessie Fauset. Edna Lewis, a Harlem socialite, Johnson believed was Piqua St. Paris, and A'Lelia Walker's secretary, Mame White, was Arabia Scribner. (Van Vechten never lost his old delight in inventing outrageous names for his characters; *Nigger Heaven's* cast only suffers by comparison with Zimbule O'Grady or Wintergreen Waterbury or Mrs. Alonzo W. Syreno, characters in other novels.) Johnson identified Montrose Esbon as a Harlem dandy named Jimmie Harris, and Russet Durwood —easily recognizable—as H.L. Mencken, editor of *The American Mercury.* Van Vechten himself appeared in the novel as Gareth Johns, a disguise he had assumed in two earlier novels as well. No one in particular served as model for Anatole Longfellow, the Scarlet Creeper, whose flashy appearance and flashier eroticism are recounted in the prologue to *Nigger Heaven,* although several sheiks would have welcomed the compliment.

The reviews were sharply divided. Most critics echoed white writer Louis Kronenberger who called the novel "a conspicuous achievement" and black writer Eric Walrond who called it "a frontier work of enduring order"; elsewhere, however, it was labeled as "vulgar," as "pure drivel," as "cheap French romance, colored light brown." Moreover, a surprising number of readers praised it or blamed it while at the same time misunderstanding Van Vechten's intention if not his accomplishment.

Probably the two most powerful figures in the Harlem Renaissance, James Weldon Johnson and W.E.B. Du Bois, best illustrate the extremes. In an extended essay in the journal of the National Urban League, Johnson called *Nigger Heaven* "the most revealing, significant and powerful novel based exclusively on Negro life yet written." Van Vechten the "satirist," he contended, had become Van Vechten the "realist":

In every line of the book he shows that he is serious. But however serious Van Vechten may be, he cannot be heavy. He does not moralize, he does not over-emphasize, there are no mock heroics, there are no martyrdoms. And, yet—Mr. Van Vechten would doubtless count this a defect—the book is packed full of propaganda. Every phase of the race question, from Jim Crow discriminations to miscegenation, is frankly discussed. Here the author's inside knowledge and insight are at times astonishing. . . . If the book has a thesis it is: Negroes are people; they have the same emotions, the same passions, the same shortcomings, the same aspirations, the same gradations of social strata as other people.[1]

Two months later, in *Crisis,* the publication of the National Association for the Advancement of Colored People, W.E.B. Du Bois countered on the basis of the superficiality of Van Vechten's "inside knowledge and insight." *Nigger Heaven* was "a caricature," he contended. "It is worse than untruth because it is a mass of half-truths." But the book's inaccuracies and exaggerations, as he judged them, disturbed Du Bois less than its pretensions as "a work of art":

Does it please? Does it entertain? Is it a good and human story? In my opinion it is not; and I am one who likes stories and I do not insist that they be written solely for my point of view. "Nigger Heaven" is to me an astonishing and wearisome hodgepodge of laboriously stated facts, quotations and expressions, illuminated here and there with something that comes near to being nothing but cheap melodrama. . . . Van Vechten is not the great artist who with remorseless scalpel probes the awful depths of life. To him there are no depths. It is the surface mud he slops about in.[2]

Both writers devoted considerable space to the title, which may explain why Johnson, in conclusion, urged people to read the book before discussing it. (Du Bois ended by advising people to burn it.) Plenty of black readers would not have opened a book called *Nigger Heaven*, certainly not one written by a white author. Langston Hughes, Walter White, and Wallace Thurman had warned Van Vechten against using it; James Weldon Johnson had suggested *Black Man's Heab'n* as an alternative. They had not misunderstood Van Vechten's intentions—"nigger heaven" was clearly explained in the narrative at least twice with sufficient irony as a name for the balcony where black audiences were forced to sit, and therefore the area of the city where they were forced to live—but the four black writers did understand the race's response to "nigger." Van Vechten's explanatory footnote early in the novel probably would not have helped had it appeared on the dust jacket:

While this informal epithet is freely used by Negroes among themselves, not only as a term of opprobrium, but also actually as a term of endearment, its employment by a white person is always fiercely resented.[3]

Early in the novel, indeed in the prologue reprinted in this anthology, a young prostitute "rapturously" calls Harlem "Nigger Heaven": "I jes' nacherly think dis heah is Nigger Heaven!" Later, however, Van Vechten's hero reacts very differently to the phrase:

Nigger Heaven! Byron moaned. Nigger Heaven! That's what Harlem is. We sit in our places in the gallery of this New York theatre and watch the white world sitting down below in the good seats in the orchestra. Occasionally they turn their faces up towards us, their hard, cruel faces, to laugh or sneer, but they never beckon. It never seems to occur to them that Nigger Heaven is crowded, that there isn't another seat, that something has to be done. It doesn't seem to occur to them either, he went on fiercely, that we sit above them, that we can drop things down on them and crush them, that we can swoop down from this Nigger Heaven and take their seats. No, they have no fear of that! Harlem! The Mecca of the New Negro! My God![4]

Van Vechten's father was disturbed by the title long before the novel was finished and urged him to change it: "If you are trying to help the race, as I am assured you are," he wrote, "I think every word you write should be a respectful one towards the black." In a subsequent letter he was firmer yet:

Some of your Negro friends agree with me. You are accustomed to "get away" with what you undertake to do; but do not *always* succeed; and my belief is that this will be another failure *if* you persist in your *"I shall use it nevertheless."* Whatever you feel compelled to say in the book, your present title will not be understood & I feel certain you should change it.[5]

The title alone, however, did not account for all of the offense taken. Most of the negative criticism came from reviewers who contended Van Vechten had only made use of the lurid aspects of Harlem life, enough to persuade black readers of the Twenties, already offended by the title, to ignore the book. A surprising number of present-day critics have dismissed *Nigger Heaven* for the same reason, and, it may be, without having read the novel themselves. Actually, two-thirds of *Nigger Heaven* is given over to the fairly bloodless affair between Mary and Byron, to sociological and aesthetic discussions among the black intelligentsia, and to Van Vechten's usual collection of catalogs of outré information and quotations; the remaining third does occur in bedchambers and Harlem nightclubs. Any reader familiar with Van Vechten's earlier novels—all four of them resolutely satirical, mannered, even frivolous—would have good reason to expect less of some pathetic little romance than of a steamy world of bolito kings and cabarets and elegant whores and Scarlet Creepers. Certainly its sensational elements helped *Nigger Heaven* to sell, but the same kind of elements had helped its predecessors to sell, too. The novel was either admired or dismissed, therefore, for several wrong reasons by many readers.

None of Van Vechten's friends seem to have misunderstood it, however, and he lost no friends because of it: Eric Walrond wrote him that the Harlem it described was "accurately, creditably, glamorously enshrined"; Alain Locke had not expected "so carefully serious and so unsatirical" a novel; Paul Robeson found it "amazing in its absolute understanding and deep sympathy"; Nella Larsen said it was "too close, too true, as if you had undressed the lot of us and turned on a strong light," and she admitted to jealousy that no black novelist had been brave enough to write it first; Charles W. Chesnutt, the first modern American black novelist, wrote of "its brilliancy and obvious honesty"; Charles W. Johnson found "no disconcerting factual jolts" and he thanked Van Vechten for his "honesty." When the *Pittsburgh Courier*, probably the most influential black newspaper outside New York, refused to run an advertisement for *Nigger Heaven*, Walter White promptly telegraphed, on behalf of the NAACP: a magnificent picture with amazing sympathy and understanding of the Negro point of view," and urged the editors to reconsider. Not only did the newspaper run the advertisement, it also carried a lengthy, sympathetic interview with Van Vechten shortly thereafter. All such rallying to his defense, however, did little to convince most black readers.[6]

Fifty years after its initial appearance, *Nigger Heaven* has finally received at least two fair evaluations. Nathan Huggins, in his *Harlem Renaissance,* pointed out its limitations but gave it a serious hearing. He concluded that it lacks "a clear moral or intellectual perspective" capable of seriously involving the reader: "Try as he might to illustrate that Negroes were much like other people, Van Vechten's belief in their essential primitivism makes him prove something else."[7] Van Vechten never denied his fascination with exoticism, of course, and plenty of evidence supports this. More recently, Mark Helbling, of the University of Hawaii, evaluated *Nigger Heaven* in the context of Van Vechten's other novels, arguing persuasively that it is "best understood not as his 'Negro novel' but as one of his novels that included people called Negroes."[8] The early novels, however, as Helbling rightly contended, were not "consciously didactic"; further, their moral or intellectual perspective, in Huggins's phrase, was also carried by the same sensational elements which helped them sell.

Published by Alfred A. Knopf, Inc., in August 1926, *Nigger Heaven* had a first printing of 16,000 copies and 205 tall paper copies; Knopf issued thirteen subsequent printings before turning the novel over to Grosset and Dunlap for a reprint edition. *Nigger Heaven* was published by Knopf in England in two separate editions; it was translated into Czech, Danish, Estonian, French, German, Hungarian, Italian, Norwegian, Polish, Swedish, and—by rumor at least—Russian; further, it was issued as a twenty-five-cent paperback by Avon Publishing Company in 1951 and apparently sold another 10,000 copies, at least on the basis of Van Vechten's royalties; Harper and Row issued it as a paperback in 1971, with W.E.B. Du Bois's review and passages about it from books by James Weldon Johnson, Langston Hughes, and Claude McKay; Octagon issued it in hard cover in 1972.

With the exception of the earliest translations, these various incarnations of *Nigger Heaven* derive from Knopf's seventh printing, the authorized version of the novel, which incorporates a number of song lyrics by Langston Hughes. Shortly after the novel was published, the American Society of Composers, Authors and Publishers threatened legal action for Van Vechten's having appropriated the words to a copyrighted song, "Shake That Thing." (He had innocently transcribed them from a phonograph record by Ethel Waters.) Hughes cheerfully agreed to the task of writing some line-for-line substitutions—not only for "Shake That Thing" but for several other songs as well, just to be safe—which avoided resetting the printer's plates or interrupting the steady flow of sales. A few of the lyrics appeared in the sixth printing, uncredited, to replace the offending song, the remainder appearing as well in the seventh printing. At the end of the book, replacing Knopf's colophon, Hughes was credited for the "songs and snatches of Blues" that he had "written especially for Nigger Heaven." To my knowledge, Hughes never collected these elsewhere, nor do they seem to be accounted for in his concordance, although they include one of his best-known phrases, indeed a familiar motto: "Harlem to duh bone!"

1. "Romance and Tragedy in Harlem," *Opportunity*, October 1926, p. 330.

2. "Books," *Crisis*, December 1926, p. 81.

3. Carl Van Vechten, *Nigger Heaven* (New York: Alfred A. Knopf, Inc., 1926), p. 26.

4. Ibid., p. 149.

5. Carl Van Vechten Collection, Manuscript Division, New York Public Library.

6. Ibid.

7. Nathan Huggins, *Harlem Renaissance* (New York: Oxford University Press, 1971), pp. 102-18.

8. "Carl Van Vechten and the Harlem Renaissance," *Negro American Literature Forum* (summer 1976), pp. 45-46.

A BELATED INTRODUCTION

"A Note by the Author," dated 21 October 1950, appeared in the Avon Publishing Company's paperback edition of *Nigger Heaven*. That version of the novel disappeared almost immediately—the title was still controversial in 1951, inspiring several letters of protest— and, with it, Van Vechten's reflections from the vantage point of a quarter of a century. Regrettably, the recent Harper Colophon Books' paperback edition, apparently designed as a text for students and scholars—it includes critical materials by W.E.B. Du Bois, Claude McKay, James Weldon Johnson, and Langston Hughes—did not reprint "A Note by the Author." Now another quarter of a century has passed; Van Vechten's naïveté regarding what he called the lack of psychological differences between races seems an oversimplification, and the "some of my best friends" attitude—however true it may have been in his case—seems superficial. His associations with blacks, however, were almost entirely limited to artists and entertainers and intellectuals. Further, the

cultural revolution of the late Sixties — a second Black
Renaissance given a black consciousness very different
from the black consciousness Van Vechten advocated
during the first — was still fifteen years away.

Carl Van Vechten called this essay "A Belated Introduction to Nigger Heaven." Avon retitled it and published
it as an afterword to the novel.

In his autobiography, *Along This Way*, the late James Weldon Johnson has this to say about the novel which precedes these notations: "The two books about Harlem that were most widely read and discussed (1926) were Carl Van Vechten's *Nigger Heaven* and Claude McKay's *Home to Harlem*. Mr. Van Vechten's novel ran through a score of editions, was published in most of the important foreign languages, and aroused something of a national controversy. For exactly opposite reasons, there were objections to the book by white and colored people. White objectors declared that the story was a Van Vechten fantasy; that they could not be expected to believe that there were intelligent well-to-do Negroes in Harlem who lived their lives on the cultural level he described, or a fast set that gave at least a very good imitation of life in sophisticated white circles. Negro objectors declared that the book was a libel on their race, that the dissolute life and characters depicted by the author were non-existent. Both classes of objectors were wrong, but their points of view can be understood.

"Negro readers of the book who knew anything knew that dissolute modes of life and dissolute characters existed in Harlem; their objections were really based on chagrin and resentment at the disclosures to a white public. Yet, Mr. McKay's book dealt with low levels of life, a lustier life, it is true, than the dissolute modes depicted by Mr. Van Vechten, but entirely unrelieved by any brighter lights; furthermore, Mr. McKay made no attempt to hold in check or disguise his abiding contempt for the Negro bourgeoisie and 'upper class.' Still, *Home to Harlem* met with no such criticism from Negroes as did *Nigger Heaven*. The lusty primitive life in *Home to Harlem* was based on truth, as were the dissolute modes of life in *Nigger Heaven*; but Mr. Van Vechten was the first well-known American novelist to include in a story a cultured Negro class without making it burlesque or without implying reservations and apologies.

"Most of the Negroes who condemned *Nigger Heaven* did not read it. They were stopped by the title. I don't think they would now be so sensitive about it; as the race progresses it will become less and less susceptible to hurts from such causes. From the first my belief has held that *Nigger Heaven* is a fine novel."

In conversation Mr. Johnson was still more explicit. He often said that the Negro race would never grow up until they ceased to be frightened by words, especially words they use freely in communication with one another.

Mr. Johnson first expressed the belief that *Nigger Heaven* is a fine novel in a review of the book, a most favorable review of the book, published in a Negro periodical called *Opportunity*, now defunct. Other important Negro writers who regarded the novel with favor when it first appeared were George S. Schuyler and Alice Dunbar Nelson, formerly the wife of Paul Laurence Dunbar. The white press was almost uniformly enthusiastic.

As a matter of fact, the plot of *Nigger Heaven* is one of the oldest stories in the world, the story of the Prodigal Son, without the happy ending of that biblical history. In my book a boy from a small town is bewitched, bothered, and bewildered by a big-time Lady of Pleasure and is unable to meet the demands made on his character by life in a big city. Paul Laurence Dunbar had previously employed this plot in a very bad novel called *The Sport of the Gods*, a title which fits *Nigger Heaven* like a glove, as Mrs. Nelson pointed out in her review of that book.

There have been those who have objected to the title. These objections have usually come from people who have not read the novel. The title is symbolic and ironic, even tragic. Before the book was published I had submitted the manuscript to two prominent Negro literary men, James Weldon Johnson and Rudolph Fisher, for their approval or disapproval and also to check up on errors. After it had passed this test successfully, it was submitted to the world.

What made the book important, what sold it in immense quantitites, what caused it to be translated into all European languages and even one Asiatic tongue, was the fact that it gave readers a microcosm of American Negro life and habits from the rich and intelligent figures at the top, to the exotic misfits at the lowest round of the ladder. And, as one reviewer sapiently pointed out, it is written about condescension. The story is related exactly as I would have written it if the characters had been white.

When I am asked how I happen to know so much about Negro character and Negro customs, I can answer proudly that many Negroes are my intimate friends. The Negro magazine *Ebony* once alluded to me as the white man who had more friends among colored people of distinction than any other white person in America. With a high degree of accuracy, I can still boast that many Negroes are still my friends.

I might state further that so far as psychology and behavior are considered in the book, Negroes are treated by me exactly as if I were depicting white characters, for the very excellent reason that I do not believe there is much psychological difference between the races. The local color was the local color to be found in Harlem in 1925. Dunbar's world of 1900 was obsolete. Even the scenes in my novel are laid in a different quarter of New York, an essential change due to the fact that Negroes had moved in the interim from one part of the city to another. Just as now in 1951, much that I discussed or pictured has also happily become obsolete.

One of the games frequently played by the public after the publication of a novel is the guessing game of the identity of the characters. In 1926, this was played with *Nigger Heaven* up to the hilt. All the characters of a novel naturally are imagined from the novelist's experience, but it should be stated sternly that any resemblance or fancied resemblance to living persons by the characters in *Nigger Heaven* is purely coincidental. A few of the characters may have possessed some of the superficial traits of persons then living, but unless an author takes his characters from books this would be true of any novel. I must repeat, however, that any fancied resemblances to be found in *Nigger Heaven* are purely accidental and coincidental. In the round the characters are imagined, and only exist in real life in certain aspects or attitudes. What is more important is that the book itself is true, at least *was* true, to actual existence in Harlem.

The rise of the Negro in this white world of ours we call the United States of America has been remarkably rapid since the days of slavery. During the past few years the pace of progress has accelerated, prodded on by new laws, new modes of thought in high places, but principally by dramatic achievements within the race itself. Segregation is being dealt severe blows from more vantage points than ever before. Negroes play tennis and baseball under the best auspices. The captain of the football team at Yale is a Negro. College fraternities invite Negroes to join their ranks and withdraw from the parent organization when protests arise. Even miscegenation is becoming more possible, and certainly it is becoming more popular. Meanwhile the list of internationally famous names grows. Few people alive are more celebrated or more loved than Marian Anderson, Joe Louis, Jackie Robinson, Ethel Waters, Richard Wright, or Ralph Bunche.

PROLOGUE

Because *Nigger Heaven* is generally available elsewhere, it is represented here only by the Prologue, but through its successive drafts, offering a unique opportunity to examine the manner in which an author — like painters and sculptors and composers — *makes* rather than *writes*. Van Vechten once said, "First drafts are already more than half the battle. They give me the form and most of the content. Everything else is either additional fact or embroidery. I love the embroidery." After a dozen leaves of notes, Van Vechten wrote the first draft of *Nigger Heaven* in six weeks; the second, adding about fifty pages, in two weeks; the third, adding another twenty pages, in three weeks — each commencing with the prologue. Its development may illustrate how serious a craftsman Carl Van Vechten was and, in this instance, how compassionate. A single example will suffice.

In a cabaret, the young prostitute Ruby voices her pleasure in Harlem: "I jes' nacherly think it Nigger Heaven." Van Vechten altered that to "I jes' nacherly think dis am Nigger Heaven!" A third version occurred in the galley proof: "I jes' nacherly think dis heah is Nigger Heaven!" From his own voice, to the dangerous interim voice of caricature, to Ruby herself. The detail is insignificant, perhaps, but telling.

Although elsewhere in this anthology I have altered punctuation, quotation marks, italics, spelling, and other stylistic devices to conform with conventional usage, I have not edited these drafts beyond correcting obvious typographical errors and beyond deleting typographical errors Van Vechten himself corrected. Van Vechten's inked holograph additions are inserted [*bracketed and printed in italics*] to approximate the location at which he wrote between lines or in his margins. Three sets of galley proofs contained various minor alterations, differing among themselves only in Van Vechten's indecision over "you" and "yo' ": from "you" in his third draft to "yo' " in his first galleys and back to "you" in the second ones. One set of galleys went to Bert Stern, a lawyer who read them for possible obscenity charges, questioning the implicit eroticism in Van Vechten's description of the dance and in the words to "Shake That Thing"; Van Vechten allowed them to stand, although elsewhere in the novel he followed Stern's advice to tone down the sexual encounters. The galley proofs for the Prologue, as corrected here, and for a section of Van Vechten's "Glossary of Negro Words and Phrases," correspond with the published version of *Nigger Heaven*.

FIRST DRAFT

First draught, started Nov. 3, 1925

Prologue

Anatole Longfellow, alias the Scarlet Creeper, sidled aimfully down the East side of Seventh Avenue. He was dressed in a tight fitting sheapher's plaid suit through which his great muscles bulged with the intended effect on all who gazed upon him, and all gazed. A diamond, or a stone which had that appearance glittered in his scarlet tie. His shoes were polished to a state which made them throw off golden gleams whenever the light from a street lamp touched them. Whenever he spoke to a friend which was often—all the street seemed to know him—his two rows of ~~yellow~~ [*pearly*] teeth gleamed from his seal-brown countenance. [*His hair was sleek under his grey derby.*]

It was the hour when promenading was popular—about eleven o'clock in the evening. The street was crowded; the shops were lighted. The air was warm, but balmy for June, not too humid. Over the broad street, up and down which taxicabs rushed, hung a canopy of indigo sky spangled with stars. Sloughing under the walls of the buildings, in front of show windows, groups of young men were congregated, talking and laughing. women, alone and in groups walked down the ample sidewalk. The street had the air of an Italian plaxa on a holiday.

Hello, Toly! A stalwart black man ~~stopped~~ [*accosted*] the ~~roller~~ [*creeper*].

Hello, Ed. How you been?

Rollin high'.

Number came out. Got sixty-seven bucks.

Holy Christ.

Yeh. Anatole's teeth gleamed.

What nummer?

Seven-Nine-Eight.

Where'd you get it?

Off'n a gal's fron' do'.

Comin' out?

Goin' in. I wen' out de back winder. Her daddy done cum home widout writin'.

You ain't sayin'!

I is indeed.

Anatole walked on with a still more self-satisfied expression. He unbuttoned his coat and exposed his much buttoned waiscoat. The Scarlet Creeper expanded his chest stretching to a dangerous limit the gold watchchain that was extended from pocket to pocket across his ~~musucualr~~ [*muscular*] belly.

Howdy!

Howdy!

He greeted Leanshanks Pescod, ~~who was~~ a coming lightweight. He had defeated two white comers in two succesive Saturday evenings at the Commonwealth Club.

You enjoyin' de air, Mr. Longfellow?

Indeed I is, Mrs. ~~Waddington~~ [*Guckeen*]. How you been?

My compliments, Mr. Longfellow, an' pretty well.

Mrs. ~~Waddington~~ [*Imogene Guckeen*] kept a beauty parlor farther up the street. Every afternoon at five o'clock Anatole came in for a manicure. As this habit of the Scarlet Creeper was well known trade increased around five. Mrs. Waddington was aware of her customer's drawing powers and never made onerous efforts to collect his always considerable bill. Occasionally Anatole would slip her five or ten dollars, with a chuck under the chin and a laugh.

At One hundred and Thirty-third Street Anatole suddenly turned about and faced North. His leisurely stroll began once more. Flipping and twisting his ebony cane with a ball of ivory at the top, ~~he began to grow~~ [assumed a] more businesslike [air], peering into the faces of the women he passed with almost an anxious expression. Once, so keen was he in his inspection of a face which offered him no encouragement in return, that he ran into an elderly black man with a long white beard, who limped supported by a cane. Anatole caught the stumbling old gentleman as he fell.

I most surtainly beg yo' pahdon, he added with his most enchanting smile.

The old gentleman smiled back. Peers to me, he squeaked, dat yo's most unnacherly perlite for dis street at dis hour.

The ~~sign~~ Scarlet Creeper's breast expanded a full two inches more which caused the watchchain, stretched to its capacity to drag a ring of jangling keys from his waistcoat pocket. Replacing the keys, the Creeper reflected that he could afford to be pleasant, even magnanimous to [a] harmless old gentleman. Was there another sheik in Harlem with his capacity for attracting the female sex? Was there another of whose muscles the brick ~~warmers~~ [pressers], with their ugly comments about passersby were more afraid? And as he was meditating in this wise, his pride was given a sudden jolt. In front of the Lafayette Theatre under the bright lights he discerned a pompous figure which caused a frown to obliterate the smile from his countenance.

Randolph Pettijohn, the Bolito King had come to Harlem a few years earlier as a hot-dog merchant. His little shop, hugged between two vast buildings, had shortly become famous. His dogs were good, his mustard and buns were fresh. In a short time, Pettijohn was doing such a trade at such slight expense that he found he had money to invest. He invested in real-estate which increased in value over night. [Soon] He opened a cabaret which became the most popular resort in Harlem. And now his Bolito game had made him so rich that he had become a powerful influence in politics. Anatole hated him, unreasoningly. He had never directly crossed the Creeper's path. Never stolen a girl from him, but somehow Anatole always felt the possibility of an occurrence of this king and he hated Randolph Pettijohn. The feeling was not reciprocated. Anatole had often been a spectacular figure in the Winter Palace, Pettijohn's cabaret. He greeted him now, warmly, if not affectionately.

How you been, Toly?

My compliments, Ran.

Out sportin'.

I'm takin' em in. The Creeper was reticent.

Yo' sairtainly are one flashy dresser, Creeper, one of the Bolito King's companions asserted.

~~The~~ Anatole's exposed his pearls.

Quit yo' kiddin'. [?]

No one like de Creeper foh close an' women, another chirped up.

The pearls almost gleamed with delight.

Come in an' see us, the Bolito King urged. My Winter Palace am open winter an' summer.

Still more at his ease, the Creeper strolled away, swinging his cane, expanding his chest, and humming to himself:

Mah man's got teeth like a lighthouse on de sea
An when he smiles he throws dem lights on me.

Howdy, Toly!

Toly was looking into the eyes of a high yellow boy, whose clothes were shiny and whose shoes showed signs of patching.

There was the mere suggestion of condescension in the Creeper's manner.

How you been, Duke?

Not so good, Toly. De show done went broke.

Dere'll be annudder.

Suh. How's I gwine live til den?

The Creeper volunteered no suggestions.

Yo' lookin' mighty lucky, Toly.

The Creeper remained silent.

[*Hush my mouff but*] I nebber did see no one had yo' gif' fo' dressin'.

The Creeper's breast came out a half inch or so.

I'se hungry, Toly. Gimme de price of a dog.

The creeper pulled a mass of loose change out of his pocket, with great deliberation chose a quarter from the pile, and handed it to his indigent friend.

Here yo' is, Duke. Now why ain't you git mo' provident?

I is, Toly, when I gits a chance. Tain't my fault duh show went broke. The boy ~~made a~~ put the quarter in his mouth and made a dash down a side street.

At the corner of One hundred and thirty-seventh Street a group of ~~boys~~ children were excercising their skill with the Charleston. Anatole stopped— he had been proceeded in this gesture by a number of others—to wtatch them. But as he watched his eyes strolled around the group of onlookers. ~~until he found what he had been looking for.~~

[*Suddenly they were arrested.*] She was a seal-brown and her skin was clear. She was as pretty a piece as he had seen around those parts for some time, and he had not happened to have seen her before. She wore a dress of coral silk over her (slender body. The short skirt exposed her (slender legs. A blue silk cloche partially covered her straight black hair. And her eyes looked at Toly and begged. ~~He~~ [*He withdrew his gaze at her but he was aware that she*] managed, without seeming to do so, without, indeed, seeming to look at ~~her~~ [*him*] at all to edge ~~him~~[*her*]self around by ~~her~~ [*his*] side, the while ~~his~~ [*her*] hands kept up the steady rhythmic clapping which assisted in accompanying the juvenile dancers. Once by ~~her~~ [*his*] side she made every pretence of being interested in nothing but the dancers. [*He paid no attention to her whatever.*]

Hello, Toly, she accosted him.

He turned, without smiling, and looked hard at her.

I don' seem to recollec' dat I got de honor o' yo' acquaintance.

You~~'~~ ain', Mr. Toly, an dat's a fac'. Ma name's ~~Ruth~~ [*Ruby*].

~~Ruth~~ [*Ruby*]?

Ruth Silver.

He was silent. Presently he began to clap his hands ~~again~~ [*for the dancers. A particularly agile lad of six was executing some pretty capers. Hey! Hey! Do dat thing!*]

Everybody knows who yo is, Mr. Toly. ~~Everybody.~~

The Creeper continued to clap.

I jes' been nacherly crazy to meet yo' all.

The Creeper was stern. Wha' fur? he shot out.

You know, Mr. Toly, I guess yo' know.

How much money yo' got?

O, I been lucky tonight. I met an ofay wanted change his luck. He gimme a tenner.

The Creeper appeared to meditate. I met a blue gal las' night who promised me fifteen.

I got another five in my lef' stockin'.

The Creeper became more affable. I do seem to remember yo' face, Miss Silver, he said. Will yo' do me de favo[*u*]r to take ma arm?

~~Winter Palace~~

As they walked down a side street his hand freely explored her body, warm and soft under the thin covering of coral silk.

Wanna dance? he said.

Luvvit, she replied.

Come across.

She stooped and fumbled in her stockings, first the right then the left. Presently she handed him two bills which he stuffed into a waistcoat pocket without examining them.

Winter Palace? she asked.

The nasty shadow flitted once more across Anatole's face.

Nah, he replied, too many ofays. Les go to Little's.

[*I ain' arnchy*]

A moment later they stood before two revolving red lights on Lenox Avenue and passed arm in arm down into the basement. As they approached the dance hall the sound of jazz, slow, wailing jazz struck their ears.

[*Charcoals, dinges, Shines an jigs. pink chaser.*]

Entering, the Creeper was warmly greeted by a group of ~~evening~~ waiters in evening clothes who stood near the door.

Why, Mr. Toly, how you been? You gwine sit at my table.

Anatole expanded his chest and looked down the room. Couples were dancing in such close proximity that their bodies tocuheched as they rocked to the sensuous blare of the brass, the barbaric beating of the drums. Across each woman's back, held tight against her shoulder blades, were the black hands of her partner.

Le~~t~~'s dance! Ruth suggested.

Le~~t~~'s sit down, Anatole countered, and he found an empty table. A waiter charlestoned towards him, holding a tray high over his head, a tray which twirled to the giddy rhythm.

A pint, Anatole hinted.

Presently the waiter came back with a bottle of transparent liquid, which he carried in his pocket. On the tray were two glasses with ice and two splits of ginger ale. He poured out the ginger ale. Anatole poured out the gin.

Tea fer two, he toasted his companion.

She drank her glassful at one swallow and then giggled, Toly, ~~I'm jujes' nacherly crazy 'bout yo'~~. [*Ah sure does luv you wid all ma haht.*]

The band was playing the second and last encore, Everybody loves my baby.

~~Ruth~~ [*Ruby*] began to sing. She rubbed his arm up an' down tenderly. Jes' once around, she begged.

[*Monkey chasers. Carry 'em I say earn em.*]

[*Ain' dis place dicty?*]

[*hefty wobble.*]

[*dance on their heels—use their knees*]

He humored her. Clutching her tightly against his lithe, taut body, he rocked her slowly around the room. ~~Ruth~~ [*Ruby*] shut her eyes. On all sides of the swaying couple bodies rocked, black bodies, brown bodies, high yellows, almost whites, a kaleidoscope of color, picturesque under the amber search light which shot from one corner of the room. The drummer threw his sticks in the air. The saxophone player drew a hat over the bowl of his instrument. Hugged tightly together the bodies rocked, rocked, closer and closer to the pulsateing rhythm. Occasionally the floor manager expostulated: Get off that dime!

Suddenly the music stopped. As if it h they had all been under some enchantment each couple stopped too. They looked dazed. Quiet. One woman let out a hysterical screech of pleasure. They all lumbered awkwardly towards their tables. Their bodies had lost the secret of the magic rhythm. There was no music. With the others, Anatole and Ruth left the floor and reseated themselves. He drew the bottle of gin from his hip pocket and poured out two more drinks.

Ruth again drained her tumblerful at one gulp. Again she caressed the arm of her partner. Again she sought his eyes out with her own.

I cert'nly does love you, daddy, she said. I certn'ly does love you.

Anatole grunted: ah.

Does yo' know what I calls dis? she went on rapturously.

Calls what?

Dis place, where I met you, all over: Harlem! Harlem! I calls it, spesherly tonight, Nigger Heaven! Nigger Heaven! I jes' nacherly think its [dis am] Nigger Heaven.

The Creeper took another sip out of his glass of gin. On the floor a tall yellow girl in a pink silk dress, sewed with bronze sequins in designs of flowers began to sing while she rocked back and forth:

My daddy rocks me with one steady roll.

[Dere ain't no stoppin when he once takes ahole hol'.]

SECOND DRAFT

[Nothin a-tall]

PROLOGUE

Anatole Longfellow, alias the Scarlet Creeper, strutted aimfully down the east side of Seventh Avenue. He wore a tight-fitting suit of shepherd's plaid through which his thoroughly revealed his lithe, sinewy figure to all who gazed upon him, and all gazed. A great diamond, or a stone less valuable stone which aped a diamond, glistened in his fuschia cravat. His boots were polished to a state which made them throw off golden gleams whenever they encountered the light from the street lamp. was entered. The uppers of these shoes were dove-coloured suède and the buttons were pale blue. His hair was sleek under his grey derby. When he saluted a friend which was often he seemed to know everybody [—a wide acquaintance—] his two rows of pearly teeth gleamed from his seal-brown countenance.

It was the hour when promenading was popular—about eleven o'clock in the evening. The air was warm, balmy for June, and not too humid. Over the broad avenue, up and down which multi-hued taxi-cabs plied, hung a
[Trees?]
canopy of indigo sky, spangled with bright stars. The shops, still open,
[dresses?]
were brilliantly illuminated. Slouching under the protecting walls of the

buildings, in front of show-windows, [or under the trees.] groups of young men congregated, talking and laughing. Women, in pairs, or with male escorts, strolled up and down the ample sidewalk.

Hello. 'Toly! A stalwart black man accosted the Creeper.

Hello, Ed. How you been?

~~Po'ly~~ Poo'ly, thank you. How you been?

No complaints. Number [1] came out. Got sixty-seven bucks.

Holy Christ.

Yeh. Anatole's teeth gleamed.

[The reader will find a glossary of all unusual Negro words and phrases employed in this novel at the end of the volume.

The reader unfamiliar with Negro words & phrases will find a glossary at the end of the novel.]

What nummer?

Seven-Nine-eight.

Where'd yo' found it?

Off'n a gal's fron' doo'.

Comin' out?

Goin' in. I went out duh back window. Her daddy done cum home widout writin'.

Hush mah mouff!

I doan mean mebbe.

~~Anatole walked~~

As Anatole walked on, the self-satisfaction on his countenance increased. Unbuttoning his coat, he expanded his chest, dangerously stretching the gold watch-chain which extended from pocket to pocket across his muscular belly.

Howdy.

Howdy.

He greeted in passing Leanshanks Pescod, a coming lightweight, who had defeated two white comers in two successive Saturday sessions at the Common-wealth Club.

Yo' enjoyin' de air, Mr. Longfellow?

Indeed ~~I~~ [Ah] is, Mrs. Guckeen. How you been? The Creeper's manner became slightly flirtatious.

My compliments, Mr. Longfellow, an' pretty well.

Mrs. Imogene Guckeen was the proprietor of a popular beauty parlour farther up the avenue. It was the invariable custom of Anatole to visit this parlour for a manicure every afternoon ~~at five~~ around five. As a wide circle of admiring women was cognizant of this habit, ~~trad~~ five was the rush hour at Mrs. Guckeen's establishment. She was fully aware of the part this customer played in this [irrational] influx ~~of trade~~ and ~~never~~, as a consequence, made no effort to collect his always considerable bill. Occasionally, moreover, the Creeper would slip her five or ten dollars on account, with a chuck under the chin and a devastating smile.

Turning about a One hundred and thirty-third [?] Street, Anatole faced North and renewed his leisurely stroll. Now, however, in spite of the apparently careless flipping and twisting of ~~the~~ his ebony cane, tipped with a ball of ivory, he assumed a more serious air, peering into the faces of the women he encountered with an expression that was almost anxious. Once, so keenly did he seek a pair of eyes which refused to return his stare, he bumped into an elderly black man with a long, white beard, who limped, supported by a cane. Old black Joe to the life! Anatole caught the senile fellow in time to prevent his falling.

I sartainly beg yo' pahdon, he implored with his most enchanting smile.

The octogenarian returned the smile. 'Pears to me, he squeaked, dat yo's mos' unnacherly perlite fur dis street at dis hour.

The Creeper's breast expanded a full two inches more, causing his watch[-]chain, stretched to capacity, to drag a ring of jangling keys from his waistcoat pocket. Replacing the keys, he reflected that he could afford to be pleasant, even magnanimous to a harmless old gentlemen. Was there another sheik in Harlem who possessed one-tenth his attraction for the female sex? Was there another of whose muscles the brick-pressers, ~~who were~~ ordinarily quite free with their audible unflattering comments about passersby, were more afraid? As he was meditating in this wise, his pride ~~was awarded~~ [*received*] a sudden jolt. Under the bright lights, in front of the Lafayette Theatre, he discerned a pompous figure whose presence obliterated the smug cheerfulness from his heart.

A few years earlier, Randolph Pettijohn had come to Harlem as a hot-dog merchant. His little one-storey shop hugged between two towering buildings, had rapidly achieved fame. His dogs were excellent; his buns were fresh; his mustard beyond reproach. In a short time, Pettijohn was doing such a trade with such slight overhead expense—he was his own cook and he personally served his customers over the counter—that he ~~found~~ he had [*saved a good deal of*] money ~~to invest.~~ He ~~put~~ [*invested*] his funds in real-estate which increased in value over-night. Then, with the proceeds of a few judicious sales, he opened a cabaret which shortly became the most popular resort in Harlem. Now, his Bolito game had made him so rich that his influence began to be powerfully exerted and felt in political circles.

Unreasoningly, Anatole hated him. He had never directly crossed the Creeper's path, never stolen a girl from him, but somehow, subconsciously, Anatole was aware that in the future such an act was by no means ~~an un-potentiality.~~ [*impossible.*] Besides, it irked the Creeper to realize that any one else had any power of whatever kind. ~~So~~ [*Therefore*] he hated the Bolito King. The feeling was not reciprocated. Anatole had frequently been a ~~pa~~ spectacular figure in the Winter Palace, Pettijohn's cabaret. He was known to be a particular favourite with jig-chasers from below the line. So the King greeted the Creeper warmly, even affectionately.

How you been, 'Toly?

Compliments, Ran.

Out sportin'?

[*Ah*]~~I~~'se takin' 'em in . The Creeper was reticent.

Yo' sartainly are one dressin' up fool, Creeper, one of the King's companions inserted.

Heavy lover too, another added.

~~Anatole exposed his pearls. Bottle it, he said.~~

The King offered his accolade: Nobody like duh Creeper for close an' women.

Anatole exposed his pearls. Bottle it, he said.

Come in an' see me, ~~the~~ Pettijohn invited. Mah Winter Palace am open winter an' summer.

Once more, completely at his ease, the Creeper strutted on, swinging his cane, expanding his chest, and humming to himself:

Mah man's got teeth ~~like~~ [*lak*] a lighthouse on duh sea,
An when he smiles he throws dem lights on me.

Howdy, 'Toly!

As ~~The Creeper~~ Anatole looked into the unwelcome eyes of a high yellow boy whose suit was shiny and whose boots showed signs of patching, ~~A~~ a suggestion of condescension crept into his manner.

How yo' been, Duke?

Not so good, 'Toly, De show done went broke.

Dere'll be annudder.

~~Suh~~ [*ho'*]. How's I gwine live till den?

The Creeper ~~made no profession of knowledge in this regard.~~ [*offered no advice.*]

Yo' lookin' mighty lucky, 'Toly.

The Creeper preserved his discreet silence.

I nebber did see no sheik what had yo' gif' for dressin'.

The Creeper's breast was the thermometer of the effect of this compliment.

~~I~~[*Ah*]'se hungry, 'Toly. Hones'. Gimme duh price of a dog.

The Creeper drew a mass of loose change from his trouser's pocket, with great deliberation selected a quarter from this heap and handed it to his indigent ~~frien~~ acquaintance.

Heah yo' is, Duke. . . He had the air of a munificent benefactor. . . Now why ain't yo' git mo' providen'?

I is, 'Toly, when I gits duh chance. T'aint mah fault duh show done went broke. The boy inserted the quarter in his mouth and made a sudden dash down a side street.

Han' full o' gimme, ~~mouth~~ mouff full o' much oblige, mused the Creeper.

At the corner of One Hundred and thirty-seventh [?] Street a crowd of urchins were executing the Charleston. They were surrounded by a numerous group of spectators, many of whom gave rhythm to the dancers by clapping their hands. Anatole, apparently carelessly, joined these pleasure-seekers, but as he did so, his eyes quickly shifted from the dancers and stole around the ring of onlookers. Suddenly, as if satisfied, they were arrested. She was a golden-brown and her skin was clear, as soft as velvet. As pretty a piece, he reflected, as he had seen around these parts for some time, and he had not happened to see her before. Her slender body was encased in coral silk, the short skirt exposing her trim legs in golden-brown stockings. A turquoise-blue cloche all but covered his [her] straight black shingled hair. Her eyes seemed to beg. Withdrawing his own gaze almost immediately, he was nevertheless aware that she was contriving without seeming to do so, without, indeed, seeming to look at him at all, to edge nearer to him. Never once, while she was carrying out this design, did her hands refrain from the rhythmic clapping which accompanied the juvenile dancers. When finally, she stood by his side, so close that he might of touched her, she continued to pretend that she was only interested in the intricate steps of the Charleston. Anatole, outwardly, gave no sign whatever that he was aware of her presence.

At last, losing patience or acquiring courage, she accosted him. Hello, 'Toly.

He turned, without a smile, and stared at her.

I doan seem to recerlec' dat I got duh honour o' yo' acquaintance.

Yo' ain', Mr. 'Toly, an' dat's a fac'. Mah name's Ruby.

He did not encourage her to go on.

Ruby Silver, she completed.

He remained silent. Presently he began to clap his hands for the dancers. A particularly agile lad of six was executing some pretty capers. Hey! Hey! Do that thing!

Everybody knows who yo am, Mr.! 'Toly, Everybody. Her voice was pleading.

The Creeper continued to clap.

I been jes' nacherly crazy to meet yo' all.

The Creeper was stern. Wha' fu[e]r? he shot out.

You' know[s], Mr. 'Toly, I guess yo' know[s].

How much yo' got?

O, I been full o' luck tonight. I met an ofay wanted change his luck. He gimmer a tenner.

The Creeper appeared to meditate. I met a gal las' night dat offer me fif-teen, he countered. Nevertheless, it could be seen that he was weakening.

I got annuder five in mah lef' stockin', [an' Ah'll show lovin' such as yo' never seen.]

The Creeper became more affable. I [Ah] do seem to remember yo' face, Miss Silver, he averred. Will yo' do me duh favour to cling to mah arm.

As they strolled, their bodies touching, down a dark side street, his hand freely explored her body, warm and soft under the thin covering of coral silk.

Wanna dance? he demanded.

Luvvit, she replied.

Come across.

She stooped and fumbled in her stockings, first the right, then the left. Presently she handed him two bills which he stuffed into his waistcoat pocket without examining them.

Winter Palace? she inquired.

A nasty shadow flitted across Anatole's face.

Nah, he replied, too many ofays ~~and~~ an' jig-chasers.

Bowie Wilcox's is dicty.

Too many monks.

Atlantic City Joe's?

Too many pink-chasers and bulldiguers.

Where den?

~~Spiffen's.~~ [*Duh Black Venus*]

A moment later they were swallowed by an entrance on Lenox Avenue, flanked by two revolving red lights. Arm in arm, they descended the steps to the basement. As they walked down the long hallway to the dance-floor, the blare of jazz, slow, wailing jazz, ~~smote~~ [*stroked*] their ears. At the door the Creeper was greeted with enthusiasm by three waiters in evening clothes.

Why, good evenin', Mr. 'Toly, Yo~~u~~' gwine sit at mah table?

Anatole expanded his chest and gazed down the length of the hall. The amber lights gave the skin of the dancers a rich colour. Couples were dancing in such close proximity that their bodies melted together as they swayed and rocked to the sensuous brass harmonies, the barbaric beating of the drum. Across each woman's back, clasped tight against her shoulder blades were laid flat the black hands of her partner. Blues, smokes, dinges, chocolate browns, shines, and jigs. The high yellows looked white under the amber light.

Le's dance, Ruby urged.

Le's set down, Anatole countered. He waved his hand to a friend as a waiter guided him to an empty table.

Hello, 'Toly!

Hello, Licey!

A pint, the Creeper commanded.

The waiter charlestoned down the floor, twirling his tray [*on palm high over head*] to the intoxicating rhythm.

Put ashes in sweet papa's bed so as he can't slip out, moaned Licey in the Creeper's ear. [*Ah knows a lady what'll be singin Wonder whah mah easy rider's gone!*]

Bottle it!

Licey chuckled. Hush mah mouff ef ~~I~~ ah don't!

The waiter came back, like a cat, tacking from one side of the room to the other, making his way through the throng of dancers. Charleston! Charleston! Do that thing! Oh, boy! ~~So's your ole man or what have you?~~

On the waiter's tray were two glasses, two splits of ginger ale and a bowl of ice. In his hip pocket a flask of a transparent liquid. He poured out the ginger ale. Anatole poured out the gin.

Tea fu[e]r two, he toasted his companion, almost jovially.

She gulped her glassful at one swallow, and then giggled, 'Toly, you'se mah daddy, an' Ah suh [ho'] does love yo' wid all mah h'aht.

The band was playing the second and last encore: Everybody loves mah baby . . .

But mah baby doan love nobody but me, Ruby chimed in. She ~~rubbed~~ touched his arm, stroked it tenderly. Jes' once 'round, she pleaded.

He humoured her. Clutching her tightly against his taut body, he rocked her slowly around the hall. Their heels rubbed the floor. Their knees clicked. On all sides of the swaying couple, bodies rocked, black bodies, brown bodies, high yellows, a kaleidescope of colour in picturesque costumes, under the amber search light which shot from one corner of the room. Scarves of bottle green, amethyst, chrysoprase, ~~scarlet,~~ crimson, lemon. The drummer in abandon tossed his sticks in the air. The saxophone player drew a delipidated derby over the bowl of his instrument. [*smothering the din*]

[*Music took ~~him~~ back to days when he worked as a boot Black in a barber-shop in the south.*]

[*hyena laughter.*]

[*toots & snorts & whistles*]

[*The banjos plunked deliriously.*]

Hugged closely together, the bodies rocked and swayed, rocked and swayed. Sometimes a rolling-eyed couple would scarcely move from one spot, caught in ~~the~~ a whirlpool of aching sound. Then the floor-manager would cry: Git offen dat dime!

Quite suddenly the musis stopped and instantly the saxophone player ~~replaced~~ [*substituted ~~for~~ a black cigar for*] the tube of his instrument. ~~with a black cigar.~~ As if they ~~were~~ [*had*] all recovered ~~suddenly~~ from some enchantment the dancing couples broke apart, dazed, and lumbered towards their tables. One woman let out a hysterical screech. There was no music and their bodies had lost the secret of the magic rhythm. With the others, Anatole and Ruby sidled off the space reserved for dancing and resumed their seats. Laughing and chatting Negroes at every table. Normal illumination. Another mood. The Creeper extracted the flask of gin from his hippocket and poured out two more drinks.

Ruby again drained her portion at one gulp. This time she had repudiated the ginger ale. Again she caressed the arm of her companion. Again she sought his eyes out with her own. Soft eyes he had, brown soft eyes, like a doe's.

Ah sartainly does love yo', mah daddy, she said. Ah sartainly does love yo'.

The Creeper grunted his approval.

Does yo' know what I calls dis? she continued rapturously.

Calls what?

Dis place, where I met yo': Harlem! Harlem! I calls it, specherly tonight, I calls it Nigger Heaven! I jes' nacherly think dis am Nigger Heaven!

The Creeper sipped his gin. On the floor a scrawny yellow girl in pink silk, embroidered with bronze sequins in designs of flowers, began to sing:

Mah daddy rocks me with one steady roll;
Dere ain't no slippin' when he once takes hol' . . .

THIRD DRAFT

PROLOGUE

[Footnote on next page]

Anatole Longfellow, alias the Scarlet Creeper, strutted aimfully down the east side of Seventh Avenue. He wore a tight-fitting suit of shepherd's plaid which thoroughly revealed his lithe, sinewy figure to all who gazed upon him, and all gazed. A great diamond, or some less valuable stone which aped a diamond, glistened on his ~~fuschia~~ fuchsia cravat. ~~His boots were polished to a state which enabled them to throw off golden gleams whenever they~~ encountered ~~a ray of light from a street lamp~~. The uppers of ~~these~~ [*his highly polished tan*] boots were dove-coloured suède and the buttons were pale blue. His black hair was sleek under his ~~grey derby~~ [*straw hat*], set at a jaunty angle. When he saluted a friend—and his acquaintanceship seemed to be wide—two rows of pearly teeth gleamed from his seal-brown countenance.

It was the hour when promenading was popular—about eleven o'clock ~~at~~ in the evening. The air was warm, balmy for June, and not too humid. Over the broad avenue, up and down which multi-hued taxi-cabs rolled, hung a canopy of indigo sky, spangled with bright stars. The shops, still open, were brilliantly illuminated. Slouching under the protecting walls of the buildings, in front of show-windows, or under the trees, groups of young men congregated, ~~talking~~ chattering and laughing. Women, in pairs, or with male escorts, strolled up and down the ~~ample~~ [*broad ample*] sidewalk.

Hello, 'Toly! A stalwart black man accosted the Creeper.

Hello, Ed. How <u>you</u> been?

Poo'ly, thank you. How <u>you</u> been?

No complaints. Nummer come out. ~~Got~~ [*Drew*] sixty-seven bucks.

Holy Christ [Kerist]!

Yeh. Anatole displayed his teeth.

What nummer?

Seven-Nine-Eight.

Whah yo' found et?

Off'n a gal's fron' doo'.

Comin' out?

Goin' in. I went out duh back winder. Her daddy done come home widout writin'.

Hush mah mouf!

Ah doan mean mebbe.

As Anatole walked on, his self [esteem flowered.] satisfied expression increased. Unbuttoning his coat, he expanded his chest, dangerously stretching the gold watch-chain which extended from pocket to pocket across his muscular belly.

Howdy.

Howdy.

He greeted in passing Leanshanks Pescod, a mulatto lightweight, who, had in two successive Saturday sessions at the Commonwealth Club, had defeated two white comers.

Is yo' enjoyin' duh [de] air, Mr. Longfellow?

'Deed, Ah is, Mrs. Guckeen. How yo' been? The Creeper's manner became slightly flirtatious.

My compliments, Mr. Longfellow, an' pretty well.

Mrs. Imogene Guckeen was the proprietor of a popular beauty parlour further up the avenue. It was Anatole's invariable custom to indulge in a manicure at this parlour every afternoon around five. As a wide circle of admiring women was cognizant of this habit, five was the rush hour at Mrs. Guckeen's establishment. She was fully aware of the important rôle this customer played in her affairs and, as a consequence, made no effort to collect his always considerable bill. Occasionally, moreover, the Creeper would slip her five or ten dollars on account, adding a chuck under her drooping chin and a devasting smile.

Turning about at One hundred and thirty-third[ieth] Street, Anatole faced north and resumed his leisurely promenade. Now, however, despite the apparently careless flipping and twisting of his ebony cane, tipped with a ball of ivory, his air was more serious. as He peered into the faces of the women he encountered with an expression that was almost anxious. Once, so eagerly did he seek a pair of eyes which obstinately refused to return his

See page (2)

Footnote

   The reader will find, at the end of this volume, a glossary of the unusual Negro words and phrases employed in this novel.

stare, he bumped into an elderly black man with a long white beard, who limped, supported by a cane. Anatole caught the old fellow only, in time to prevent his falling.

I sartainly beg yo' pahdon, he said with his most enchanting smile.

The octogenarian returned the smile.

'Pears to me, he squeaked, dat yo's mos' unnacherly perlite f[o'] dis street at dis hour.

The Creeper's breast expanded a full two inches, causing his watch-chain, stretched to capacity, to drag a ring of jangling keys from his waistcoat pocket. Replacing the keys, he reflected that he could afford to be agreeable, even magnanimous, to harmless old gentlemen. Was there another sheik in Harlem who possessed one-tenth his attraction for the female sex? Was there another of whose muscles the brick-pressers, ordinarily quite free with their audible, unflattering comments about passers-by, were more afraid? As he meditated in this wise, his pride received an unexpected jolt. Under the bright lights in front of the Lafayette Theatre, he discerned a pompous figure whose presence obliterated the smug cheerfulness from his heart.

A few years earlier Randolph Pettijohn had made his start in Harlem as a merchant of hot-dogs. His little one-storey shop, hugged between two towering buildings, had rapidly become popular. His ~~dogs~~ [*frankfurters*] were excellent; his buns were fresh; his mustard beyond reproach. In a short time Pettijohn's ~~was doing such trade with such slight~~ [*business was so successful, the*] overhead expense [*so light*]—he was his own cook and he personally served his customers over the counter—that he had saved a sufficient sum of money to invest in real-estate, an investment which increased in value over-night. Next, with the proceeds of a few judicious sales, he opened a cabaret which shortly became the ~~most popular~~ [*favourite*] resort in Harlem. Now, his Bolito game had made him so rich that his powerfully exerted influence began to be felt in political circles.

Unreasoningly, Anatole hated him. He had never inimically crossed the Creeper's path, but somehow, subconsciously, Anatole was aware that such ~~ancondition~~ [*eventuality*] was by no means impossible. Besides, it irked the Creeper to realize that any one else possessed power of whatever kind. Therefore he hated the Bolito King. The feeling was not reciprocated. Anatole was frequently a spectacular figure at the Winter Palace, Pettijohn's cabaret, [*where he was welcome because*] He was known to be a particular favourite with jig-chasers from below the line.

How you been, 'Toly? The King greeted the Creeper warmly, even affectionately.

Compliments, Ran.

~~Out sportin'?~~ [*Lookin' 'em over?*]

Ah'm taking' 'em in. The Creeper was reticent.

Yo' sartainly are one dressin' up fool, Creeper, one of the King's companions inserted.

Heavy lover, too, another added.

The King offered his accolade: Nobody like duh Creeper fo' close an' women, nobody a-tall.

Anatole exposed his pearls. Bottle it, he suggested.

Come in an' see me, Pettijohn invited. Mah Winter Palace am open winter an' summer.

Completely at his ease again, the Creeper strutted on, swinging his cane, expanding his chest, and humming to himself:

Mah man's got teeth lak a lighthouse on duh sea,
An' when he smiles he throws dem light son me.

Howdy, 'Toly!

As Anatole looked into the unwelcome eyes of a high yellow boy whose suit was shiny and whose boots were patched, his manner became a trifle patronizing.

How yo' been, Duke?

Not so good, 'Toly. Duh show done went broke.

Dere'll be annudder.

Sho'. How's Ah gwine live till den?

The Creeper proffered no advice.

Yo' lookin' mighty lucky 'Toly. The Duke's tone was one of whining admiration.

The Creeper preserved his discreet silence.

I nebber did see no sheik what had no' gif' fo' dressin'.

The Creeper's chest was the thermometer of the effect of this compliment.

Ah'se hungry, 'Toly. Hones'. Gimme duh price of a dog.

~~The Creeper drew~~ [*Drawing*] a handful of loose change from his trouser-pocket, ~~and~~ with great deliberation [*the Creeper selected*] ~~selecting~~ a quarter from this heap [*and*] passed it to his indigent acquaintance.

Heah yo' is, Duke. . . He had the air of a munificent benefactor. . . Now why ain' yo' mo' providen'?

Ah is, 'Toly, when Ah gits duh chance. 'T'ain' mah fault duh show done went broke. Inserting the quarter in his mouth, the boy made a sudden dash down a side-street.

Han' full o' gimme, mouf full o' much oblige, mused the Creeper.

At the corner of One hundred and thirty-seventh Street, surrounded by a numerous group of spectators, many of whom clapped their hands rhythmically, a crowd of urchins executed the Charleston. Apparently without intent, Anatole joined these pleasure-seekers. ~~As he At the same time, however,~~ His eyes, [*however,*] quickly shifted from the dancers and stole around the ring of onlookers, in hasty but accurate inspection. Suddenly he ~~saw~~ [*found*] what he had been searching.

She was a golden-brown and her skin was clear, as soft as velvet. As pretty a piece, he reflected, as he had seen around these parts for some time, and he had not happened to see her before. Her slender body was encased in coral silk, the skirt sufficiently short to expose her trim legs in golden-brown stockings. A turquoise-blue cloche all but covered her straight black shingled hair. Her soft brown eyes seemed to be begging. Withdrawing his own gaze almost immediately, so swift had been his satisfactory appraisal, he was nevertheless aware that she was contriving, without appearing to do so, without, indeed, appearing to look at him at all, to edge nearer to him. Never once, while she carried out her design, did her hands refrain from the rhythmic clapping which accompanied the juvenile dancers. When at last, she stood by his side, so close that he might touch her, she continued to pretend that she was only interested in the intricate steps of the Charleston. Anatole, outwardly, gave no sign whatever that he was aware of her presence.

After they had played this game of mutual duplicity for some time, she, losing patience or acquiring courage, accosted him.

Hello, 'Toly.

He turned, without a smile, and stared at her.

I doan seem to recerllec' dat I got duh honour o' yo' acquaintance.

Yo' ain', Mr. 'Toly, an' dat's a fac'. Mah name's Ruby.

He did not encourage her to proceed.

Ruby Silver, she completed.

He remained silent. Presently, in an offhand way, he began to clap ~~for the dancers~~ [*his hands*]. A particularly agile lad of six was executing some pretty capers. Hey! Hey! Do that thing!

Everybody knows who yo' is, Mr. 'Toly, everybody! Her voice ~~was pleading~~ [*implored his attention.*]

The Creeper continued to clap.

I been jes' nacherly crazy to meet yo'.

The Creeper was stern. Wha' fo'? he shot out.

Yo' knows, Mr. 'Toly. I guess yo' knows.

~~How much yo' got? They stepped a little back~~

He drew her a little apart from the ring.

How much yo' got?

Oh, I been full o' luck tonight. I met an ofay wanted to change his luck. He gimmer a tenner.

The Creeper appeared to be taking the matter under consideration. ~~I m~~ Ah met a gal las' night dat offer me fifteen, he countered. Nevertheless, it could be seen that he was weakening.

Ah got annuder five in mah lef' stockin', an' Ah'll show yo' lovin' such as yo' never seen.

The Creeper became more affable. Ah do seem to remember yo' face, Miss Silver, he averred. Will yo' do me duh favour to cling to mah arm.

As they strolled, their bodies touching, down a dark side-street, his hand freely explored her body, soft and warm under the thin covering of coral silk.

Wanna dance? he demanded.

Luvvit, she replied.

She stooped to fumble in her stockings, first the right, then the left. Presently she handed him two bills which he stuffed into his waistcoat pocket without the formality of examination.

Winter Palace? she inquired.

A nasty shadow flitted across Anatole's face.

Naw, he retorted. Too many ofays an' jig-chasers.

Bowie Wilcox's is dicty.

Too many monks.

Atlantic City Joe's?

Too many pink-chasers an' bulldi[k]guers.

Where den?

Duh Black Venus.

A few moments later they were swallowed by an entrance on Lenox Avenue, flanked by two revolving green lights. Arm in arm, they descended the stairs to the basement. As they walked down the long hallway which led to the dance-floor, the sensuous blare of jazz, slow, wailing jazz, stroked their ears. At the door three waiters in evening clothes greeted the Creeper with enthusiasm.

Why, dat's sartainly Mr. 'Toly.

Good evenin'.

Gwine sit at mah table?

Mine?

Mine, Mr. 'Toly?

Expanding his chest, Anatole gazed down the length of the hall. Couples were dancing in such close proximity that their bodies melted together as they swayed and rocked to the tormented howling of the brass, the barbaric beating of the drum. Across each woman's back, clasped tight against her shoulder blades the black hands of her partner were flattened. Blues, smokes, dinges, charcoals, chocolate browns, shines, and jigs. The high yellows looked white under the amber searchlight.

Le's dance hoof, Ruby urged.

Le's set down, Anatole commanded. Passing his straw hat to the hatcheck girl he followed a waiter to an empty table, pushing Ruby ahead of him.

Hello, 'Toly! A friend from greeted him from an adjoining table.

Hello, Licey.

A pint, the Creeper commanded [ordered].

The waiter charlestoned down the floor to the intoxicating rhythm, twirling his tray on palm [held] high overhead.

Put ashes in sweet papa's bed so as he can' slip out, moaned Licey in the Creeper's ear. Ah knows a lady what'll be singing' Wonder whah mah easy rider's gone!

Bottle it.

Licey chuckled. Hush mah mouf ef I doan!

The waiter came back, like a cat, tacking ingeniously from one side of the room to the other, in and out of the throng of dancers. Charleston! Charleston! Do that thing! Oh boy!

On ~~the waiter's~~ [*his*] tray were two glasses, two splits of ginger ale, and a bowl of cracked ice. In his hip pocket a ~~glass flask~~ [*bottle*] containing a transparent liquid. He poured out the ginger ale. Anatole poured out the gin.

Tea fo' two! he toasted his companion, almost jovially.

She gulped her glassful in one swallow, and then giggled, 'Toly, yo's mah sho' 'nough daddy an' Ah sho' does love yo' wid all mah h'aht.

Everybody loves mah baby, tooted the cornet.

But mah baby doan love nobody but me, Ruby chimed in. She [*tentatively*] touched ~~his~~ [*the Creeper's*] arm, ~~tentatively.~~ [*As*] ~~H~~e did not [*appear to*] object [*to this attention*], ~~and~~ she stroked it tenderly.

Jes' once 'roun', she pleaded.

He humoured her. Embracing her closely, he rocked her slowly around the hall. Their heels shuffled along the floor. Their knees clicked [*amorously.*] On all sides of the swaying couple, bodies [*in picturesque costumes*] rocked, black bodies, brown bodies, high yellows, a kaleidoscope of colour ~~in picturesque costumes,~~ transfigured by the amber searchlight. Scarves of bottle green, cerise, amethyst, vermillion, lemon. The drummer in complete abandon tossed his sticks in the air ~~and~~ [*while he*] shook his head like a wild animal. The saxophone player drew a dilapidated derby over the bowl of his instrument, smothering the din. The banjos planked deliriously. The ~~music~~ [*band*] tooted and snorted and whistled and laughed like a hyena. ~~It~~ [*This music*] reminded ~~T~~ the Creeper of the days he had worked as a bootblack in a Memphis barber-shop. Hugged closely together, the bodies rocked and swayed, rocked and swayed. Sometimes a rolling-eyed couple, caught in the whirlpool of aching sound, would scarcely move from one spot. Then the floor-manager would cry, Git off dat dime!

Suddenly it was over. The saxophone player substituted the stub of a black cigar for the tube of his instrument. As if they had ~~all recovered~~ [*been released*] from some subtle enchantment, the dancing couples broke apart, dazed, and lumbered towards their tables. ~~Wi~~ Now that music was lacking their bodies had lost the secret of the magic rhythm. ~~A woman shrieked hysterically.~~ With the others, Anatole and Ruby found their places at table. Normal illumination. A new mood. Laughter and chatter. [*A woman shrieked hysterically.*] The Creeper extracted the ~~flask of gin~~ [*bottle*] from his hip-pocket and poured out two more drinks.

Again Ruby drained her portion at one gulp. This time she had repudiated the ginger ale. Again she caressed her companion's arm. Again she sought his eyes, his great brown eyes, like a doe's.

Ah sho' will show yo' some lovin', daddy, she promised.

The Creeper grunted his approval.

Does yo' know what Ah calls dis? she continued rapturously.

Calls what?

Dis place, where Ah met yo'—Harlem. Ah calls et, specherly tonight, ~~I~~ Ah ~~calls it~~ et Nigger Heaven! I jes' nacherly think dis am Nigger Heaven!

~~The Cre~~

On the floor a scrawny yellow girl in pink silk, embroidered with bronze sequins in floral designs, began to sing:

Mah daddy rocks me with one steady roll;

Dere ain' no slippin' when he once takes hol' . . . .

The Creeper sipped his gin meditatively.

GALLEY PROOF

PROLOGUE

Anatole Longfellow, alias the Scarlet Creeper,[1] strutted aimfully down the east side of Seventh Avenue. He wore a tight-fitting suit of shepherd's plaid which thoroughly revealed his lithe, sinewy figure to all who gazed upon him, and all gazed. A great diamond, or some less valuable stone which aped a diamond, glistened on his fuchsia cravat. The uppers of his highly polished tan boots were dove-coloured suède and the buttons were pale blue. His black hair was sleek under his straw hat, set at a jaunty angle. When he saluted a friend—and his acquaintance seemed to be wide—two rows of pearly teeth gleamed from his seal-brown countenance.

It was the hour when promenading was popular—about eleven o'clock in the evening. The air was warm, balmy for June, and not too humid. Over the broad avenue, up and down which multi-hued taxi-cabs rolled, hung a canopy of indigo sky, spangled with bright stars. The shops, still open, were brilliantly illuminated. Slouching under the protecting walls of the buildings, in front of show-windows, or under the trees, groups of young men congregated, chattering and laughing. Women, in pairs, or with male escorts, strolled up and down the ample sidewalk.

Hello 'Toly! A stalwart black man accosted the Creeper.

Hello, Ed. How you been?

Poo'ly, thank you. How *you* been?

No complaints. Nummer come out. Drew sixty-seven bucks.

Holy Kerist!

Yeh. Anatole displayed his teeth.

[1]The reader will find, at the end of this volume, a glossary of the unusual Negro words and phrases employed in this novel.

What nummer?

Seven-Nine-Eight.

What you found et?

Off'n a gal's fron' do'.

Comin' out?

Goin' in. +[*Ah*] went out duh back winder. Her daddy done come home widout writin'.

Hush mah mouf!

Ah doan mean mebbe.

As Anatole walked on, his self-esteem flowered. Unbuttoning his coat, he expanded his chest, dangerously stretching the gold watch-chain which extended from pocket to pocket across his muscular belly.

Howdy.

Howdy.

He greeted in passing Leanshanks Pescod, a mulatto lightweight, who, in successive Saturday sessions at the Commonwealth Club, had defeated two white comers.

Is you enjoyin' de air, Mr. Longfellow?

'Deed, Ah is, Mrs. Guckeen. How you been? The Creeper's manner became slightly flirtatious.

~~My compliments~~ [*Thank you*], Mr. Longfellow, an' pretty well.

Mrs. Imogene Guckeen was the proprietor of a popular beauty parlour further up the avenue. It was Anatole's custom to indulge in a manicure at this parlour every afternoon around five. As a wide circle of admiring women was cognizant of this habit, five was the rush hour at Mrs. Guckeen's establishment. She was fully aware of the important role this customer played in her affairs and, as a consequence, made no effort to collect his always considerable bill. Occasionally, moreover, the Creeper would slip her five or ten dollars on account, adding a chuck under her drooping chin and a devastating smile.

Turning about at One hundred and ~~thirtieth~~ [*twenty-seventh*] Street, Anatole faced north and resumed his leisurely promenade. Now, however, despite the apparent [*copy ly*] careless flipping and twisting of his ebony cane, tipped with a ball of ivory, his air was more serious. He peered into the faces of the women he encountered with an expression that was almost anxious. Once, so eagerly did he seek a pair of eyes which obstinately refused to return his stare, he bumped into an elderly black man with a long white beard, who limped, supported by a cane. Anatole caught the old fellow only in time to prevent his falling.

+[*Ah*] sartainly beg yo' pahdon, he said with his most enchanting smile. The octogenarian returned the smile.

'Pears to me, he squeaked, dat you's mos' unnacherly perlite fo' dis street at dis hour.

The Creeper's breast expanded a full two inches, causing his watch-chain, stretched to capacity, to drag a ring of jangling keys from his waist-coat pocket. Replacing the keys, he reflected that he could afford to be agreeable, even magnanimous, to harmless old gentlemen. Was there another sheik in Harlem who possessed one-tenth his attraction for the female sex? Was there another of whose muscles the brick-pressers, ordinarily quite free with their audible, unflattering comments about passers-by, were more afraid? As he meditated in this wise, his pride received an unexpected jolt. Under the bright lights in front of the Lafayette Theatre, he discerned a pompous figure whose presence obliterated the smug cheerfulness from his heart.

A few years earlier Randolph Pettijohn had made his start in Harlem as a merchant of hot-dogs. His little one-storey shop, hugged between two towering buildings, had rapidly become popular. His frankfurters were excellent; his buns were fresh; his mustard beyond reproach. In a short time Pettijohn's business was so successful, the overhead expense so light—he was his own cook and he personally served his customers over the counter—that he had saved a sufficient sum of money to invest in real-estate, an investment which increased in value over-night. Next, with the proceeds of a few judicious sales, he opened a cabaret which shortly became the favourite resort in Harlem. Now, his Bolito game had made him so rich that his powerfully exerted influence began to be felt in political circles.

Unreasoningly, Anatole hated him. He had never inimically crossed the Creeper's path, but somehow, subconsciously, Anatole was aware that such an eventuality was by no means impossible. Besides, it irked the Creeper to realize that any one else possessed power of whatever kind. ~~Therefore he hated the Bolito King.~~ The feeling was not reciprocated. Anatole was frequently a spectacular figure at the Winter Palace, Pettijohn's cabaret, where he was welcome because he was known to be a particular favourite with jig-chasers from below the line.

How you been, 'Toly? The [*Bolito*] King greeted the Creeper warmly, even affectionately.

~~Compliments~~ [*Hello*], Ran.

Lookin' 'em over?

Ah'm takin' 'em in. The Creeper was reticent.

You sartainly are one dressin' up fool, Creeper, one of the King's companions inserted.

Heavy lover, too, another added.

The King offered his accolade: Nobody like duh Creeper fo' close an' women, nobody a-tall.

Anatole exposed his pearls. Bottle ~~it~~ [*et*], he suggested.

Come in an' see me, Pettijohn invited. Mah Winter Palace ~~am~~ [*is*] open winter an' summer.

Completely at his ease again, the Creeper strutted on, swinging his cane, expanding his chest, and humming to himself:

Mah man's got teeth lak a lighthouse on duh sea,
An' when he smiles he throws dem lights on me.

Howdy, 'Toly!

As Anatole looked into the unwelcome eyes of a high yellow boy whose suit was shiny and whose boots were patched, his manner became a trifle patronizing.

How you been, Duke?

Not so good, 'Toly. Duh show done went broke.

Dere'll be annudder.

Sho'. How's Ah gwine live till den?

The Creeper offered no advice.

You lookin' mighty lucky 'Toly. The Duke's tone was one of whining admiration.

The Creeper preserved his discreet silence.

~~I~~ [*Ah*] nebber did see no sheik what had yo' gif' fo' dressin'.

The Creeper's chest was the thermometer of the effect of this compliment.

Ah'se hungry, 'Toly. Hones'. Gimme duh price of a dog.

Drawing a handful of loose change from his trouser-pocket, with great deliberation the Creeper selected a quarter from this heap and passed it to his indigent acquaintance.

Heah you is, Duke. . . . He had the air of a munificent benefactor. . . . Now why ain' you git mo' providen'?

Ah is, 'Toly, when Ah gits duh chance. 'T'ain' mah fault duh show done went broke. Inserting the quarter in his mouth, the boy made a sudden dash down a side-street.

Han' full o' gimme, mouf full o' much oblige, mused the Creeper.

At the corner of One hundred and thirty-seventh Street, surrounded by a numerous group of spectators, many of whom clapped their hands rhythmically, a crowd of urchins executed the Charleston. Apparently without intent, Anatole joined these pleasure-seekers. His eyes, however, quickly shifted from the dancers and stole around the ring of onlookers, in hasty but accurate inspection. Suddenly he found ~~what~~ [*that for which*] he had been searching.

She was a golden-brown and her skin was clear, as soft as velvet. As pretty a piece, he reflected, as he had seen around these parts for some time, and he had not happened to see her before. Her slender body was encased in coral silk, the skirt sufficiently short to expose her trim legs in golden-brown stockings. A turquoise-blue cloche all but covered her straight black shingled hair. Her soft brown eyes seemed to be begging. Withdrawing his own gaze

almost immediately, so swift had been his satisfactory appraisal, he was
nevertheless aware that she was contriving, without appearing to do so,
without, indeed, appearing to look at him at all, to edge nearer to him.
Never once, while she carried out her design, did her hands refrain from the
rhythmic clapping which accompanied the juvenile dancers. When at last,
she stood by his side, so close that he might touch her, she continued to
pretend that she was only interested in the intricate steps of the Charleston.
Anatole, outwardly, gave no sign whatever that he was aware of her presence.

After they had played this game of mutual duplicity for some time, she,
losing patience or acquiring courage, accosted him.

Hello, 'Toly.

He turned, without a smile, and stared at her.

+[Ah] doan seem to recerllec' dat I got duh honour o' yo' acquaintance.

You ain', Mr. 'Toly, an' dat's a fac'. Mah name's Ruby.

He did not encourage her to proceed.

Ruby Silver, she completed.

He remained silent. Presently, in an offhand way, he began to clap his
hands. A particularly agile lad of six was executing some pretty capers.
Hey! Hey! Do that thing!

Everybody knows who you is, Mr. 'Toly, *everybody*! Her voice implored
his attention.

The Creeper continued to clap.

+[Ah] been jes' nacherly crazy to meet you.

The Creeper was stern. What fo'? he shot out.

You knows, Mr. 'Toly. I guess you knows.

He drew her a little apart from the ring.

How much you go?

Oh, +[Ah] been full o' luck tonight. I [prosperity dis evenin'. Ah] met an
ofay wanted to change his luck. He gimmer a tenner.

The Creeper appeared to be taking the matter under consideration. Ah
met a gal las' night dat offer me fifteen, he countered. Nevertheless, it could
be seen that he was weakening.

Ah got annudder five in mah lef' stockin', and Ah'll show you lovin' such
as you never seen.

The Creeper became more affable. Ah do seem to remember yo' face,
Miss Silver, he averred. Will you do me duh favour to cling to mah arm.

As they strolled, their bodies touching, down a dark side-street, his hand
freely explored[ing] her body [flesh], soft and warm under the thin covering
of coral silk.

Wanna dance? he demanded.

Luvvit, she replied.

She stooped to fumble in her stockings, first the right, then the left. Presently
she handed him two bills which he stuffed into his waistcoat pocket without
the formality of examination.

Winter Palace? she inquired.

A nasty shadow flitted across Anatole's face.

Naw, he retorted. Too many ofays an' jig-chasers.

Bowie Wilcox's is dicty.

Too many monks.

Atlantic City Joe's?

Too many pink-chasers an' bulldikers.

Where den?

Duh Black Venus.

A few moments later they were swallowed by an entrance on Lenox Avenue, flanked by two revolving green lights. Arm in arm, they descended the stairs to the basement. As they walked down the long hallway which led to the dance-floor, the sensuous[sual] blare of jazz, slow, wailing jazz, stroked their ears. At the door three waiters in evening clothes greeted the Creeper with enthusiasm.

Why, dat's sartainly Mr. 'Toly.

Good evenin'.

Gwine sit at mah table?

Mine?

Mine, Mr. 'Toly?

Expanding his chest, Anatole gazed down the length of the hall. Couples were dancing in such close proximity that their bodies melted together as they swayed and rocked to the tormented howling of the brass, the barbaric beating of the drum. Across each woman's back, clasped tight against her shoulder blades[,] the black hands of her partner were flattened. Blues, smokes, dinges, charcoals, chocolate browns, shines, and jigs.

Le's hoof, Ruby urged.

Le's set down, Anatole commanded. Passing his straw hat to the hat-check girl[,] he followed a waiter to an empty table, pushing Ruby ahead of him.

Hello, 'Toly! A friend greeted him from an adjoining table.

Hello, Licey.

A pint, the Creeper ordered.

The waiter Charlestoned down the floor to the intoxicating rhythm, twirling his tray on palm held high overhead.

Put ashes in sweet papa's bed so as he can' slip out, moaned Licey in the Creeper's ear. Ah knows a lady what'll be singin' Wonder whah mah easy rider's gone!

Bottle it [et].

Licey chuckled. Hush mah mouf ef I [Ah] doan!

The waiter came back, like a cat, tacking [shuffling] ingeniously from one side of the room to the other, in and out of the throng of dancers. Charleston! Charleston! Do that thing! Oh boy!

On his tray were two glasses, two splits of ginger ale, and a bowl of cracked ice. ~~In~~ [*From*] his hip-pocket [*he extracted*] a ~~glass-flask~~ [*bottle*] containing a transparent liquid. He poured out the ginger ale. Anatole poured out the gin.

Tea fo' two! he toasted his companion, almost jovially.

She gulped her glassful in one swallow, and then giggled, 'Toly, you's mah sho' 'nough daddy an' Ah sho' does love you wid all mah h'aht.

Everybody loves mah baby, tooted the cornet.

But mah baby doan love nobody but me, Ruby chimed in. She tentatively touched the Creeper's arm. As he did not appear to object to this attention, she stroked it tenderly.

Jes' once 'roun', she pleaded.

He humoured her. Embracing her closely, he rocked her slowly around the hall. Their heels shuffled along the floor. Their knees clicked amorously. On all sides of the swaying couple, bodies in picturesque costumes rocked, black bodies, brown bodies, high yellows, a kaleidoscope of colour transfigured by the amber searchlight. Scarves of bottle green, cerise, amethyst, vermillion, lemon. The drummer in complete abandon tossed his sticks in the air while he shook his head like a wild animal. The saxophone player drew a dilapidated derby over the bowl of his instrument, smothering the din. The banjos planked deliriously. The band ~~tooted~~ [*snored*] and snorted and whistled and laughed like hyena. The music reminded the Creeper of the days ~~he had~~ [*when he*] worked as a bootblack in a Memphis barber-shop. Hugged closely together, the bodies rocked and swayed, rocked and swayed. Sometimes a rolling-eyed couple, caught in the whirlpool of aching sound, would scarcely move from one spot. Then the floor-manager would cry, Git off dat dime!

~~Suddenly~~ [*Unexpectedly*] it was over. The saxophone player substituted the stub of a black cigar for the tube of his instrument. As if they had been released from some subtle enchantment, the dancing couples broke apart, dazed, and lumbered towards their tables. Now that music was lacking their bodies had lost the secret of the magic rhythm. ~~With the others, Anatole and Ruby found their places at table.~~ Normal illumination. A new mood. Laughter and chatter. A woman shrieked hysterically. The Creeper ~~extracted~~ [*drew*] the bottle from his hip-pocket and poured out two more drinks.

Again Ruby drained her portion at one gulp. This time she had repudiated the ginger ale. Again she caressed her companion's arm. Again she sought his eyes, his great brown eyes, like a doe's.

Ah sho' will show you some lovin', daddy, she promised.

The Creeper grunted his approval.

Does you know what Ah calls dis? she continued rapturously.

Calls what?

Dis place, where Ah met you—Harlem. Ah calls et, specherly tonight, Ah calls et Nigger Heaven! I jes' nacherly think dis ~~am~~ [*heah is*] Nigger Heaven!

On the floor a scrawny yellow girl in pink silk, embroidered with bronze sequins in floral designs, began to sing:

Mah daddy rocks me with one steady roll;
Dere ain' no slippin' when he once takes hol' . . .

The Creeper sipped his gin meditatively.

from the *Glossary of Negro Words and Phrases*

blue: a very black Negro. Not to be confused with the Blues, Negro songs of disappointment and love.
Bolito: see Numbers.
bottle it: equivalent to the colloquial English *shut up*.
brick-presser: an idler; literally one who walks the pavement.
bulldiker: Lesbian.
charcoal: Negro.
creeper: a man who invades another's marital rights.
daddy: husband or lover.
dicty: swell, in the slang sense of the word.
dinge: Negro.
high yellow: mulatto or lighter.
hoof: to dance. A hoofer is a dancer, and hoofing is dancing.
jig: Negro.
jig-chaser: a white person who seeks the company of Negroes.
monk: see monkey-chaser.
monkey-chaser: a Negro from the British West Indies.
Numbers: a gambling game highly popular in contemporary Harlem. The winning numbers each day are derived from the New York Clearing House bank exchanges and balances as they are published in the newspapers, the seventh and eighth digits, reading from the right, of the exchanges, and the seventh of the balances. In Bolito one wagers on two figures only.
ofay: a white person.
papa: see daddy.
pink: a white person.
pink-chaser: a Negro who seeks the company of whites.
shine: Negro.
smoke: Negro.

James Weldon Johnson, 1932

3

James Weldon Johnson

MY FRIEND: JAMES WELDON JOHNSON

The method employed in preparing this composite essay on James Weldon Johnson is illustrative of similar examples elsewhere in the anthology. The first part is an open letter for the *New York Amsterdam News*, perhaps never printed there but written at the time of Johnson's death and dated only "1938" in a manuscript version among Van Vechten's papers in the New York Public Library. The second part is the first section of "My Friend: James Weldon Johnson," in *James Weldon Johnson*, a pamphlet privately printed at Fisk University in memory of the writer. The third part is the "Introduction to Mr. Knopf's New Edition" of Johnson's *The Autobiography of an Ex-Coloured Man*, printed in the "Blue Jade Library" series of Alfred A. Knopf, Inc., in 1927, deleted from a subsequent edition, and reprinted in a new edition in 1970. The fourth part is the opening section of Van Vechten's album notes for Harold Scott's recorded version of Johnson's *God's Trombones* (UAL 4039), issued in 1959, the closing section of which repeats part of the Fisk pamphlet and is therefore deleted here. The fifth part is the concluding section of the Fisk pamphlet, interspersed with such additional information as the 1959 record album notes contained.

I feel a selfish grief over the death of James Weldon Johnson because one of my dearest friends has passed away, but, more than that, it is easy to realize that the world has lost one of its great men. Putting aside his work as an artist, which is very important, I think it can be said that no one ever has done more for interracial understanding (and when I say interracial I am referring to ALL races) than James Weldon Johnson. He had a genius for tactful decisions and on many occasions his mere presence has been sufficient to make new friends for his race. He was widely known from coast to coast in America and he will be missed and remembered as long as anyone in American history is missed and remembered.

It has always been my belief that my father was a thoroughly good man: kind, gentle, helpful, generous, tolerant of unorthodox behavior in others, patriarchal in offering good advice, understanding in not expecting it to be followed, moderate in his way of living, and courageous in accepting the difficulties of life itself. Of all the men I have encountered since I was born, I can think of but one other, James Weldon Johnson, who could be measured by this high standard. Furthermore, I am sure, if Jim's friends and acquaintances could be brought together to vote on the truth of this blanket assertion, there would be no dissenting voice. As a matter of fact, Jim possessed at least two other desirable qualities which were lacking in my father: tact and discretion.

I am aware that it would seem almost impossible to continue, at least in any enlivening manner, an essay which begins with such a complete statement of faith, but in Jim's case such a statement is unavoidable. It just happens to be true. I fully realize that a man who was unpredictable, undependable, and inefficient, an atheistic opportunist with a hankering for liquor and a variety of odd ideas about sex, would contribute livelier material for a paper of this kind, but I have no intention of writing fiction in order to satisfy any inherent craving for gossip in my readers. What I have said of Jim is the truth, the simple truth, perhaps a little understated at that.

So warm was his humanity, so deep his knowledge of the history of mankind, and the human heart, so complete his tact, and so amazing his social skill that he was the master of any situation in which he found himself. Time and again I have observed him emerging from a room, which earlier had bristled with prejudice, having conquered this bad feeling by the breadth of his understanding and the charm of his personality, actually holding his opponents, no longer to be so described, in the palms of his hands. His distinction, his tact, his powers of diplomacy would have made him a peerless envoy. He would have been, I always believed, an excellent choice for ambassador to the Court of St. James. I am convinced that only his color prevented his fellow citizens, the American people, from enjoying the honor that such a brilliant appointment would have bestowed on them. Not that he regarded his color as a disadvantage. Quite the contrary. He was very proud of his race and not at all ignorant of the fact that his standing as a Negro gave him, in many important particulars, a certain superiority over white men who were, in some respects, his equals.

It is my conviction that he would have endowed any diplomatic mission, which did not require the practice of chicanery, with an especial effulgence, that he would have emerged from any contest of international bargaining with colors flying and banners waving. He actually knew a good deal about this world and its ways and what he didn't know he seemed to comprehend instinctively. As a writer, as a lecturer, for this reason and others, he had a special niche. Since Addison no one has written a better prose style than Jim. *Along This Way* will remain a perfect pattern for future writers of autobiography for many years to come. His poetic sermons, *God's Trombones*, express many angles of his many-faceted personality. Their striking imagery, their brilliantly conceived metaphors, their emotional intensity perhaps form a monument to the memory of James Weldon Johnson.

The Autobiography of an Ex-Coloured Man is, I am convinced, a re-markable book. I have read it three times and at each rereading I have found it more remarkable. Published in 1912, it then stood almost alone as an inclusive survey of racial accomplishments and traits, as an interpretation of the feelings of the Negro towards the white man and towards the members of his own race. Written, I believe, while Mr. James Weldon Johnson was U.S. Consul to Nicaragua, it was issued anonymously. The publishers attempted to persuade the author to sign a statement to the effect that the book was an actual human document. This he naturally refused to do. Nevertheless, the work was hailed on every side, for the most part, as an individual's true story.

The *Autobiography*, of course, in the matter of specific incident, has little enough to do with Mr. Johnson's own life, but it is imbued with his own personality and feeling, his *views* on the subjects discussed, so that to a person who has no previous knowledge of the author's own history, it reads like *real* autobiography. It would be truer, perhaps, to say that it reads like a composite autobiography of the Negro race in the United States of America in modern times.

It is surprising how little the book has dated in fifteen years. Very little that Mr. Johnson wrote then is not equally valid today, although in those remote times he found it necessary when he mentioned Negroes in evening clothes to add that they were not hired! On the other hand, it is cheering to discover how much has been accomplished by the race in New York alone since the book was originally published. Then there was no Harlem—the Negro lived below Fifth-ninth Street. To encounter the cultured, respectable class of Negro one was obliged to visit Brooklyn. In the very few years since this epoch the great city beyond the [Central] Park has sprung into being, a city which boasts not only its own cabarets and gamblers, but also its intelli-gentsia, its rich and cultured group, its physicians, its attorneys, its educa-tors, its large, respectable middle class, its churches, its hospitals, its theatres, its library, and its business houses. It would be possible to name fifty names such as those of Paul Robeson, Langston Hughes, Charles Gilpin, Walter White, Rudolph Fisher, Countée Cullen, Florence Mills, Ethel Waters, Aaron Douglas, Taylor Gordon, and Jean Toomer, all of whom have made their mark in the artistic world within the past five years.

When I was writing *Nigger Heaven* I discovered the *Autobiography* to be an invaluable source book for the study of Negro psychology. I believe it will be a long time before anybody can write about the Negro without con-sulting Mr. Johnson's pages to advantage. Naturally, the *Autobiography* has its precursors. Booker T. Washington's *Up From Slavery* (1900) is a splendid example of autobiography, but the limitations of his subject matter made it impossible for Dr. Washington to survey the field as broadly as Mr. Johnson, setting himself no limitations, could. Dr. Du Bois's important work, *The Souls of Black Folk* (1903), does, certainly, explore a wide territory, but these essays lack the insinuating influence of Mr. Johnson's calm, dispassionate tone, and they do not offer, in certain important respects, so revealing a portrait of Negro character. Charles W. Chesnutt, in his interesting novel, *The House Behind the Cedars* (1900), contributed to literature perhaps the first authentic study on the subject of "passing," and Paul Laurence Dunbar, in *The Sport of the Gods*, described the plight of a young outsider who comes to the larger New York Negro world to make his fortune, but who falls a victim to the sordid snares of that world, a theme I elaborated in 1926 to fit a newer and much more intricate social system.

Mr. Johnson, however, chose an all-embracing scheme. His young hero, the ostensible author, either discusses (or lives) pretty nearly every phase of Negro life, North and South and even in Europe, available to him at that period. That he "passes" the title indicates. Miscegenation in its slave and also its more modern aspects, both casual and marital, is competently treated. The ability of the Negro to mask his real feelings with a joke or a laugh in the presence of the inimical white man is here noted, for the first time in print, I should imagine. Negro adaptability, touchiness, and jealousy are referred to in an unself-conscious manner, totally novel in Negro writing at the time this book originally appeared. The hero declares: "It may be said that the majority of intelligent coloured people are, in some degree, too much in earnest over the race question. They assume and carry so much that their progress is at times impeded and they are unable to see things in their proper proportions. In many instances a slight exercise of the sense of humour would save much anxiety of soul." Jim Crow cars, crap-shooting, and the cakewalk are inimitably described. Color snobbery within the race is freely spoken of, together with the economic pressure from without which creates this false condition. There is a fine passage devoted to the celebration of the Negro Spirituals and there is an excellent account of a southern camp meeting, together with a transcript of a typical oldtime Negro sermon. There is even a lynching.

But it is chiefly remarkable to find James Weldon Johnson in 1912, five or six years before the rest of us began to shout about it, singing hosannas to ragtime (jazz was unknown then). It is simply astonishing to discover in this book, issued the year after "Alexander's Ragtime Band" and the same year that "The Memphis Blues" were published, such a statement as this:

"American musicians, instead of investigating rag-time, attempt to ignore it, or dismiss it with a contemptuous word. But that has always been the course of scholasticism in every branch of art. Whatever new thing the *people* like is pooh-poohed; whatever is *popular* is spoken of as not worth the while. The fact is, nothing great or enduring, especially in music, has ever sprung full-fledged and unprecedented from the brain of any master; the best that he gives to the world he gathers from the hearts of the people, and runs it through the alembic of his genius." So the young hero of this

Autobiography determines to develop the popular music of his people into a more serious form, thus foreseeing by twelve years the creation of the *Rhapsody in Blue* by George Gershwin.

Sherman, French and Co. published the *Autobiography* in Boston in 1912. When, a few years later, they retired from business it was out of print and, although constantly in demand and practically unprocurable, it has remained out of print until now when Alfred Knopf, justifiably, I believe, has seen fit to include it in his Blue Jade series. New readers, I am confident, will examine this book with interest: some to acquire through its mellow pages a new conception of how a colored man lives and feels, others simply to follow the course of its fascinating history.

In his youth, James Weldon Johnson had listened to the old Negro preachers whose sermons were frequently brilliant examples of the art of the expounder. He admired vastly the thunderous and confident way in which these orators appealed to the emotions of their auditors. Some of these sermons were so successful that they were frequently repeated by their creators (crowds revisited his church in Richmond, Virginia, to hear John Jasper deliver his celebrated discourse entitled, "The Sun Do Move") and imitated widely by rival reverends. Mr. Johnson came to believe that these sermons were as much folk material as the Spirituals and the Blues and early in his career he determined to revive these sermons in poetic form. His first attempt in this direction was called "The Creation" (written in 1919 and first published in *The Freeman*). From its very inception he had decided not to use dialect, despite the fact that dialect seemed superficially to be appropriate. He recalled that the old preachers themselves were so imbued with the language of the Bible and the majesty of their calling that they only resorted to dialect occasionally. Also, Mr. Johnson had long since discovered that dialect had only two stops: humor and pathos; hence it could awaken no other emotions.

I was introduced to James Weldon Johnson in 1924 and we became intimate friends almost immediately. It was not long before I heard him recite (this is certainly not the word; probably intone would be better) "The Creation," his first sermon in poetic form. This performance was repeated many times: one evening after dinner at HIS apartment before the enthusiasm of Clarence Darrow and Newman Levy; several times at my apartment; certainly on one occasion when Paul Robeson sang "Let My People Go" and "Little David, Play on Your Harp" (my favorite Spiritual at this epoch and one which I liked so much that Mr. Robeson invariably sang it whenever he encountered me in any group where he was singing). In addition George Gershwin had played his recently composed *Rhapsody in Blue*. Just as often I had listened to Mr. Johnson intone "The Creation" in other people's houses.

The other sermons followed shortly: "Go Down, Death," my own favorite, "Listen, Lord," "The Prodigal Son," "Noah Built the Ark," "The Judgment Day," and "Let My People Go." I have heard Jim on various occasions intone several of these and I have heard some of them arranged for a chorus of human voices. Indeed certain of them in this new form were sung by Eva Jessye's choir at Jim's funeral.

In the introduction to *God's Trombones*, the title of the volume which included these sermons, Jim dictates: "These poems had better be intoned than read; . . . This intoning is always a matter of crescendo and diminuendo in the intensity—a rising and falling between plain speaking and wild chanting. And often a startling effect is gained by breaking off suddenly at the highest point of intensity and dropping into the monotone of ordinary speech." This opinion exactly describes Jim's technique in the delivery of these sermons, at which he was expert. He held the memory of the voices of the old-time preachers in his ears and made an attempt, with certain important modifications, to approximate their tone to reach modern ears. . . .

In his magnificent autobiography, *Along This Way*, Mr. Johnson informs us that he wrote "Go Down, Death," the second sermon to reach completion, on Thanksgiving Day, 1926. It received its initial publication in *The American Mercury*, edited by [H.L.] Mencken and [George Jean] Nathan. Between Thanksgiving Day and Christmas he had written "Listen, Lord." The others followed swiftly and were published under the title, *God's Trombones*, by the Viking Press in 1927. The book was received with enthusiasm by the reviewers and since that day the public has had an opportunity to enjoy the poems in various ways, even as accompaniments to the dance, a fact not difficult to explain when it is recalled that the Church was the first theatre to employ the dance and in some churches (notably the Cathedral in Seville, where the Sevillana is still danced at Easter) dancing is a permanent occasional feature.

If all this touches a little on the side of solemnity I think it is time to warn the reader that Jim himself was seldom solemn. Nobody ever enjoyed a better sense of humor. Nobody ever was able to laugh more freely. It was one of his more frequently expressed theories, indeed, that the Negro race would be well on its way to complete emancipation when it could laugh at derogatory epithets. Furthermore, Jim liked good music, good pictures, good books, and good food. He knew how to find pleasure in their sustenance; moreover, he knew how to communicate this pleasure, through description, to others.

As I look back over our many meetings, it is perhaps the memory of the dinners we enjoyed together which seems to recapture the most characteristic and personal moments. As a host he was unrivalled and never in better form than when carving a roast at his own well-laden board while he tossed comments across his shoulder to his Venezuelan friend, Lorita the parrot.

There wasn't a mean streak in him. He was even fair to his enemies, giving them credit for all the good qualities they possessed. Even when he disliked the man, he could see good in his poem or symphony. He could be very stern, however, and when occasion demanded, he could be strong. Once or twice I have observed him when a shadow passed over his mobile face as he realized that necessity obliged him to say something disagreeable. He passed through the ordeal, no doubt with acute personal discomfort.

But more often his disposition was sunny. Happy in his family life, for he deeply loved his wife and his brother, comfortable in his relations with the two races between which he was compelled to live, he struggled with no neuroses, betrayed no signs of irritability or impatience. The Negro probably learned to be patient in the dim reaches of Time, and while Jim had intelligently unlearned this lesson, he was skillful in concealing this impatience before observers.

Myself, I loved him warmly. My wife loved him. I don't know anybody who really knew him who didn't love him. Deep in our hearts we knew this was more than a personal affection: it was also the respect due to dignity and distinction, the appreciation won by true nobility of character. It is because he was like that that Jim can never die.

A JAMES WELDON JOHNSON MEMORIAL

> When James Weldon Johnson died in 1938, a group of his friends determined to commemorate him through a memorial statue. As one of his most intimate friends, Carl Van Vechten wrote "The James Weldon Johnson Memorial Project" for *Crisis* and "The Proposed James Weldon Johnson Memorial" for *Opportunity*, both appearing in the February issues in 1940, to publicize the endeavor. In combining the two pieces into a single essay, I have made a number of deletions to eliminate several nearly verbatim passages.

The announcement of the death, by accident, of James Weldon Johnson in the summer of 1938 came as a great shock to his personal friends of several races and was felt as an irremediable loss by many who never knew the man himself at all, but who had experienced his influence and inspiration. He was, I might say without any of that exaggeration which is considered permissible when one is speaking of the dead, a well-nigh perfect human being who had consecrated his whole existence to the elevation and celebration of the race to which he was proud to belong. He sought, in all quarters, towards a better understanding for that race. Sometimes it was by the exam, le f his own acts that he set a high standard; at other times, it was by word o ath, spoken or written, that he released his noble thought. But, in one way or another, almost from the moment he arrived in New York from Florida, he envisioned as his ideal a glorious future for the Negro, as readers of that magnificent autobiography, *Along This Way*, which he was fortunate enough to complete and see published before he died, will be well aware.

From the beginning of his own career he realized the value of cultural development as a means of advancing the dignity of the American Negro in national life, a belief in which he never wavered. Almost as soon as he wrote at all, he championed the cause of the Spirituals, challenging other American races to adduce on their part anything nearly as valuable in the way of native folk culture. Naturally, he foresaw they would be unable to do so. In fact, instead of attempting anything of the sort, his readers of other races for the most part were happy to join with him in singing the praises of those "Black and Unknown Bards," in the words of his immortal poem, who had created the Spirituals:

> O black and unknown bards of long ago,
> How came your lips to touch the sacred fire?
> How, in your darkness, did you come to know
> The power and beauty of the minstrel's lyre?
> Who first from midst his bonds lifted his eyes?
> Who first from out the still watch, lone and long,
> Feeling the ancient faith of prophets rise
> Within his dark-kept soul, burst into song?

It was to be expected that many would seek ways to immortalize the memory (and more particularly the *purpose*) of this great Negro citizen, who had foreseen one way himself—that is, in the writing and publication of his books, which will be alive and an inspiration for many years to come, not only to Negroes but to other races as well. Some of these projects for a memorial have already come to fruition and others no doubt will eventually do so. Schools with which he was associated, institutions which he fostered, in some instances will wish to organize their own personal memorials.

A few of his friends, however, felt that in many cases this disconnected striving after a perpetuation of the name of the author of the American Negro Anthem, and indeed all that this name stands for in our national life, might be realized more successfully if those of both races who have suggested isolated plans might be persuaded to join in a concerted action, if different sections of the country, schoolchildren and college presidents, workmen, newspaper editors, musicians and poets, ministers of God, might be brought together and united in fundamental harmony on the subject of what form the memorial would take. . . . When I began to talk about my own ideas on the subject to Walter White, I discovered that he, too, had spent a good deal of time cogitating and that in his official capacity as secretary of the NAACP he had received many letters either offering suggestions towards a memorial or asking his advice in regard to the particular shape a memorial should assume. In a short time Walter and I added Arthur Spingarn to our conferences and shortly thereafter invited a group of Jim's friends to meet and confer officially on the matter. We organized this group under the title of the James Weldon Johnson Memorial Committee.

Several matters pertaining to the memorial were settled almost at once. It was obvious to all of us, for instance, that . . . James Weldon Johnson himself would have approved no scheme whereby he was celebrated merely as an individual. . . . The memorial, it was felt, must include some kind of testimonial to the Negro race. . . . A scholarship at some institution of learning had been frequently suggested as an excellent manner of preserving the memory of the poet. But it was pointed out that a scholarship, at most, benefits only one man a year, while the title of a scholarship and indeed its real meaning are often forgotten by the very men who are educated under its provisions. Besides, it was argued sensibly, scholarships in the name of Mr. Johnson are sure to come sooner or later anyway, under the conditions in wills of friends or in other ways.

The idea which finally crystallized after many alternatives had been discussed and rejected, was a monument in bronze, not *of* James Weldon Johnson, but *to* his Black and Unknown Bards, the creators of the Spirituals which Mr. Johnson so much admired, their arms and faces uplifted to heaven, an inspiration to their race, a challenge to the defamers of that race. On the marble base of this memorial would appear on one side a bas-relief of Mr. Johnson's head, while on the other would be carved a stanza from the verses of the poet which had inspired the monument. The committee . . . recommended that it should be erected on a prominent site in the city of New York, the mayor of that city having already committed himself as being highly favorable to the project. The particular site which the committee would prefer is the island in the center of Seventh Avenue, immediately above One hundred and tenth Street, the monument facing the entrance to Central Park, so that anyone who emerged from the park at that point— and many thousands do in the course of a week—would meet the statue face to face. On the other hand, schoolchildren and their elders on their way to the park from Harlem would pass it by from the other direction.

Many good reasons dictated the choice of New York City as the proper location for such a memorial. One of the best reasons is that no Negro memorial of any kind whatever exists at present on the island of Manhattan (which cradles the largest Negro community in the world) while Boston (with both Crispus Attucks and Robert Gould Shaw and his Negro soldiers honored in marble on the Common), Philadelphia, Washington, and other American cities already can boast one or more such memorials. The decid-

ing factor, however, in the selection of New York is contained in the poet's
own words:

> When I come down to sleep death's endless night,
> The threshold of the unknown dark to cross,
> What to me then will be the keenest loss,
> When this bright world blurs on my fading sight?
> Will it be that no more shall I see the trees
> Or smell the flowers or hear the singing birds
> Or watch the flashing streams or patient herds?
> No. I am sure it will be none of these.
>
> But, ah! Manhattan's sights and sounds, her smell,
> Her crowds, her throbbing force, the thrill that comes
> From being of her a part, her subtle spells,
> Her shining towers, her avenues, her slums—
> O God! The stark, unutterable pity,
> To be dead, and never again beyond my city.

Once the committee had determined that the work would be awarded to
a Negro sculptor, it was almost inevitable that Richmond Barthé should be
chosen to be the recipient of the commission. He is, perhaps, the best-known
sculptor of his race and as an artist he can stand comparison (and has stood
this comparison at an indefinite number of art shows throughout the United
States) with the best sculptors of other races who have exhibited in this
country. Moreover, for a considerable period before he died, James Weldon
Johnson had tried to find the time to keep a promise to sit for Barthé, and
Mrs. Johnson therefore cherished a sentimental interest, quite apart from
her artistic interest, in hoping he would be chosen to shape the memorial.

Mr. Barthé was born in New Orleans thirty-seven years ago and studied
painting at the Art Institute in Chicago to emerge later as a sculptor. Three
examples of his work are in the permanent collection of the Whitney Museum
of American Art in New York City and there are many other examples in
private collections here. His work has been shown at art exhibitions in
Chicago, Nashville, Washington, Dallas, New Orleans, Pittsburgh, Philadelphia, and Baltimore. In New York he has held three one-man shows,
the latest at the Arden Galleries on Park Avenue last winter. He has also
exhibited at one-man shows in Grand Rapids, Michigan; Washington,[D.C.];
Madison, Wisconsin; and Chicago. . . .

The Black and Unknown Bards should offer Barthé an excellent opportunity for the search and for the eventual capture of spiritual values. Indeed,
the complete success of the undertaking, from any point of view, rests on
the assumption that he will do just that. . . . His group of Negroes with

uplifted faces should simulate an honest pride in the achievements of their race, in Negro youth for generations to come, while it should also bring it about that others, at present not fully aware of the cultural contributions the Negro has made to America, will seek to learn more about this race.

It is not true, as some have said, that New York has enough statues. It is true that we have enough bad statues, but no great city can have too many works of art. Lest we forget that works of art can exist in public places as well as in museums or in private collections, it is well to recall the *David* of Michelangelo which has been standing in its classic grace, to be admired by hundreds of thousands, in the Piazza della Signoria in Florence since the early sixteenth century. It is to be hoped then that the carver of *Mother and Son*, on view in the Contemporary Arts Building at the New York World's Fair, and the newer *Boy with Flute*, which may be seen in the current show of the Whitney Museum of American Art in New York, will be sufficiently inspired by the subject which has been offered him to create a work of art which will stimulate young Negroes for many generations to come and awaken in their white brothers a desire to learn more about the race which has produced the Spirituals and a sculptor great enough to celebrate their spirit in a singing bronze group. . . .

The James Weldon Johnson Memorial Committee solicits gifts towards the termination of this project and directs that they may be sent to the committee at 69 Fifth Avenue, New York. Checks may be made payable either to Theodore Roosevelt, chairman, or to Gene Buck, treasurer. It is the hope of the committee that interest in the project will be sufficiently widespread so that contributions will be sent in from all parts of America, not only in dollars, but also in nickels and dimes, and even in pennies. The James Weldon Johnson Memorial Committee is composed of close friends of the great Negro. This is a list of its members: Theodore Roosevelt, chairman; Hon. Fiorello H. LaGuardia, honorary chairman; Gene Buck, treasurer and chairman of the executive committee; Walter White, secretary; and the following vice-chairmen: Sterling A. Brown, Harry T. Burleigh, Elmer A. Carter, W.C. Handy, J. Rosamond Johnson, E. George Payne, Arthur B. Spingarn, and Carl Van Vechten.

THE JAMES WELDON JOHNSON MEMORIAL COLLECTION OF NEGRO ARTS AND LETTERS

At about the same time, Van Vechten established The James Weldon Johnson Memorial Collection of Negro Arts and Letters at Yale University. I have used this title for a single essay combining "The J.W. Johnson Collection at Yale," from *Crisis*, March 1942, and "How the Theatre

is Represented in the Negro Collection at Yale," from
Theatre Annual 1943 (New York: Theatre Annual, 1944).
   In these essays, to avoid repetition, I have freely re-
arranged sections of the original versions—and silently
so—for purposes of coherence. Elipses, of course, indicate
my deletions.

For a very long time I pondered, in my own mind, the question of what
would be my ultimate disposal of my collection of Negro books, manuscripts, letters, photographs, phonograph records, and music; not a large
collection, perhaps, but an extremely interesting and valuable one, since it
has been my privilege during the past two decades to know intimately many
of the most prominent members of the race. In this quandary, and spurred
on by world conditions to arrive at my decision in some haste, I was invited
by Bernhard Knollenberg, the librarian of Yale University, to deposit this
material to the Yale Library. Fortuitously, he employed precisely the right
words to convince me that Yale was the place for it: "We haven't any Negro
books at all."

It seemed to me then that this collection of mine could not only be made
immediately useful at Yale (the first white college in the North, I believe, to
make any determined effort to secure such material) but also might become
an active and growing source of propaganda, for no student hitherto unin-
formed on the subject could read these letters, these inscriptions in the
books, or even the books themselves, without asking himself, and others,
many questions.

There are other advantages connected with New Haven as a depository
for research material. It is near New York, Boston, and other cultural centers,
and in the very heart of the thickest section of the collegiate world. It is
sufficiently close to the largest Negro community on the globe, which itself
already boasts one of the most remarkable collections of Negro material,
that of Arthur A. Schomburg in the New York Public Library. The new
Yale building offers more elastic space to the collection than can be found in
most other college library buildings. Further, the material has been accepted
on my own terms and with an enthusiasm from the librarian and his staff
which speaks well for the future.

The official title of this gift is The James Weldon Johnson Memorial
Collection of Negro Arts and Letters, founded by Carl Van Vechten. It
seemed most appropriate to couple the name of my friend James Weldon
Johnson with material of which his advice had been so important an element
in its selection. My love and respect for the dead poet actually demanded
that I do so. Furthermore, I was frank in hoping that this title would serve
to induce others to make valuable additions to the collection. This already
has proved to be the case.

Mr. Knollenberg agrees with me that any manuscripts or books written by any one with Negro blood, and the best books about Negroes written by white men, belong in this collection. Further, interesting photographs, rare first editions of music (I wish somebody would give us the "St. Louis Blues" in this form!), phonograph records, programs of plays or concerts, and especially letters, should find a fitting, permanent resting place here. Incidentally, at some time to be appointed in the not too distant future, the collection will be officially opened with a showing of some of the more interesting material already in hand.

My own Negro library, which forms the nucleus of the collection, is not rich in the work of the past, although it does contain a first edition of Phillis Wheatley's *Poems on Various Subjects*, several books by William Wells Brown and Frederick Douglass, and many antislavery pamphlets and slave narratives. Beginning, however, with the early twentieth century and continuing to date, it assembles an almost complete accumulation of the literary work of the period, mostly represented in association items, together with a quantity of letters from the authors themselves. Charles W. Chesnutt, for example, has written long autobiographical inscriptions in all his books. Unfortunately, I didn't know Paul Laurence Dunbar, but he is fully represented by first editions, and in one of them is laid a letter from his wife with his autograph enclosed. James Weldon Johnson himself is represented by a complete set of his books, presentation copies of first editions, with long personal inscriptions, for the most part in mint condition in the original dust jackets, by phonograph records, by pamphlets, by clippings, by musical settings of his poems, by photographs, and by a fine series of letters and manuscripts.

Among the authors who are solidly represented (often in pamphlet form and by letters as well as by books) on the Yale Library shelves, in first editions in superb condition, and for the most part by association items, are the following: Jean Toomer, Wallace Thurman, George Schuyler, Eric Walrond, Zora Neale Hurston, C.L.R. James, Nella Larsen, Sterling Brown, Georgia Douglass Johnson, Claude McKay (including the very rare *Constab Ballads*), Alain Locke, Rudolph Fisher, William Stanley Braithwaite, W.E.B. Du Bois, Arna Bontemps, Richard Wright, Walter White, Booker T. Washington, William Attaway, and Waters E. Turpin.

Langston Hughes, through my own library, and by his own gifts to Yale, is so fully represented here that no other library will ever be able to compete with Yale in this respect. All his books, with personal inscriptions, songs set to his words, inscribed to me, photographs, a quantity of letters, most of his magazine and newspaper appearances, his inclusions in anthologies, translations of his work (into Spanish, French, Yiddish, Russian, Swedish, and German) together with eight large boxes of manuscripts (partly my gift, partly his) are already stored on the shelves at New Haven. Manuscripts of all of the several drafts of *Not Without Laughter*, of many of his poems, of all his plays, are in the collection. Countée Cullen is only less fully represented, but by important and unique items. Through separate gifts from Roberta Bosley, Harold Jackman, and myself, we have succeeded in putting together the complete series of manuscripts of *The Lost Zoo*, in several drafts, beginning with Mr. Cullen's original notes. The manuscript of Countée Cullen's play, *One Way to Heaven*, derived from his novel of the same name, is in the collection. So is the manuscript of the play he wrote with Arna Bontemps, *God Sends Sunday*. So is the manuscript of the prologue and epilogue to Mr. Cullen's version of the *Medea*, which were not yet written when the play was published, written in his own hand, with corrections, in a Paris notebook, all preserved at Yale for posterity to examine.

The collection contains the published books of W.C. Handy, most of his music, all of it inscribed to me, and a good deal of it in first editions, a great many letters, photographs, and phonograph records, and several extremely interesting manuscripts, including the full score in parts of an arrangement of "The Basement Blues" for band. J. Rosamond Johnson is equally fully represented and some of his songs are also signed by his poet brother, James Weldon Johnson. There is a large group of Spirituals, arranged by Henry T. Burleigh, inscribed to me, and Mr. Burleigh has also given me for the collection two manuscripts from the cycle, *Passionale*, with corrections in the hand of James Weldon Johnson who wrote the words. Another of the more interesting items in this department of the collection is the manuscript orchestral score of William Grant Still's ballet, *Sahdjii*, in which is laid autobiographical comment in longhand by Alain Locke and Bruce Nugent, who collaborated on the scenario for this dance-drama. From Hall Johnson has come the manuscript of the original songs in *Run, Little Children*, and William Dawson and Clarence Cameron White have been generous with their musical manuscripts. Clarence Cameron White has presented us with the manuscript score of the prelude to his opera, *Ouanga*.

On the shelves at New Haven stand many famous books about Negroes by white authors, including Du Bose Heyward's novel, *Mamba's Daughters* (accompanied by an inscribed presentation copy of the first edition of the play from Ethel Waters), Leonard Merrick's *The Quaint Companions*, Dorothy Baker's *Young Man with a Horn*, W.D. Howells's *An Imperative Duty* (a most amazing book for the year 1892!), George W. Cable's *The Silent South and the Negro*, Gilmore Millen's *Sweet Man*, the extremely rare first edition of Joel Chandler Harris's *Uncle Remus*, and other books by Mr. Harris, *The Key to Uncle Tom's Cabin*, Ellen Glasgow's *On Barren Ground* and *In This Our Life*, novels and stories by Julia Peterkin, Willa Cather's *Sapphira and the Slave Girl*, Vachel Lindsay's *The Congo*, and a mass of material . . . by and about Nancy Cunard. An inscribed copy of Eugene O'Neill's *The Emperor Jones* and copies of such other of this author's plays as deal with Negroes are in the collection in first editions. So are such other celebrated plays as *The Green Pastures, Goat Alley,* the plays of Ridgely Torrence, *In Abraham's Bosom* and other plays by Paul Green, William Du Bois's *Haiti,* Richard Wright's *Native Son,* Edward Sheldon's *The Nigger,* and *Stevedore* [by George Sklar and Paul Peters]. Pamphlets, manuscripts, books relating to the Negro in the theatre abound in the collection. A great many of these books are association items. Further, the manuscripts I possess of my own work concerning the Negro, together with the first appearances of this material, have been given to the collection.

There is a fund of books dealing with sociological subjects and there are many books and pamphlets connected with the Negro's dealings with Communism and the Catholic church. . . . There are files of several periodicals, of which those of *Challenge, Phylon,* etc., are complete. The file of *Opportunity* begins with Volume II; that of *Crisis* with the year 1925, Volume XXX. We have Volume VIII (1926) complete of *The Messenger;* the first three numbers of 1925 and the last eight of 1927 are missing. We haven't the other years of this magazine at all. It would be a splendid thing if somebody would make the collection of a gift of any of the missing years of these periodicals. . . .

The James Weldon Johnson Memorial Collection of Negro Arts and Letters is certainly only incidentally devoted to theatrical materials, but just as certainly, we are passionately interested in every scrap of matter which concerns the Negro in the theatre. I daresay that many persons, when the Negro theatre is mentioned, think of *Uncle Tom's Cabin* or at best, *Porgy* or *The Emperor Jones,* forgetting that three of the most famous playwrights of the modern stage had Negro forbears. Actually, the Negro theatre might boast as many ancient traditions as the theatre of other races, for assuredly it was born in the dance-dramas of prehistoric Africa. The Negro was the inspiration for the American Minstrel Show and many of the best minstrel performers (James C. Bland, the composer of "Carry Me Back to Ole Virginny," for example) were colored men. For what we once called ragtime, which has been developed into what we call jazz and swing and hot music, we are also indebted to the Negro, as these sounds were first blown into the world by black lips in the basements of Memphis and New Orleans. The Negro theatre has its classical traditions, too: the Negro tragedian, Ira Aldridge, toured Europe in *Othello* and other classical plays in the middle of the nineteenth century; Sissieretta Jones (the "Black Patti") rivalled Sofia Scalchi as a concert singer in the nineties; and the playwrights referred to above, Alexandre Dumas, father and son, and Alexander Pushkin, in their respective periods, dominated the stages of Europe and, in the case of *La Dame aux Camelias,* of the entire western world.

It is not generally known, perhaps, that another playwright with Negro blood, Victor Sejour, born in New Orleans, was a successful writer of melodrama in Paris from 1841 to 1861, contemporary with the younger Dumas, and is buried in the famous Paris cemetery of Père Lachaise. There are about seventeen of his very bad plays in the Yale Library and I have taken the trouble to read one or two. Completely divorced from reality (or even poetry or fantasy) the plays possessed the glamour of the spectacular and the speeches in them were endowed with the ephemeral charm of flamboyant rhetoric. The fact to be noted is that a Negro from New Orleans made such a profound impression on the theatre world of Paris that he had twenty-one of his plays successfully produced there in the principal theatres at a time when notable French playwrights were almost as common as blueberries in Maine during the month of August.

The James Weldon Johnson Collection is not lacking in reminders of the two Dumas (it even contains autographed letters of the elder Dumas) or of Pushkin or of Sejour. The plays of these men may be studied here, but up to this time the collection has been more concerned with the writers of the present century. It is already possible for a student to examine in the Yale Library, either in book form or in manuscript, almost any play by or about Negroes produced since 1900. For instance, all of Langston Hughes's plays exist in the collection in manuscript (usually in several drafts) and they comprise a much more extensive list than playgoers in general are aware of, because, while the public has seen *Mulatto* and *Don't You Want to Be Free?*, the latter script is almost unique among this author's plays in achieving publication, while *When the Jack Hollers, Little Ham, Joy to My Soul,* and *Outshines the Sun* have been performed by the Gilpin Players at the Karamu Theatre in Cleveland, and *The Sun Do Move* has been produced only in Chicago. A future investigator will discover that he may examine at New Haven not only the various scripts of Hughes's pageant, *For This We Fight*, recently enacted at Madison Square Garden, but also programs, dodgers, posters, and even tickets for this event.

Owen Dodson is another Negro playwright abundantly represented here by his manuscripts. Mr. Dodson was formerly an undergraduate at Yale where, in succeeding years, two of his plays were presented by the white students: *Divine Comedy* (built around the career of Father Divine) and *Garden of Time*, an arrangement of the Medea legend. Mr. Dodson subsequently became the head of the drama department at Atlanta University, where he produced *The Cherry Orchard*, and still later he headed the drama department at Hampton Institute, where he produced *Hedda Gabler*. Until recently he has been a sailor in the American navy, stationed at the Great Lakes Station in Illinois where his superior officers availed themselves of his experience and talent by putting him in charge of the "Happy Hours" program at Camp Robert Smalls, a program designed to entertain the drafted and enlisted sailors at this spot. Seaman Dodson took full advantage of his opportunity to do a great deal more than entertain the boys. He wrote and produced a series of "Pageants of Freedom," one devoted to the story of

Dorie Miller, Negro hero of Pearl Harbor, another devoted to the wonder of George Washington Carver ("Climbing to the Soil"). "Everybody Join Hands" publishes the passionate faith of the Chinese folk, while "Freedom the Banner" is an attempt to express the contemporary feeling of the Russians. While he was stationed there, new dramas were offered to the sailors in this camp nearly every month, while the more popular older pieces were repeated. The manuscripts of these miniature dramas, intended for the consumption of sailors often hitherto unfamiliar with the theatre and thereby tempting the author to employ experimental forms, have been presented to the collection in their several drafts, together with invitations, programs, and posters, frequently designed by the Negro painter, Charles Sebree. One of the most interesting of Mr. Dodson's manuscripts is that of his play *Amistad*, written for and produced at Talledega College in Alabama in 1939. The title is taken from the name of a slave ship with a curious history of which the denouement, the trial of the escaped slaves, fortuitously occurred in the courts of New Haven. Preserved in the library at Yale, further, is a series of portraits of these slaves.

The collection is rich in photographs. My own collection of photographs of Negro celebrities was extensive before I dreamed of giving it to Yale, although it consisted largely of portraits of contemporaries or those more recently dead. When Mrs. [Edith] Isaacs invited me to become a member of the committee which planned the Negro number of *Theatre Arts*, published in August 1942, I discovered, along with the other members of the committee and the editors of the magazine, that photographs of Negroes so recently deceased as Florence Mills and Bert Williams did not exist in any considerable quantity, while photographs of stage celebrities as well known as George Walker, Aida Overton Walker, and Ernest Hogan, almost might be said not to exist at all. It isn't that these dancers and actors and singers were not frequently photographed in their day. It is that, generally speaking, few persons had taken the trouble to collect and to preserve their photographs. I have since made a determined effort to dislodge from their hiding places as many photographs, lithographs, or pictures in any reproduced form, of as many Negro stage celebrities as can be found.

One of the unique features of the collection is a set of photographs of Negroes which I have made myself and these have become an impressive group, perhaps the largest group of photographs of notable Negro personalities ever made by one man, including not only James Weldon Johnson and his brother, J. Rosamond Johnson (who wrote words and music for Klaw and Erlanger extravaganzas at the turn of the century, long before they became famous in other fields), but also Langston Hughes (whose *Mulatto* may have received more performances than any other play by a dramatist with Negro blood save the dramas of the two Dumas!). There are also photographs of Rose McClendon, including pictures of her in the *Medea* of Counté̈e Cullen, although she died too early to create this role in the theatre; and Ruby Elzy, the touching singer of the role of Serena in *Porgy*; of Maxine Sullivan who probably can sing "Loch Lomond" in her sleep; of Joe Louis whose legitimate position in a theatre collection derives from the fact that he appears in the motion-picture version of *This Is the Army* and in another cinema or two; of Elisabeth Welch, better known in London and Paris than in New York, where she originally sang Cole Porter's "Love for Sale"; of the principal singers of Virgil Thomson's setting of Gertrude Stein's *Four Saints in Three Acts*; of Oscar Polk, Marian Anderson, Canada Lee, Georgette Harvey, Lena Horne, Katherine Dunham, Bill Robinson, Ethel Waters, W.C. Handy, Cab Calloway, Bricktop, William L. Dawson, Aaron Douglas, Paul Williams, Taylor Gordon, Zora Neale Hurston, Rex Ingram, Nella Larsen, Claude McKay, Horace Pippin, Henry Armstrong, Avon Long, Richard Wright, Dean Dixon, Richmond Barthé, Counté̈e Cullen, Jimmie Daniels, Fredi Washington, Dorothy Maynor, Paul Robeson, and many others. I am still taking photographs of Negro celebrities, so this branch of the collection will continue to grow automatically.

There are photographs, mostly inscribed, from other lenses in the collection, of James Weldon Johnson, Paul Robeson (including many pictures of Mrs. Robeson), Adelaide Hall, A'Lelia Walker, Josephine Baker, Richard B. Harrison, Charles W. Chesnutt, Nora Holt, and countless others. There is also a group of photographs of celebrated paintings which include Negroes, from the public and private galleries of Europe and America. Further, there are several original paintings, decorations, and prints by Charles Sebree, Zell Ingram, Hale Woodruff, Aaron Douglas, and others.

In the matter of phonograph records the collection finds itself in the propitious position of possessing almost complete sets of the records of the "Empress of the Blues," Bessie Smith (of whom Hugues Panassié has written in *Hot Jazz*, "She is so perfect she defies all description and all praise"), and of the superb Ethel Waters, including not only her suave deliveries of the melodies she has made famous ("Dinah," "Am I Blue?," "Stormy Weather," etc.) but also her early raucous and obscene plaints ("Maybe Not at All," "Shake That Thing," "Go Back Where You Stayed Last Night," and the like). Paul Robeson, Duke Ellington, Louis Armstrong, and Cab Calloway are also well represented, while the voices of other well-known Negro singers, Clara, Mamie, and Trixie Smith, "Ma" Rainey, Sloppy Henry, Lena Wilson, Gertrude Saunders, Victoria Spivey, Joshua White, Billie Holliday, Blind Lemon Jefferson, and many more are preserved on discs in the collection.

The modern theatre has many branches and in every one of these the Negro occupies an important niche. In moving pictures, not only is he an important member of the cast in many big productions (*Gone with the Wind, Imitation of Life, In This Our Life*, and many another film) but also a few pictures, such as the early *Hallelujah* and the later *Cabin in the Sky*,

have been devoted entirely to the Negro. He is often a feature of radio entertainment. He sings in opera. Many operas, such as *L'Africaine, Aïda,* and
Jonny Spielt Auf have Negro protagonists; still others, such as *Lakmé,
Salomé, Samson et Dalila,* and even *Carmen* and *Cavalleria Rusticana,* may
be performed appropriately by dark-skinned singers. Dean Dixon has made
a name for himself as a conductor of symphonic works. The Negro is a figure
in ballet, notably in *Petrouchka* and *Scheherazade.* Agnes de Mille composed and produced, for the Ballet Theatre, an entire ballet, *Dark Ritual,*
danced by Negroes. Katherine Dunham, Pearl Primus, Belle Rosette, Feral
Benga, are all Negro dancers who have won applause on the boards. In the
legitimate theatre it is the rule rather than the exception to discover Negroes
in the cast; the concert stage is studded with Negro stars and Marian Anderson
shines brighter than any white star in this particular firmament.

One of the more interesting features of the James Weldon Johnson Collection at Yale is the series of boxes, indexed and catalogued, devoted to the
Negro in the theatre, ballet, opera, concert, and the motion picture. These
boxes contain programs, clippings of reviews and interviews, photographs,
even personal notes and letters. This miscellany is fluid, of course, and is
constantly growing both into the past and during the present. As often as
sufficient material accumulates, further boxes are added. A specimen box is
devoted to Paul Robeson material. It contains over seventy-five photographs
and over thirty programs of plays and concerts signed by Mr. Robeson,
occasionally with explanatory notes; pamphlets and leaflets, over forty
leaves of clippings, articles about Mr. Robeson, and other items. Another
box contains twenty-two Marian Anderson programs together with twenty-
four pages of mounted clippings concerning the contralto; Taylor Gordon
and J. Rosamond Johnson materials; Dorothy Maynor programs; items
dealing with *Four Saints in Three Acts;* Clarence Cameron White's Negro
opera, *Ouanga; La Belle Hélène* as given by Negroes at Westport; *Porgy
and Bess;* and the concert and opera appearances of Caterina Jarboro who
has sung *Aïda* in New York.

I have been amazed and endlessly delighted by the response which the
announcement of the founding of the collection has met from Negroes and
others who possess Negro material. From the very beginning they have been
of the greatest assistance to me in planning additions to the collection.
Dorothy Peterson, for instance, has secured for us many interesting volumes
by Puerto Rican Negroes, and the second volume of *Opportunity* not on my
own shelves. She has successfully solicited many gifts from others. Walter
White gave me carte blanche to take any books from his personal library
not already in the collection. I availed myself literally of this opportunity
and confiscated a great many, a number of which are association items. Mr.
White has further furnished the James Weldon Johnson Collection with a
complete set of pamphlets (many written by Mr. Johnson himself) issued by

the NAACP from 1912 to date and has been instrumental in securing much material from others. Harold Jackman likewise has permitted me to pillage his library to my heart's content and further has turned over many important letters and manuscripts and has been endlessly and continuously valuable in unearthing other buried treasures. It has already been suggested that Langston Hughes has presented the collection with practically everything he possesses relating to himself or to Negroes in general. Claude McKay has given us the manuscript of *Home to Harlem* and other material. Arthur Spingarn has given most generously from his own superb Negro library. The Misses Helene Grant and Georgia Washington have presented to the collection the manuscript of *Aunt Hagar's Children*, an unpublished book by Wallace Thurman, also four pages of the manuscript on which Thurman was writing when he died, and letters and photographs of this writer. Fannie Hurst has given the collection a first edition of *Imitation of Life*, stills from the picturization of this story, and other material.

In the matter of letters the collection has also been fortunate. I am a prolific letter writer myself and frequently my letters are answered. My Negro correspondence has all been presented to the collection. Letters have also poured into the New Haven library from other sources so that now the collection contains hundreds of autographed letters from (and to) James Weldon Johnson, Ethel Waters, Langston Hughes, Richard B. Harrison ("de Lawd" of *The Green Pastures*), Roland Hayes, Paul and Essie Robeson, Rose Mc-Clendon, Florence Mills, and others. Dean E. George Payne of New York University has presented us with several fine letters from James Weldon Johnson, and Amy Spingarn has given us Langston Hughes's letters to her and letters from James Weldon Johnson, J. Rosamond Johnson, and others to Joel Spingarn. Dorothy West has given us the manuscripts of two short stories. Further gifts have been received from Robert C. Weaver, Dr. Louis Wright, Henry W. Greene, and others. Donald G. Wing of the accessions department at the Yale Library has put the cream on the other gifts by adding to the collection by purchasing a fine letter from Toussaint L'Ouverture. I hope we shall be able to announce in the future the acquisition of manuscript material, letters, or photographs of the two Dumas and Pushkin.

And I hope to be able to announce more, lots more. Anyone who has letters, manuscripts, photographs of prominent Negroes, please be assured they will be welcome and safer and more permanently preserved and of greater service than they would be at home. So will rare books and association copies. So will theatre programs and phonograph records when they are in fine condition and do not duplicate material already at hand.

There is nothing then pertaining to the Negro too important or too unimportant to fit into this collection. Certainly welcome, as they come in, are Pushkin and Dumas letters, manuscripts, and first editions, Ira Aldridge programs, photographs, prose descriptions of African tribal dances and phonograph records of the music which accompanies them; welcome also are Bob Cole's laundry bills, posters of nineteenth-century minstrel shows, stills of Louise Beavers, Hattie McDaniel, Clarence Muse, Butterfly McQueen, or other prominent Negro picture actors, dodgers advertising Sissieretta Jones, or songs written by Will Marion Cook to be sung by Abbie Mitchell, or pamphlets or books in any form relating to the Negro. Their arrival is always the cause of great interest for they add to this collection of Negro material that is meant to be as useful to future students as enthusiastic accumulation, careful explanation, and arrangement can make it.

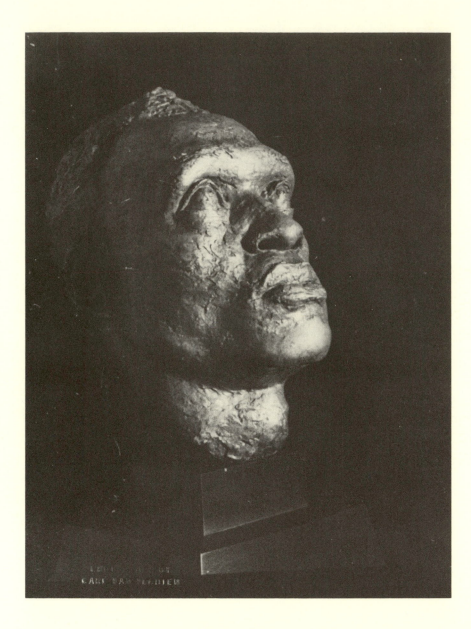

Paul Robeson, bronze by Jacob Epstein, photograph by
Carl Van Vechten, 1933

4

Portrait Memoirs

WALTER WHITE

At a 1944 banquet, given in honor of Walter White by the National Association for the Advancement of Colored People, Carl Van Vechten spoke briefly. The notes for his comments, roughly typed on half a sheet of paper, are now among his papers at Yale and are published here for the first time.

Elsewhere, in the Columbia Oral History which Van Vechten did not intend to publish, he was more candid, indicating without the slightest malice or apology that he and White had forced their friendship for largely practical reasons. "I was never completely sold on Walter," he admitted. "He wasn't all there really." As the Twenties ran out, they "grew more and more apart. This was partly on his side too. Walter knew, after a while, that I was no particular use to him and he was less to me too as far as that goes." In the beginning, Van Vechten had afforded White access to a particular white intelligentsia and, in turn, White had introduced Van Vechten to Harlem's intellectuals. They were on friendly terms, however, until White's death even though their contacts were largely involved with business matters after the Harlem Renaissance.

Van Vechten once said that White's first novel, *The Fire in the Flint*, was bad fiction perhaps, but good propaganda. He endorsed it, nevertheless, and its successor, *Flight*, with enthusiasm. His review of the latter, "A Triumphant Negro Heroine," appeared in the *New York Herald Tribune Books*, 11 April 1926. It is here appended to Van Vechten's notes for his speech.

I am asked to speak of Walter White in his capacity as author. Walter has written and published two successful novels, *The Fire in the Flint* and *Flight*. Further, he is responsible for *Rope and Faggot*, the authoritative work on lynching. He has written innumerable propaganda articles for magazines and periodicals and an incredible number of pamphlets on the race question. He writes a weekly column for the *Chicago Defender* and contributes a monthly editorial to the NAACP *Bulletin*.

As a novelist Walter burns with as much righteous indignation as he does as a propagandist. In fact, his novels are propaganda novels—no one can read them without sharing to some extent his horror of the conditions they expose.

His family were sufferers in the Atlanta race riots and Walter has described this riot with such fury in *Flight* that any reader would believe he actually witnessed the riot itself. I was so moved and impressed by a reading of *The Fire in the Flint* that I asked my publisher, also Walter's publisher, . . . for an introduction to the young man who wrote it. This was in 1924. Since then we have become warm friends and he was of the greatest assistance to me in accumulating some material for my novel, *Nigger Heaven*, published two years later. We have indeed been associated in several projects, so much so that at one time he dubbed my apartment, situated halfway between 695 Seventh Avenue and his Harlem home, the midtown office of the NAACP.

Walter has such a gift for making people see and feel what he sees and feels about bad race relations that anything he writes is valuable. In Germany his books undoubtedly would be burned, but in America it is his books that burn his readers.

It may be interesting to record the fact that Mr. Walter White is the third American of African descent to see two novels in print. Several American Negroes have had one novel published, but previous to the appearance of *Flight* only Paul Laurence Dunbar and Charles W. Chesnutt could claim more than one.

Mr. White's first novel, *The Fire in the Flint*, issued by Mr. Knopf in September 1924, was immediately and widely hailed as a work of grim power. Dealing as it does with peonage, rape, and lynching in Georgia, certain of its scenes are executed with a force sufficiently elemental to efface the memory of some amateurish writing in other passages.

It is a pleasure to be able to state that Mr. White's second novel is much better than his first. It is written with a calm detachment of which *The Fire in the Flint* contains no hint. Furthermore, in Mimi Daquin, a Negro Creole girl with ivory skin and hair of reddish gold, the author has drawn a character entirely new to Afro-American fiction. Instead of the persecuted figure with which books on this general subject have made us so familiar, we are presented with a heroine who is mistress of her own fate, a woman whose ultimate acts are governed by her will. Mimi does not long permit herself to be hampered by the restrictions of Negro life and she is equally independent in her relations with the two men who play important parts in her career. She refuses to marry the father of her child; later, she leaves her white husband to return to the heart of her own race.

The subject of passing (that is, passing for white) has infrequently been utilized by Negro authors. Charles W. Chesnutt dwelt on its tragic aspects in *The House Behind the Cedars* (1902) and James Weldon Johnson contributed a more suave study of the theme in that human document, *The Autobiography of an Ex-Coloured Man* (1912), an invaluable source book for all and sundry who deal in the future with the problems of color. Both these books are at present out of print.

Mr. White approaches the subject from a new and sufficiently sensational point of view. Mimi Daquin does not leave the colored world because she has been insulted or humiliated by white people; she leaves it because of her momentary dissatisfaction with Negroes. In the end, as has been stated, realizing that both races have their peculiar faults and virtues, she decides for purely logical reasons that she is happier with her colored brethren and she deserts her white husband to return to Harlem.

This, then, is the distinguishing merit of this novel, that it focuses attention upon a Negro character who is not materially hindered in her career by white prejudice. It is the simple chronicle of a beautiful, intelligent, dignified, self-supporting Negro girl. There is, indeed, a curious resemblance between Mimi and the self-reliant heroines of Miss Ellen Glasgow.

The story takes the reader from the Creole quarter in New Orleans through the race riots of Atlanta (1906), in which Mimi as a child acquires her race consciousness, through a brief episode in Philadelphia where her child is born, on to Harlem, and finally into white Manhattan. The incidental Negro characters are in no wise depicted as paragons of propriety and good taste. In fact, occasionally the author deals with them even a little cruelly. The petty gossip, the small meannesses, the color snobbery of Negro society (Mimi's father, Jean, says of the group in Atlanta: "Colored people here are always talking about prejudice, and they're just about as full of prejudice against Catholics, Jews and black Negroes as white people themselves") are fully described, but Mr. White makes it plain that in these respects there is little to choose between the two worlds.

In short, an excellent novel which should be read with increasing wonder by those who are unfamiliar with the less sordid circles of Negro life, and which others may read simply as a story without thought of propaganda. Indeed, with this second book Mr. White takes on quite a new stature. There is little doubt but that he will be heard from further.

COUNTÉE CULLEN

Vanity Fair first published the poems of Countée Cullen
in June 1925, at Carl Van Vechten's instigation. For that
appearance he prepared a brief note of introduction.

Subsequently, however, Cullen rejected Van Vechten's
offers of assistance. Within a decade, Countée Cullen had
nearly completed his career as a writer. Some juvenile
stories followed, but his poetry — exquisitely turned on
conventional forms and pretty images — finally suffered
from what Van Vechten had praised as "haunting, lyric
loveliness." He also wrote an interesting novel about
Harlem, *One Way to Heaven*, in which Van Vechten appears
as Walter Dervent. Cullen spent the last decade of his life
as a high school English teacher, and two years before his
death in 1947 he had already arranged the contents of
On These I Stand, the "collected poems" of Countée Cullen.

What the colored race needs to break its bonds is a few more men and
women of genius. This is a theory recently promulgated by the Negro intelligentsia. Providence, apparently, is willing to test the theory, for genius,
or talent, is pouring prodigally out of Harlem, and out of other cities' black
belts as well. Such young writers as Jean Toomer, Jessie Fauset, Walter
White, Claude McKay, Eric Walrond, Langston Hughes, Rudolph Fisher,
and Alain Locke; such young musicians, actors, and dancers as Roland
Hayes, Paul Robeson, Julius Bledsoe, Lawrence Brown, Eddie Rector,
Florence Mills, and Johnny Hudgins (I am naming only a few of the many)
are sufficiently earnest of what the "gift of black folk" (to employ Dr.
Du Bois's poetic phrase) will be in the immediate future.

One of the best of the Negro writers, Countée Cullen, is the youngest of
them all. He was barely twenty-one when "The Shroud of Color" (published
in the November 1924 issue of *The American Mercury*) created a sensation
analogous to that created by the appearance of Edna St. Vincent Millay's
"Renascence" in 1912, lifting its author at once to a position in the front rank
of contemporary American poets, white or black. "The Shroud of Color"
was emotional in its passionate eloquence, but Countée Cullen sometimes,
as on this page, for instance, strikes the strings of his inspirational lyre
more lightly, although a satiric or bitter aftertaste is likely to linger in his
most ostensibly flippant verse. All his poetry is characterized by a suave,
unpretentious, brittle, intellectual elegance; some of it—"To John Keats,
Poet, at Spring Time" is an excellent example—by a haunting, lyric loveliness.
It is to be noted that, like any distinguished artist of any race, he is able to
write stanzas which have no bearing on the problems of his own race. In
this respect his only Negro forebear, so far as I can recall at the moment, is
the poet Pushkin, whose verses dwelt on Russian history and folklore,
although he was the great-grandson of a slave.

LANGSTON HUGHES

Carl Van Vechten met Langston Hughes and Countée Cullen through James Weldon Johnson. Shortly thereafter, he arranged for publication of their poems in *Vanity Fair*. Those of Hughes appeared in two installments, September 1925 and May 1926. In between, Hughes's first volume of poems, *The Weary Blues*, was published by Alfred A. Knopf, also at Van Vechten's instigation. I have incorporated the brief introductory notes Van Vechten prepared for *Vanity Fair* into his introduction to *The Weary Blues*, "Introducing Langston Hughes to the Reader." Unlike Cullen, who demurred, Hughes was delighted to be able to turn to Van Vechten for advice — and Van Vechten to him — during the long friendship that ensued. To these early pieces about the poet, I have appended two book reviews Van Vechten prepared for the *New York Times* about two of the *Simple* collections. Langston Hughes first prepared these short stories, dialogues, and observations for the *Chicago Defender*, about Jesse B. Semple, better known as "Simple," a black folk hero for the Fifties. Van Vechten's "Simple Speaks His Mind" was published 7 May 1950; "In the Heart of Harlem" appeared 31 May 1953.

Langston Hughes's forty-year career produced a richly varied, astonishingly productive range of verse, fiction, plays, edited collections, autobiography (in which he paid affectionate tribute to Van Vechten), and criticism, all from a black perspective that his promising contemporary, Countée Cullen, could not or would not, perhaps, call upon.

At the moment I cannot recall the name of any other person whatever who, at the age of twenty-three, has enjoyed so picturesque and rambling an existence as Langston Hughes. Indeed, a complete account of his disorderly and delightfully fantastic career would make a fascinating picaresque romance which I hope this young Negro will write before so much more befalls him that he may find it difficult to capture all the salient episodes within the limits of a single volume.

Born on February 1, 1902, in Joplin, Missouri, he had lived, before his twelfth year, in the City of Mexico; Topeka, Kansas; Colorado Springs; Charleston; Indiana; Kansas City; and Buffalo. He attended Central High School, from which he graduated, at Cleveland, Ohio; while in the summer, there and in Chicago, he worked as delivery- and dummy- boy in hat stores. In his senior year he was elected class poet and editor of the year book.

After four years in Cleveland, he once more joined his father in Mexico, only to migrate to New York where he entered Columbia University. There, finding the environment distasteful, or worse, he remained till spring, when he quit, broke with his father and, with thirteen dollars in cash, went on his own. First he worked for a truck-farmer on Staten Island; next, he delivered flowers for Thorley; at length he partially satisfied an insatiable craving to go to sea by signing up with an old ship anchored in the Hudson for the winter. His first real cruise as a sailor carried him to the Canary Islands, the Azores, and the West Coast of Africa, of which voyage he has written: "Oh, the sun in Dakar! Oh, the little black girls of Burutu! Oh, the blue, blue bay of Loanda! Calabar, the city lost in a forest; the long, shining days at sea, the masts rocking against the stars at night; the black Kru-boy sailors, taken at Freetown, bathing on deck morning and evening; Tom Pey and Haneo, whose dangerous job it was to dive under the seven-ton mahogany logs floating and bobbing at the ship's side and fasten them to the chains of the crane; the vile houses of rotting women at Lagos; the desolation of the Congo; Johnny Walker, and the millions of whisky bottles buried in the sea along the West Coast; the daily fights on board, officers, sailors, everybody drunk; the timorous, frightened missionaries we carried as passengers; and George, the Kentucky colored boy, dancing and singing the Blues on the after-deck under the stars."

Returning to New York with plenty of money and a monkey, he presently shipped again—this time for Holland. Again he came back to New York and again he sailed—on his twenty-second birthday: February 1, 1924. Three weeks later he found himself in Paris with less than seven dollars. However, he was soon provided for: a woman of his own race engaged him as doorman at her *boîte de nuit*. Later he was employed, first as second cook, then as waiter, at the Grand Duc, where the Negro entertainer, Florence, sang at this epoch. Here he made friends with an Italian family who carried him off to their villa at Desenzano on Lago di Garda where he passed a happy month, followed by a night in Verona and a week in Venice. On his way back across Italy his passport was stolen and he became a beachcomber in Genoa. He has described his life there to me: "Wine and figs and *pasta*. And sunlight! And amusing companions, dozens of other beach-combers roving the dockyards and waterfront streets, getting their heads whacked by the Fascisti, and breaking one loaf of bread into so many pieces that nobody got more than a crumb. I lived in the public gardens along the waterfront and slept in the Albergo Populare for two lire a night amidst the snores of hundreds of other derelicts. . . . I painted my way home as a sailor. It seems that I must have painted the whole ship myself. We made a regular 'grand tour': Livorno, Napoli (we passed so close to Capri I could have cried). Then all around Sicily—Catania, Messina, Palermo—the Lipari Islands, miserable little peaks of pumice stone out in the sea; then across to Spain, divine Spain! My buddy and I went on a spree in Valencia for a night and a day. . . . Oh, the sweet wine of Valencia!"

He arrived in New York on November 10, 1924. That evening I attended a dance given in Harlem by the National Association for the Advancement of Colored People. Some time during the course of the night, Walter White asked me to meet two young Negro poets. He introduced me to Countée Cullen and Langston Hughes. Before that moment I had never heard of either of them.

I have merely sketched a primitive outline of a career as rich in adventures as a fruitcake is full of raisins. I have already stated that I hope Langston Hughes may be persuaded to set it down on paper in the minutest detail, for the bullfights in Mexico, the drunken gaiety of the Grand Duc, the delicately exquisite grace of the little black girls at Burutu, the exotic languor of the Spanish women at Valencia, the barbaric jazz dances of the cabarets in New York's own Harlem, the companionship of sailors of many races and nationalities, all have stamped an indelible impression on the highly sensitized, poetic imagination of this young Negro, an impression which has found its initial expression in the poems assembled in this book.

And also herein may be discerned that nostalgia for color and warmth and beauty which explains this boy's nomadic instincts.

> We should have a land of sun,
> Of gorgeous sun,
> And a land of fragrant water
> Where the twilight
> Is a soft bandanna handkerchief
> Of rose and gold,
> And not this land where life is cold,

he sings. Again, he tells his dream:

> To fling my arms wide
> In the face of the sun,
> Dance! whirl! whirl!
> Till the quick day is done.
> Rest at pale evening. . . .

A tall, slim tree. . . .
Night, coming tenderly,
    Black like me.

More of this wistful longing may be discovered in the poems entitled "The
South" and "As I Grew Older." His verses, however, are by no means limited
to an exclusive mood; he writes caressingly of little black prostitutes in
Harlem; his cabaret songs throb with the true jazz rhythm; his sea-pieces
ache with a calm, melancholy lyricism; he cries bitterly from the heart of
his race in "Cross" and "The Jester"; he sighs, in one of the most successful of his
fragile poems, over the loss of a loved friend. Always, however, his stanzas
are subjective, personal. They are the (I had almost said informal, for they
have a highly deceptive air of spontaneous improvisation) expression of an
essentially sensitive and subtly illusive nature, seeking always to break
through the veil that obscures for him at least in some degree, the ultimate
needs of that nature.

To the Negro race in America, since the day when Phillis Wheatley indited
lines to General George Washington and other aristocratic figures (for
Phillis Wheatley never sang "My way's cloudy," or "By an' by, I'm goin' to
lay down dis heavy load") there have been born many poets. Paul Laurence
Dunbar, James Weldon Johnson, Claude McKay, Jean Toomer, Georgia
Douglas Johnson, Countée Cullen, are a few of the more memorable names.
Not the least of these names, I think, is that of Langston Hughes, and perhaps
his adventures and personality offer the promise of as rich a fulfillment as
has been the lot of any of the others.

Readers of the Washington newspapers were astonished a few weeks ago
by the report that Vachel Lindsay, during the course of a lecture he delivered
at the Wardman Park Hotel, had read five poems written by Langston Hughes,
a Negro busboy working in the same hotel. Readers of *Vanity Fair* would
not have been amazed because several poems of Mr. Hughes appeared in
the September 1925 issue of this magazine. Alfred A. Knopf has recently
published Langston Hughes's first volume of poetry, *The Weary Blues.* It
may also be stated that this boy, who was twenty-four years old on February first, is at present in attendance at Lincoln University in Pennsylvania.
The poems below represent an attempt that no other Negro poet has made—
none other, certainly very successful—to recapture the spirit of Negro folklore. The Blues are not yet as famous as the Spirituals, but all the world is
now learning about their beauty.

On frequent occasions, the late James Weldon Johnson, Negro author,
was heard to observe: "There is no doubt in my mind that the solution to
the 'race problem' depends on a sense of humor." Then he would say that

persons who would permit Negroes to prepare their food, to lave their garments, to suckle their children, and then refuse to allow these same Negroes to sit next to them in streetcars or buses (although they often sat next to them in their carriages and motor cars) must be a trifle cracked. "The only way to make these benighted souls see the light," he would continue, "is to convince them that their conduct is a huge joke."

Langston Hughes, the poet, may be performing this very service in a book which is perhaps not new in form ("Mr. Dooley" comes to mind as a similar creative effort) but which presents the Negro in a new way. Jesse Semple is wise, witty, as mad as the Madwoman of Chaillot—and invariably race-conscious. He is the naïve propagandist, through a series of dialogues.

Since these papers were originally written for a Negro newspaper and consequently an exclusively Negro audience, there is no attempt at obfuscation. The papers probably exhibit the Negro in bedroom slippers and pajamas—that is, as nearly himself as it would be possible to show him. Simple is completely frank in his opinions about white people; he dislikes them intensely. The race problem is never absent, but the flow of the book is lighthearted and easy.

This is a sane approach to the real insanity and I wouldn't be surprised if this book reaches more people and has a wider audience than any volume on a similar subject since *Uncle Tom's Cabin*. *Simple Speaks His Mind* will start a lot of people thinking hard. For those who have to swallow bitter pills it provides a sugar coating of humor. Only a Negro could have written this book, and only a Negro as wise as Langston Hughes.

It is not generally known as it should be that Langston Hughes laughs with, speaks with, and cries for the Negro (in all classes) more understandingly, perhaps, than any other writer. Harlem is his own habitat, his workshop, and his playground, his forte and his dish of tea. He is so completely at home when he writes about Harlem that he can afford to be both careless and sloppy. In his *Simple* books he is seldom either, and *Simple Takes a Wife* is a superior achievement to the first of the series, *Simple Speaks His Mind*. This new book is more of a piece, the material is more carefully and competently argued, more unexpectedly presented; it is more brilliant, more skilfully written, funnier, and perhaps just a shade more tragic than its predecessor.

The genre has been employed extensively by other writers: by Finley Peter Dunne in "Mr. Dooley," by A. Neil Lyons in "Arthurs," and by Joel Chandler Harris in "Uncle Remus"; it is not too far, indeed, from the scheme of Gorky's "The Lower Depths." The locale, however, is original, the taste truly Harlem, the matters disclosed pertinent to the inhabitants and the effect prevailing evocative. The question-and-answer formula is used throughout the book, but frequently Simple's replies are somewhat protracted. The views expressed for the most part have a sane basis, and it is probable that at least a modicum of these are the beliefs of Mr. Hughes himself, although they find expression on Simple's tongue.

It would be easy to refer to the author as the Molière of Harlem who has just got around to writing his *School for Wives* (or is it his *School for Husbands*?). At any rate, Mr. Hughes (himself a bachelor) seems to be as cynical in his report as Colette, when he deals with the war between the sexes. Here and there he suggests that he is writing the Harlem version of Colette's *Cheri*.

There are several women in this book. The first is Mabel, "the woman like water." "Do you want me to tell you what that woman was like? Boy, I don't know. She was like some kind of ocean, I guess, some kind of great big old sea, like the water at Coney Island on a real hot day, cool and warm all at once—and company like a big crowd of people—also like some woman you like to be alone with, if you dig my meaning. Yet and still, I wasn't in love with that woman."

Simple passes on to other conquests and to discussions of other ideas. For instance, in chapter seven there is a long and cheerful lesson in English grammar and usage. Chapter two is an addition to the folklore of Harlem, in which Simple describes the custom under which each roomer in a house is alloted a different ring. " 'Joyce's landlady objects to my ringing her bell late. Seven rings is a lot for ten or eleven o'clock at night. So I go at six-thirty or seven. Then, I have only to ring once, which is seven times. If I go later, and nobody hears me, I have to ring twice, which is fourteen times. And, if I ring three times, which is three times seven, twenty-one times is too much for the landlady's nerves.'

" 'Colored rooming houses certainly have a lot of different bell signals,' I commented.

" 'You told that right,' said Simple. 'I lived in a house once that had up to twenty-one rings, it were so full of roomers. Mine was twelve. I often used to miss count when somebody would ring. One time I let in another boy's best girl friend—she were ringing eleven. He had his second best girl friend in his room.' "

Somewhat further on there is a learned discussion of Bebop, which Simple declares has its origin in the police habit of beating up Negroes' heads. " 'Everytime a cop hits a Negro with his billy club that old club says Bop! Bop! . . . BEBOP! . . . MOP! . . . BOP!' "

In chapter sixteen Simple and Joyce, his lady friend, warmly discuss the disturbing subject of miscegenation. There is a touch of Mr. Hughes's special kind of poetry in his description of night: " 'Night, you walk easy, sit on a stoop and talk, stand on a corner, shoot the bull, lean on a bar, ring a bell and say "Baby, here I am." ' " In chapter fifty-seven Simple dilates on the unpleasant connotations of the word *black*. " 'What I want to know,' asks

Simple, 'is where white folks gets off calling everything bad *black*? If it is a dark night they say it's *black* as hell. If you are mean and evil, they say you got a BLACK heart. I would like to change all that around and say that the people who Jim Crow me have a WHITE heart. People who sell dope to children have got a WHITE mark against them. And all the gamblers who were behind the basketball fix are the WHITE sheep of the sports world.'"

This is true humor with a bite to it, spoken in the authentic language of 135th Street, and set down good-naturedly in a book which tells us more about the common Negro than a dozen solemn treatises on the "race question."

ZORA NEALE HURSTON

One of Van Vechten's warmest associations began in 1926 when he first met Zora Neale Hurston, the raffish novelist-anthropologist. It ended with her sudden disappearance in 1948. When he wrote briefly about her, in "Some 'Literary Ladies' I Have Known" for the *Yale Gazette* in January 1952, Van Vechten did not know she was working in Florida as a housekeeper. She died there in a welfare home in 1960, completely out of touch with her friends from the Harlem Renaissance.

Zora Neale Hurston's letters suggest that she was genuinely fond of Van Vechten: "If Carl was a people instead of a person, I could then say, these are my people," Fannie Hurst reported her saying.[1] Some years later, indeed shortly before her disappearance, she wrote for permission to write Van Vechten's biography: "You have had such a tremendous influence on the arts of the last twenty-five years, that I think it ought to be precipitated out of the mass of lies that are now growing up. People are now brazenly claiming credit for the many things that you were responsible for."[2]

Zora Neale Hurston wrote three volumes of folklore, one of them dedicated to Van Vechten; three novels, including *Their Eyes Were Watching God*, perhaps the finest novel written by a member of the Harlem Renaissance; and a delightful, if unreliable, memoir, *Dust Tracks on a Road*. Robert Hemenway's recent exhaustive biography should do much to bring this gifted writer the attention she deserves.

1. "Zora Neale Hurston: A Personality Sketch," *Yale University Library Gazette*, July 1960, p. 19.

2. Carl Van Vechten Collection, the Beinecke Rare Book and Manuscript Library, Yale University.

Fannie [Hurst] and I (to be sure we meet only occasionally) have an inexhaustible subject for conversation: Zora Neale Hurston, the Negro novelist published by Scribner's, who began her fantastic career as Fannie's secretary. Zora is picturesque, witty, electric, indiscreet, and unreliable. The latter quality offers material for discussion; the former qualities induce her friends to forgive and love her. No engagement, no matter with whom, is sacred to Zora; nor does she find it important to advise you that she intends to break it. Very often she is consumed by a new plan or argument. When next you see her, perhaps twelve months hence, very likely she will not even mention the former project so dear to her heart, but assuredly, she will have a new one. Her unconventional behavior extends to her mode of dressing. She once appeared at a party we were giving attired in a wide Seminole Indian skirt, contrived of a thousand patches; still another time in a Norwegian skiing outfit, with a cap over her ears. Her conversation, never smutty, is as breezy and natural as the West Wind. It was Zora who invented the sobriquet "Niggeratti" to describe the young writers of the so-called Negro Renaissance. Indeed, Fannie and I always have plenty to talk about with Zora as our subject. Even her complete disappearance from circulation attracts attention. Under such a condition no one has the remotest notion where or how she may be living, whether as an anthropologist in Haiti, as a cook in Alaska, or as a teacher of folk dancing in Florida (she once sponsored an exhibition in New York of Caribbean folk dancing in which she herself appeared).

W.C. HANDY

This paper on W. C. Handy originated as a review of his autobiography, *Father of the Blues*, entitled "W. C. Handy, Dean of Negro Composers." More a memoir than a critical evaluation of the book, it appeared in the *New York Herald Tribune Books*, 6 July 1941.

The following year, when Handy read Van Vechten's *Crisis* article about the James Weldon Johnson Memorial Collection of Negro Arts and Letters, he wrote to say it was

"a relief to know that some one cares," and to offer to send
things to the collection from time to time.[1] Van Vechten's
photographs of W. C. Handy were already in the collection,
of course. The musician posed against an American flag
since, Van Vechten insisted, he had written the truly
authentic national anthem, "The Saint Louis Blues."

1. Carl Van Vechten Collection, Manuscript and Archives Division, New York Public Library.

W. C. Handy, if he doesn't mind my saying so, is the dean of Negro
composers, almost, indeed, the dean of Negro celebrities. He has lived to
see the work, with which he set out honestly and modestly to make a living,
acclaimed as an art; moreover, he has lived to see the folk art of his race
appreciated and admired. On every hand he himself is regarded as an important contributor to the art of the nation and at least one of his songs,
"The St. Louis Blues," has become as popular all the world over, as any other
song America ever produced, ranking in this respect with the compositions
of Stephen Collins Foster. Mr. Handy has lived, indeed, to see a park named
after him in Memphis where he spent his early days. In the circumstances
his autobiography is both welcome and valuable.

Through the years, an important series of Negro autobiographies has
been offered to the public, beginning with that of Frederick Douglass. W.E.B.
Du Bois has written several books with an autobiographical slant; Booker
T. Washington contributed *Up From Slavery*; James Weldon Johnson,
Along This Way, and Langston Hughes, *The Big Sea*. All these autobiogra-
phers, however, have been poets, publicists, and race-leaders. The "Father
of the Blues" is perhaps the first important Negro musician to tell his story.

It happens to be an important story. The history of the Spirituals has been
related many times in many ways, but here we have the history of the Blues,
the mourning songs of the Negro folk, of which, quite rightly, Mr. Handy
is held to be the "father." It isn't that he actually created the Blues or that,
singlehandedly, he made them popular with the public, a public which has
been retained, thanks to the persistent popularity of his own compositions
in this line.

Mr. Handy confesses that he took up with folk music hesitantly. When
he was playing for a dance in Cleveland, Mississippi, he had a lesson he
never forgot. The request was for some of our "native music." The request
baffled him. The men in his band could not "fake" or "sell it." They were
musicians who bowed to the authority of the printed notes. So they com-
promised by playing a well-known southern song. A few moments later a

second request was handed him. Would his band object if a local organization played a few dances? Glad to take a rest, his band obliged, and the new-comers entered:

"They were led by a long-legged chocolate boy, and their band consisted of just three pieces, a battered guitar, a mandolin and a worn-out bass. The music they made was pretty well in keeping with their looks. They struck up one of those over-and-over strains that seem to have no very clear beginning and certainly no ending at all. The strumming attained a disturbing monotony, but on and on it went, a kind of stuff that has long been associated with cane rows and levee camps. Thump-thump-thump went their feet on the floor. Their eyes rolled. Their shoulders swayed. And through it all that agonizing strain persisted. It was not really annoying or unpleasant. Perhaps 'haunting' is a better word, but I commenced to wonder if anybody besides town rounders and their running mates would go for it. The answer was not long coming. A rain of silver dollars began to fall around the outlandish stomping feet. The dancers went wild. Dollars, quarters, halves—the shower grew heavier and continued so long I strained my neck to get a better look. There before the boys lay more money than my nine musicians were being paid for the entire engagement. Then I saw the beauty of primitive music. They had the stuff the people wanted. It touched the spot. That night a composer was born, an *American* composer. Those country boys at Cleveland had taught me something that could not possibly have been gained from books."

Later, Mr. Handy discovered that the tunes he contrived, based on a few notes, an idea, or words he picked up here and there from blackfolk's lips, would conquer not only a southern group of dancers, but also would delight more sophisticated ears everywhere in the world. Although he let his first piece, "The Memphis Blues," go to a publisher for little or nothing, he acquired the glory of the great success it made.

Everywhere he went, in fact, he found to his surprise that his fame had preceded him. Soon money from phonograph records began to roll in by the thousands of dollars. He never forgot the source of his inspiration and in later years when he might have visited Europe with pleasure, instead he returned again and again to the Deep South and wherever he went he listened to Negro singing.

Other successes followed the "Memphis Blues," of course: the "Jogo Blues," the "St. Louis Blues" (1914), the "Yellow-Dog Blues," the "Beale Street Blues," "Loveless Love," the "Harlem Blues," and many others. . . . From these songs rose the great Blues singers, Bessie and Clara Smith, and, to some extent in her earlier days, Ethel Waters. These voices recorded these songs in the manner in which they were sung in the Deep South.

The story of how these songs were composed is written down in *Father of the Blues*. Further, there is an immensely valuable account of early Negro minstrel troupes, with descriptions of their parades, the routine of performances, and some account of the individual performers. Mr. Handy entered the music racket with the curses of his mother, his father, and his schoolteacher ringing in his ears and he describes with gusto how religious Negroes of this earlier period felt about the deviltries of the stage and concert platform. In the end they all came round and nobody was more proud of the boy's eventual success than his preacher-father. In fact, so accurately does this book fall into the groove of the Cinderella story, that it easily might have been called "From Cabin Boy to President," only this cabin boy came from a cabin with a dirt floor (packed down like asphalt by his father) and his presidency was based on the warm feelings of his public, rather than their actual votes. . . . There are bits of folklore, too, in the book which are interesting and instructive: his grandmother's cures, for example, and how to get rid of a hoot owl by putting a poker in the fire, and Uncle Whit's complicated stomping, which brought heel and toe of each foot into separate play.

More serious matters are discussed, although not bitterly. A lynching is described and Mr. Handy's account of how Negroes are treated on American railroads and in American hotels does not make pleasant reading for anyone who believes he is living in a democracy. It is not news, perhaps, but probably many people will learn for the first time that the theatre, unless it be a colored motion-picture house, is entirely closed to Negroes in the capital of the United States at Washington. Perhaps because it is told with great repression, more than usually moving is the description of how Mrs. Handy, fatally ill, lay for an hour outside the door of a prominent hospital in New York where a room had been engaged for her by a physician, because somebody "was sure" the hospital couldn't take a Negro in a private room. There are those who will be curious to inquire the name of this hospital. . . . There is criticism of Negroes, too. Mr. Handy's own band eventually became so unruly that he decided to conduct no more of them. So the Negro banks in his own town treated him in scurvy fashion until large cheques began to roll in, when he put his money in a white man's bank to teach them a lesson.

The book contains many anecdotes. One of the best was told Mr. Handy by Bessie Smith, the great Blues singer, now dead. Returning to New York from Beale Street in Memphis, she spoke to him about Handy Park, where shade trees had been grown.

" 'Mr. Handy, you ain't seen that park since they fixed it up, has you?'

" 'No,' I replied.

" 'They sit out there and sleep day and night,' she said.

" 'Is that so?'

" 'Yes,' she concluded. 'One fellow was sitting on a bench asleep when a passing policeman tapped him under the feet and said, "Wake up and go home." The lounger brushed his eyes, looked at the officer and said, "Y'all white folks ain't got nothin' to do with me sleepin' here. This is Handy's Park." ' "

A'LELIA WALKER

Although the *New Yorker* urged Van Vechten to write a
profile of A'Lelia Walker in 1927, and again in 1931 when
she died, he left only this incomplete fragment, undated.
In 1927 Van Vechten's interests had shifted — temporarily,
at least — from Harlem to Hollywood. In 1931 he was in
Europe, missing not only the *New Yorker's* invitation but also
A'Lelia Walker's celebrated funeral. As one of the regular
attendants at her soirées, Van Vechten surely would have
made the guest list — the funeral was by invitation only —
for this elaborate show. The trappings of her life certainly
suggested that some degree of opulence attend her death.
The "house in Irvington" Van Vechten refers to was a
cream-stucco Georgian mansion at exclusive Irvington-on-
Hudson, built in 1917 at a cost of half a million dollars —
by the time it was fully furnished with a twenty-four carat
gold piano, a pipe organ, Hepplewhite furniture, Persian
carpets, and a Japanese prayer tree. The black male
servants wore not only doublet-and-hose but white wigs.
Later, A'Lelia Walker turned a floor of her Harlem townhouse into the "Dark Tower," where black artists and writers
were supposed to gather for intellectual stimulation but
where, instead, white visitors — Van Vechten included —
predominated. A'Lelia Walker greeted her guests as they
climbed the stairs to her "Dark Tower," and charged them
fifteen cents apiece to check their hats. Still, her short-lived
salon did bring young black intellectuals — the "Niggerati,"
Zora Neale Hurston called them — into contact with influential white writers and publishers. By the time of her
death, A'Lelia Walker had gone through the two-million-
dollar legacy from her remarkable mother who had invented
the hair-straightening process. "That was really the end of
the gay times of the New Negro era in Harlem," Langston
Hughes later observed, coinciding more or less with the
stock market crash. As part of the funeral services, the
Chocolate Bon Bons sang "I'll See You Again," swinging it
gently with an implication Noël Coward did not intend.

Van Vechten appended a note to his initial sketch thirty
years later, in 1957. Also at Yale, it has not been previously
published.

The death of A'Lelia Walker removes another of the picturesque personalities in which New York was at one time so rich, figures like Diamond Jim

Brady, Mrs. Philip Lydig, Oscar Hammerstein. Born the daughter of a poor washerwoman, A'Lelia became through her mother's energy and ambition a symbol for luxurious Negro life. To her own race she became an example of what could be done; to such of the white race as did not know her personally she was that rich colored woman who lived in a palace in Irvington-on-Hudson.

She was not, as has so often been said in print in both the white and the Negro press, a social leader. She took no part in organizing the great charity balls beyond buying a box in which she might appear surrounded by her satellites. She made no effort to limit society in any strict sense. She invited whom she pleased to her own apartment when she entertained, and frequently they invited whom they pleased. Her parties were not exclusive and they in no sense represented the best of the Negro intellectual and social world. Some of the people in that world had never set foot across her threshold. Others had, to be sure, and the theatrical set and what would be known as the "fast" set in another community swarmed around her.

A'Lelia adored her mother and her mother in return had spoiled her completely. Madame C.J. Walker beginning her life most humbly lived to see herself acclaimed as one of the most prominent members of her race. Through her invention of a process for the straightening of kinky hair and her other beauty preparations, she built her house in Irvington, named Villa Lewaro by Caruso after early syllables in the name A'Lelia Walker Robinson, and she erected her splendid townhouse on West 136th Street, now owned by the city as a health center.

A'Lelia was not a businesswoman; nor was she a good housekeeper. Responsibility irked her. She hired a housekeeper to take charge of the Villa Lewaro and she rented her townhouse out to dances. Eventually, she established the "Dark Tower," intended as a rendezvous for poets, on the top floor. She installed herself in a modest, though luxuriously furnished apartment on Edgecombe Avenue. Here with the occasional aid of Ernest, her butler, whom she imported from Irvington, she lived the kind of existence that appealed to her: an existence in which she was surrounded by friends and sycophants.

Nearly every day of her life she played poker and so nearly every afternoon a group gathered at her apartment to play poker with her. After the game she went to dinner, frequently downtown, for she had scores of white friends and was asked many places. Frequently, when she was not invited out to dinner she cooked it herself. She liked to cook and cooked well. In the evening she usually went to a round of parties and often went to a nightclub to dance to round off the night. She was a good dancer and she loved dancing. Connie's Inn was her favorite club. She also loved the theatre and attended anything from which she believed she could derive pleasure. The last time I saw her was coming out of the Follies at the Ziegfeld Theatre.

Like many another woman in her position she was suspicious and had a horror of being done. This sometimes led her into making mistakes with people who were really her friends and it seldom protected her from those who were not, as she was no judge of character and could be easily won by flattery.

She looked like a queen and frequently acted like a tyrant. She was tall and black and extremely handsome in her African manner. She often dressed in black. When she assumed more regal habiliments, rich brocades of gold or silver, her noble head bound in a turban, she was a magnificent spectacle. I have been told that her appearance in a box at an opera season at Covent Garden was so spectacular that the singers were put completely out of countenance. She bought her dresses at Wanamaker's and her shoes. I should imagine that many other of her possessions came from there, including her linen sheets, heavily embroidered with her monogram. But her most cherished possession was a gold shoehorn presented to her by one of her husbands as a wedding gift.

In love and in marriage she was unsuccessful as was but natural. She was too spoiled, too selfish, too used to having her own way to make any kind of compromise.

A'Lelia died on a weekend at Atlantic City after she had consumed a chocolate cake and a whole lobster in the middle of the night. The food, of course, had been washed down with champagne.

PAUL ROBESON AND LAWRENCE BROWN

"All God's Chillun Got Songs" appeared in *Theatre Magazine* in August 1925, introducing readers to Paul Robeson and Lawrence Brown. Earlier that year, Van Vechten had organized their first public recital, and even before it occurred he had written a program note for a second recital. These were presented at the Greenwich Village Theatre in April and May; both were good examples of Van Vechten's unpaid press agentry on behalf of young black artists. By 1925 his wide circle of acquaintances included a number of influential literary and musical figures, through his own writing career, and a number of celebrated people connected with the theater, through his wife, in addition to knowing Harlem's intelligentsia through Walter White and James Weldon Johnson. It was easy to muster a good audience for the first recital; its success, of course, ensured an audience for the second. Eschewing any credit for himself, Van Vechten accounts only for the brilliance

of the performers when, in point of fact, he financed the
first recital and helped fund the second. The program
note, here appended to his essay, is dated 3 May 1925.

A few years ago—to be precise, it was November 1919—a young Negro,
Lawrence Brown, attended a concert given by the Boston Symphony Orchestra, at which the soloist, Povla Frijsh, sang Ernest Bloch's settings of
the 114th and 137th psalms. The boy listened to "the very voice of the
rejoicing over the passage of the Red Sea, the very lusty blowing on ox
horns, the very hieratic dance." He read the statement of the composer in
the program notes: "In my music I have tried to express the soul of the
Jewish people as I feel it."

On that day race pride was born in the young Negro's breast. Himself a
musician, he determined never again to compose, play, or sing anything
but the music of his own people. Shortly afterwards he went to London as
accompanist for Roland Hayes. There, keeping his aim constantly in mind,
he studied harmony and composition. Born in Florida, he had visited many
other of the southern states and, wherever it was possible, he had jotted
down notes of the Spirituals as he heard them sung in the churches or on
the plantations, or the work songs of the Afro-Americans, as he listened to
them in the factories or in the fields. These he now undertook to harmonize
for voice and piano. Several of his arrangements were published. At length
he succeeded in interesting London musicians in his aspirations and gave
several concerts of Negro music, not only with singers but with instrumental
virtuosi as well, for the broad melody of "Deep River" flows as sweetly
from the cello as it does from the human throat.

In America, in the meantime, another Negro boy, Paul Robeson, had
graduated from Rutgers College, where he had not only been chosen All-
American end for two seasons by Walter Camp, but where he had been
elected to Phi Beta Kappa as well. He now entered Columbia Law School,
with the intention of becoming an attorney. His voice and his magnificent
physique, however, [had] attracted the attention of a playwright who was
producing a play dealing with Negro life, [and] he was engaged to appear.
. . . Other histrionic opportunities came his way until, at last, Eugene O'Neill
wrote his drama, All God's Chillun Got Wings, with this actor in mind.
After All God's Chillun had run its course, The Emperor Jones was revived
for him.

Nevertheless, Robeson was not altogether satisfied with the prospect of
the limited career that the theatre offered him. Not many Negro plays were
being written and not all that were written were suitable for a black man
over six feet tall. Fortunately, his gifts were abundant. Aside from his ath-
letic and scholastic prowess and his talent for acting, he was the possessor of
a natural bass voice, clear, resonant, and of an exceptionally pleasant

quality and of considerable range. Before his appearance in O'Neill's plays, he had for a period substituted for the bass singer with the Four Harmony Kings in *Shuffle Along*. A little later, at the Plantation, where Florence Mills was the star, he had sung Rosamond Johnson's "L'il Gal." He might have gone on indefinitely singing ballads in cabarets, but he aimed higher. It was his ambition to sing Negro Spirituals. He studied a number of them and sang them, without accompaniment, for his friends, who urged him to announce a concert. He desired to follow this advice, but hesitated, modestly doubtful if he alone could enlist the attention of an audience throughout an entire evening.

At this psychological moment Lawrence Brown, the Florida boy who had spent four years in London, returned to New York. Paul Robeson had already met him when the actor had visited London to play Mary Hoyt Wilborg's *Taboo* with Mrs. Patrick Campbell. On their reunion, discovering their ideals to be identical, they questioned one another: Why should they not work together? They began to practice immediately, and a little over a month later, very unpretentiously, without any advertising save a printed announcement sent to a few friends, they gave their first concert at the Greenwich Village Theatre. The result was unexpectedly gratifying. Not only were all the seats sold, scores of prospective listeners were turned away. That was in April of the current year. Two weeks later, in May, they offered a second program with similar success. Still a third concert was given in a larger auditorium. It was evident that the public was prepared to receive them.

What causes had contributed to this success? They had consistently followed their original idea. The program was composed entirely of Negro music, including three groups of Spirituals and one of secular songs. The auditors, who reasonably may have expected that the result would be monotony, must have been amazed at the variety in the entertainment, for the program embraced such expressions of wistful resignation as "By an' By" and "Steal Away," such tragic utterances as "Go Down, Moses"; such joyously abandoned melodies as "I'll Be a Witness for My Lord" and "Joshua Fit de Battle of Jericho," and such examples of sardonic, secular humor as "Scandalize My Name":

> I met my sister the other day;
> I gave her my right han'
> An' jes' as soon as my back was turned,
> She sca-andalize my name.
> You call dat a sister?
>   No! No!
> You call dat a sister?
>   No! No!

> You call dat a sister?
> No! No!
> Sca-andalize my name!

Furthermore, the performers made an attempt to capture as much of the traditional evangelical rendering of the Spirituals as would be consistent with the atmosphere of the concert hall. Not only did they sing in dialect—in contradistinction to the refined English renderings heard not only from white singers but also from too many Negroes—but they likewise indulged in the characteristic vocal peculiarities of Negro inflection. The Negro Spirituals were—and still are under primitive conditions—sung in harmony by a chorus, one voice leading with a verse to which the chorus reponds. In the concerts I am discussing Paul Robeson undertook the solo parts while Lawrence Brown sang the choral responses, the piano filling in the harmonies.

Paul Robeson, I think, is a fine artist, as fine an artist in his way as Yvette Guilbert. There are times when he reminds me, in the poignant simplicity of his art, of Chaliapin. It is typical of his acting that he never appears to be using his full prepotence. His postures and gestures and the volume of his voice are under such complete control and such studied discipline that he always suggests the possession of a great reserve force. He is a fine actor, as anyone will testify who saw him in *The Emperor Jones*, in the role of the Negro porter pursued by racial fears. In singing, his voice retains its beautiful quality and the same sense of reserve power inherent in his acting manifests itself. His enunciation is impeccable—one never misses a word—and his interpretation is always clearly thought out and lucidly expressed.

Lawrence Brown's versions of the Spirituals are in many instances remarkable. I would call attention especially to the evangelical abandon of his transcription of "Every Time I Feel the Spirit," entirely at variance with the slow-footed arrangements made by other musicians. Mr. Brown's voice is quite adequate to the uses to which he puts it, and his spirit in the responses is so accurately just that the effect of Robeson's singing is doubly enhanced by his vital cooperation.

I can never sufficiently record my admiration for the Negro Spirituals. The music of these simple, spontaneous outpourings from the heart of an oppressed race ranks with the best folk music anywhere and with a good deal of the second-best art music. The melodies have a strange, haunting appeal to which it is very difficult to remain indifferent. Indeed, once they become incorporated in the memory, they are there to stay. The words, too, crude though they often are, have the substance of true poetry.

It is not generally realized that the folksongs of the Negro are still in the process of creation. Their invention did not end with the passing of slave days. Conditions in the South for the Negro are still sufficiently oppressive to keep him in a state of emotional ferment extremely favorable for the inspiration of religious folksong. So, even today, in little Negro churches or at camp meetings, they come into spontaneous utterance. One man throws out a line, another tosses him a response, and soon the congregation is rocking with a mighty, harmonized chorus. Furthermore, it may be stated that the religious songs are but a small part of the gift of black folk in the department of music. There are the work songs, the songs of the cotton pickers on the plantation, the songs of the corn huskers in the fields, the songs of the roustabouts on the levee, and there are the Blues which spring up in the disreputable quarters of the southern cities.

It is the desire of Lawrence Brown to travel through the Southland for the purpose of adding new examples of this material to that already collected. It is to be hoped that this altruistic ambition may be satisfied, for it may safely be stated that folksongs of the Negro constitute America's chief claim to musical distinction. Every song that can be added to the list makes that claim stronger.

To those who are accustomed to hear Negro Spirituals delivered in a sanctimonious, lugubrious manner, or yet worse, with the pseudo-refinement of the typical concert singer, the evangelical, true Negro rendering of Paul Robeson and Lawrence Brown will come as a delightful surprise. It is the avowed purpose of Paul Robeson, and of Lawrence Brown, as the arranger of these folksongs, to restore, so far as they are able, the spirit of the original primitive interpretation to these Spirituals. In realizing this purpose, which apparently no other public singer has hitherto entertained, they have been markedly successful. Aside from recognizing the unquestioned artistry of the performance, their audiences will doubtless exhibit considerable amazement over the degree of variety that these two young Negroes have been able to introduce into their all-Negro programs. . . . The beauty of these simple songs of the Negro people is celebrated the world over: I have listened to no other interpreters who so vividly reveal this beauty. At the present moment, I believe I'd rather hear Robeson and Brown sing that quaintly charming air, "Little David, Play on Your Harp," than hear anyone else sing anything.

TAYLOR GORDON

Taylor Gordon's *Born to Be* appeared in 1929, dedicated to Carl Van Vechten, although the dedication page only made the second printing. Van Vechten wrote the foreword to Gordon's autobiography, for which Muriel Draper had

supplied some editorial help. A witty woman who had kept
a musical salon in prewar London, Muriel Draper was an
enemy rather than a friend of Van Vechten until the Harlem
Renaissance when their mutual interest in black writers
fostered a firm affection. Robert Hemenway, who recently
edited a new edition of *Born to Be* (University of Washington Press, 1975), labels Van Vechten's foreword "patronizing,"
but without specifying why he thinks so.

Something new has happened in this book. It is not easy to explain what,
but obviously something new has happened. I suspect that a new kind of
personality has succeeded in expressing itself. It is a type of personality that
many writers have tried to express—one of the earliest examples perhaps is
Mark Twain's Jim in *Huckleberry Finn*—but no one has been entirely successful until Taylor Gordon somehow got himself on paper, lanky six-feet, falsetto
voice, molasses laugh, and all the rest of him, including a brain that functions
and an eye that can see. The result is probably a "human document" of the
first order, to be studied by sociologists and Freudians for years to come.
Fortunately, for you who have purchased *Born to Be*, it is something more
than that: it is an extremely amusing book.

The pictures of the big-hipped sporting women of White Sulphur Springs,
Montana, the account of the adventures of the Pullman porter and the
chauffeur to John Ringling, and especially, perhaps, the descriptions of
parties in the homes of the great, are about as good as anybody could make
them. Very little is related in this volume about Taylor Gordon's career as a
singer. Save for a few brief passages this side of his life is scarcely referred
to. The emphasis, certainly, is placed on his career as a servant. I fancy a
great many people who will read this book are going to find it rather disconcerting to discover just how much an intelligent servant can observe.
They will be the more perturbed by the realization that Taylor Gordon
has usually been fairly amiable in his report: constantly you suspect him of
concealing the most monstrous facts. On the whole, it is just as well for
those subjects that the man actually liked Big Maude, Mr. Ringling, and
most of the others. I hesitate to imagine what Taylor Gordon would be
capable of thinking about anyone he didn't like!

Mr. Gordon has written just as frankly about his own race. Indeed, it is
probably that he has even been a little more frank in dealing with the Negro.
Some of his criticism is doubtless justified; some of it has been made by
others before him. All of it, I should think, may be read with interest, and
possibly profit. It is a pleasure to be able to state that snobbery, racial or
social, is lacking from this book. Big Maude, who ran the principal sporting
house in White Sulphur Springs, Montana, traced her lineage back to the
English nobility. When, many years later in London, Mr. Gordon was

introduced to members of the English nobility, he immediately became aware that Big Maude had told the truth!

Anyone acquainted with the lyrics of the Blues will not be astonished to learn that one so unskilled in the art of belles-lettres as Taylor Gordon still writes with accurate observation and a poetic use of metaphor. Certain phrases in this book are unforgettable: "When I sing to people, ten thousand sing to me." Has ever the effect upon an artist of an audience, with its warring factors, been better expressed? Describing John Ringling concocting an omelet, he writes: "He could make an egg look like the froth on frozen milk." How exactly he has set down the essential difference between American and French sporting crowds in the following sentence: "The people in Paris would empty the large grandstand like a fire drill in the public schools between the races." And there is a paragraph about Queen Mary that will make one forever weep for royalty.

Taylor Gordon has herein given his account of his first meeting with me. The date was October 3, 1925. I was interested from the first tone the boy produced, and Meda came out of the kitchen to listen—an excellent sign in the matter of Spirituals. The first song I heard him sing was "Done Found My Lost Sheep." I remember wondering at the time if he had ever really lost them.

BESSIE SMITH

Van Vechten's two pieces about Bessie Smith, written twenty years apart—the first as part of "Negro 'Blues' Singers" in *Vanity Fair*, March 1926, and the second, "Memories of Bessie Smith" in *Jazz Record*, September 1947—form a coherent essay with some slight reordering of information. In the second of these, for example, Van Vechten incorporated a good deal of material from the first, revising it slightly in that process, and I have of course used its revised version. Neither paper, however, accounted for the full evening's activities when Bessie Smith came to the Van Vechten apartment to sing. Van Vechten did not welcome the story's public disclosure because it was embarrassing to his wife. Chris Albertson did tell it, in his biography of the singer, but through the distorted memories of Bessie Smith's companion. Both Van Vechten and Fania Marinoff recounted the incident often enough in private conversation, when there would have been no reason for distortion, even though one person cannot always see clearly through another's eyes. Still, the number of other,

minor, factual errors in Albertson's narrative — Fania
Marinoff's profession, the apartment's decor, the liquor —
encourage one general correction: Fania Marinoff attempted
to kiss Bessie Smith, in conventional actressy fashion, out
of gratitude. Bessie Smith, who had had enough of both her
host's bootleg golden gin and his ofay guests, turned on
Fania Marinoff, muttered some obscenities, and pushed
her away with sufficient force to knock her down.

Bessie Smith spent most of her youth singing in the Deep South, where, when she felt like it, she could fill a big tent with colored people from all the surrounding farms and towns, but she made a profusion of records and I was very early aware of these. I had boxes and boxes of them which I played and played in the early Twenties and everybody who came to my apartment was invited to hear them. As a matter of fact, musicians arriving from Europe called on me especially to listen to these records. Eventually I deposited them with the James Weldon Johnson Memorial Collection of Negro Arts and Letters which I founded at Yale University Library, together with the records of that other great Blues singer, Clara Smith, and the early records of Ethel Waters, one of which, "Maybe Not at All," concludes with Ethel imitating the styles and personalities and tones of the two great Smith girls, who were NOT sisters.

It was not, however, until Thanksgiving Day night, 1925, when she was appearing in Newark, that I actually had my first opportunity to hear Bessie Smith sing on the stage. A trip to Newark is a career, and so I was forced to rise from the dinner table shortly after eight o'clock if I wished to hear Bessie Smith sing at the Orpheum Theatre in that New Jersey city at a quarter to ten. I rose with eagerness, however, and so did my guests. Bessie Smith, the "Empress of the Blues," whose records sold into figures that compete with the circulation of the *Saturday Evening Post*, was to sing in Newark and Bessie Smith, who made long tours of the South where her rich voice reached the ears of the race from which she sprang, had not been heard in the vicinity of New York, save through the horn of the phonograph, for over a year.

The signs and tokens were favorable. When we gave directions to the white taxicab driver at Park Place, he demanded, "Going to hear Bessie Smith?" "Yes," we replied. "No good trying," he assured us. "You can't get in. They've been hanging on the chandeliers all the week." Nevertheless, we persevered, spurred on perhaps by a promise on the part of the management that a box would be reserved for us. We arrived, however, to discover that this promise had not been kept. It had been impossible to hold the box: the crowd was too great. "Dey jes' nacherly eased into dat box," one of the ushers explained insouciantly. However, my friend, Leigh Whipper, who will easily be recalled as the Crabmeat Man in *Porgy*, was manager of this theatre at this epoch and he eased them out again. I must say all of us enjoyed the mood of the highest anticipatory expectation. It would be no exaggeration to assert that we felt as we might have felt before going to a Salzburg Festival to hear Lilli Lehmann sing Donna Anna in *Don Giovanni.*

Once seated, we looked out over a vast sea of happy black faces—two comedians were exchanging jokes on the stage. There was not a mulatto or a high yellow visible among these people who were shouting merriment or approval after every ribald line. Where did they come from? In Harlem the Negroes are many colors, shading to white, but these were all chocolate browns and "blues." Never before had I seen such an audience save at a typical Negro camp meeting in the far South.

The comedians were off. The lights were lowered. A new placard, reading BESSIE SMITH, appeared in the frames at either side of the proscenium. As the curtain lifted, a jazz band, against a background of plum-colored hangings, held the full stage. The saxophone began to moan; the drummer tossed his sticks. One was transported involuntarily, inevitably, to a Harlem cabaret. Presently, the band struck up a slower and still more mournful strain. The hangings parted and a great brown woman emerged. She was at this time the size of Fay Templeton in her Weber and Fields days, which means very large, and she wore a crimson satin robe, sweeping up from her trim ankles, and embroidered in multicolored sequins in designs. Her face was beautiful with the rich ripe beauty of southern darkness, a deep bronze-brown, matching the bronze of her bare arms. Walking slowly to the footlights, to the accompaniment of the wailing, muted brasses, the monotonous African pounding of the drum, the dromedary glide of the pianist's fingers over the responsive keys, she began her strange, rhythmic rites in a voice full of shouting and moaning and praying and suffering, a wild, rough Ethiopian voice, harsh and volcanic, but seductive and sensuous too, released between rouged lips and the whitest of teeth, the singer swaying slightly to the beat, as is the Negro custom:

> Yo' treated me wrong,
> I treated yo' right;
> I wo'k fo' yo' full day an' night.
>
> Yo' brag to women
> I was yo' fool,
> So den I got dose sobbin' h'ahted Blues.

And now, inspired partly by the lines, partly by the stumbling strain of the accompaniment, partly by the power and magnetic personality of this elemental conjure woman and her plangent African voice, quivering with pain and passion, which sounded as if it had been developed at the sources of the Nile, the crowd burst into hysterical shrieks of sorrow and lamentation. "Amens" rent the air. Little nervous giggles, like the shivering of Venetian glass, shocked the nerves.

It's true I loves yo', but I won't take mistreatments any mo'.

"Dat's right," a girl cried out from under our box.

All I wants is yo' pitcher in a frame;
All I wants is yo' pitcher in a frame;
When yo' gone I kin see yo' jes' duh same.

"O, Lawdy! Lawdy!" The girl beneath us shook with convulsive sobbing.

I'se gwine to staht walkin' cause I got a wooden pah o' shoes;
Gwine to staht walkin' cause I got a wooden pah o' shoes;
Gwine keep on walkin' till I lose dese sobbin' h'ahted Blues.

The singer disappeared, and with her her magic. The spell broken, the audience relaxed and began to chatter. The band played a gayer tune.

Once again, Bessie Smith came out, now clad in a clinging garment fashioned of beads of silver steel. More than ever she was like an African empress, more than ever like a conjure woman.

"I'm gwinter sing dose mean ornery cussed *Wo'khouse Blues*," she shouted.

Everybody's cryin' de wo'khouse Blues all day,
All 'long,
All 'long. . . .

A deep sigh from the gallery.

Been wo'kin' so hard—thirty days is long,
long, long,
long, long . . .

The spell once more was weaving its subtle sorcery, the perversely complicated spell of African voodoo, the fragrance of chinaberry blossoms, the glimmer of the silver fleece of the cotton field under the full moon, the spell of sorrow: misery, poverty, and the horror of jail.

I gotta leab heah.
Gotta git duh nex' train home . . .

Way up dere, way up on a long lonesome road;
Duh wo'khouse ez up on a long lonesome road . . .

Daddy used ter be mine, but look who'se got him now;
Daddy used ter be mine, but look who'se got him now;
If yo' took him keep him, he don't mean no good nohow.

After the curtain had fallen, Leigh Whipper guided us backstage where he introduced us to Bessie Smith and this proved to be exactly the same experience that meeting any great interpreter is likely to be: we paid homages humbly and she accepted them with just the right amount of deference. I believe I kissed her hand. I hope I did.

A few years later, Porter Grainger brought her to my apartment on West Fifty-fifty Street. Fania Marinoff and I were throwing a party. George Gershwin was there and Marguerite d'Alvarez and Constance Collier, possibly Adele Astaire. The drawingroom was well filled with sophisticated listeners. Before she could sing, Bessie wanted a drink. She asked for a glass of straight gin, and with one gulp she downed a glass holding nearly a pint. Then, with a burning cigarette depending from one corner of her mouth, she got down to the Blues, really down to 'em, with Porter at the piano. I am quite certain that anybody who was present that night will never forget it. This was no actress; no imitator of a woman's woes; there was no pretence. It was the real thing: a woman cutting her heart open with a knife until it was exposed for us all to see, so that we suffered as she suffered, exposed with a rhythmic ferocity, indeed, which could hardly be borne. In my own experience, this was Bessie Smith's greatest performance.

Again, she came to my apartment on Fifty-fifth Street in February 1936, a year or two before her tragic death in Memphis, brought this time by my friend Al Moore, so that I might photograph her. She was making one of her final appearances (although we were not aware of this fact) at a downtown nightclub and she came to see me between shows, cold sober and in a quiet reflective mood. She could scarcely have been more amiable or cooperative. She was agreeable to all my suggestions and even made changes of dress. Of course, on this occasion she did not sing, but I got nearer to her real personality than I ever had before and the photographs, perhaps, are the only adequate record of her true appearance and manner that exist.

It is pretty generally forgotten that Bessie made a film of the "St. Louis Blues." It is a short and so poignantly effective that it was not immediately acceptable to the wider moving-picture public, as the characters were sordid and the story relentless in its depiction of the way men and women who are in and out of love behave, but it is a wonderful memorial to the artistry of Bessie Smith and, if a copy of this film can be discovered, it should be revived to prove what a great singer she was and what a great actress she might have been, given the opportunity.[1] Anybody in the future who sees this film (and hears it) will be able to understand in some degree how we felt in that room on West Fifty-fifth Street, when cigarette depending but never falling from one corner of her mouth, she moaned: "Duh wo'khouse ez up on a long lonesome road."

1. The film *St. Louis Blues* was subsequently discovered and proved Van Vechten's recollections of its value absolutely accurate. A print is in the film library of the Museum of Modern Art in New York.

ETHEL WATERS

The second section of the essay, "Negro 'Blues' Singers," in *Vanity Fair*, March 1926, was devoted to Ethel Waters. It is here combined with Van Vechten's review of her performance in *Mamba's Daughters*, published in *Opportunity* in February 1939; with the notice he wrote for publication as an advertisement in the *New York Times* in September 1938; and with a speech he made at a dinner given in the singer's honor by the Harlem Business Women at the Park Sheraton Hotel, on 29 October 1950. The speech, of course, has not been previously published. Once again, I have freely reorganized these materials to make a chronological memoir.

If Bessie Smith is crude and primitive, she represents the true folk spirit of the race. She sings Blues as they are understood and admired by the colored masses. Of the artists who have communicated the Blues to the more sophisticated Negro and white public, I think Ethel Waters is the best. In fact, to my mind, as an artist, Miss Waters is superior to any other woman stage singer of her race.

She refines her comedy, refines her pathos, refines even her obscenities. She is such an expert mistress of her effects that she is obliged to expend very little effort to get over a line, a song, or even a dance. She is a natural comedienne and not one of the kind that has to work hard. She is not known as a dancer, but she is able, by a single movement of her body, to outline for her public the suggestion of an entire dance. In her singing she exercises the same subtle skill. Some of her songs she croons; she never shouts. Her methods are precisely opposed to those of the crude coon shouter, to those of the authentic Blues singer, and yet, not for once, does she lose the veridical Negro atmosphere. Her voice and her gestures are essentially Negro, but they have been thought out and restrained, not prettified, but stylized. Ethel Waters can be langourous or emotional or gay, according to the mood of her song, but she is always the artistic interpreter of the many-talented race of which she is a conspicuous member.

Some of you, who have learned to admire Miss Waters through her performance in *The Member of the Wedding*, may wonder why I have been invited to talk about her on this occasion. Perhaps some of you are under the delusion that I was introduced to her in the same way, at the same time.

Nothing could be further from the truth. It may surprise any of my auditors who cherish such an idea, to discover that Ethel and I grew up together. She visited me at my big house and I visited her in her shack. I am not a fair-weather friend who blew in when success began to toss purple orchids in her direction. I knew her when!

I knew her when Harlem society condemned her as beneath its notice. To upper-class Harlem, she was simply that Waters woman who sang naughty songs. I knew her when she sang "You Can't Do What My Last Man Did," "Shake That Thing," and "Go Back Where You Stayed Last Night" (which she sang with a good deal of conviction):

> Go back where you stayed last night,
> Get away from my door,
> Charley's elected now,
> I don't want you no more.

Or "Maybe Not at All," in which she gave lifelike imitations of the famous Blues sisters, Bessie and Clara Smith. Most of these songs are recorded and along with my other Ethel Waters recordings—I had nearly a complete set, ranging over a long period of time and including her most recent long-playing record—they repose in the James Weldon Johnson Memorial Collection of Negro Arts and Letters in the Yale University Library. For, don't forget, Ethel was always an artist. It was during these early years that I wrote to her, comparing her art with that of Yvette Guilbert, who also, it may be remembered, sang off-color songs in HER early career. Maybe Ethel still has that letter.

I didn't know her or her art when she sang at Edmond's on upper Fifth Avenue, but Edna Thomas and many of my other friends did, and they have told me that she was never greater than when she sang in this lovely dive. My first encounter, even with her name, occurred at a Sunday night benefit performance at the Lafayette Theatre, at which I was the guest of

James Weldon Johnson. She sang "Georgia Blues" that night and a new world was opened to me.

It was a year after that before I met her, and meeting her wasn't easy. To her, I was as good as nobody, and she had very good reasons for mistrusting any white person. Besides, she didn't need white people. She had a life of her own, with her own, which she preferred. Earl Dancer felt differently about it and perhaps it was he who persuaded her to see me, to invite me and my wife to dine in Harlem. At any rate it was not too long before we became great friends. I broke down part of her prejudice against pink people and I broke down part of social Harlem's prejudice against her.

I pointed out to them that she sang ribald songs in an objective and not an obscene or personal way, and when she was permitted to sing "Shake That Thing" at the Palace Theatre, I felt I had made my point sufficiently. She is an artist, I reiterated constantly, to all and sundry. The subject of her material is immaterial. She is a great artist and she moulds whatever she sings into great art.

I am probably the only person in America, pink or brown, connected with her early life in any way, who doesn't claim that he discovered her. There are actually hundreds who make this claim. Some of them have made it to me. She is correct when she states in her autobiography that it was the public who discovered her.

She was a busy woman in the early days—she is still a busy woman—and we saw each other by fits and starts. Whenever she appeared on Broadway or in Harlem on One hundred and twenty-fifth or One hundred and thirty-fifth Street, I was there, cheering. Occasionally, she came to our apartment for dinner or for a party. Much later, I began to photograph her and I have made photographs of her in many of her great moments in some of her great parts. These also are in the Yale collection. Unfortunately, I have not yet photographed her in *The Member of the Wedding*, but that is not MY fault.

Do you recall as many of those first nights as I do? *Africana*, in which she sang "I'm Coming, Virginia," was one of the first of her shows. Aside from Ethel, it was conventional Negro stage humor and not very inspiring dancing, but her incandescent presence lifted it out of the run-of-the-mill rut. At any rate she was on Broadway at last and it was a start. Everything has to have a beginning.

For some reason which I have forgotten (perhaps I was in Paris), I missed her appearances at the Plantation, but I have heard her sing "Dinah" since, literally hundreds of times, and have worn out several recordings of that ear-tickling song. After *Africana*, my chronology becomes a little confused (my programs are all at Yale), but I didn't miss much. There were music hall and nightclub and picture house appearances. There were fly-by-night revues. There was Lew Leslie's *Blackbirds* (I have forgotten the year) in which she delivered her great monologues of the scrubwoman with the tired arms and the nightclub hostess with the tired feet, good folk material in themselves, and forerunners of her later dramatic appearances. There was certainly "Stormy Weather" at the Cotton Club, one of her great numbers. There was *At Home Abroad* with Beatrice Lillie. There was "Am I Blue?" in a Hollywood picture, *On with the Show*, and *Tales of Manhattan* with Paul Robeson, and there were other songs and pictures, culminating in her recent appearance in *Pinky* in which she acted with that other fine player, Ethel Barrymore. I have heard her sing in Chicago. I have heard her at a benefit in the Savoy Ballroom where she was obliged to sing with scarcely anyone directly in front of her, but with auditors at either end of this long room. Without forcing her tones, singing in her ordinary manner, she held them. She can always hold them. For a time she sang over the radio into thousands of hearts and homes. I was Ethel's first escort in Paris, in which she was disappointed, as you will recall Oscar Wilde said he was with the Atlantic [Ocean]. I have heard her sing "Eili Eili" in what I have been told was impeccable Hebrew, although she actually doesn't know a word of this language and learned this lament, as is her invariable custom, as she doesn't read music either, by ear. I knew Pearl Wright, her longtime accompanist and her great friend. At first suspicious of me, later when she was certain I was Ethel's true friend there was nothing she wouldn't do for me.

The number of songs Ethel has made her own is legion. The number of songs she has made famous could not be counted on the fingers of two hands. I have mentioned some and will mention others later. Here are a few more: "St. Louis Blues," "Sleepy Time Down South," "West End Blues," "Georgia on My Mind," "Miss Otis Regrets," "My Special Friend Is Back in Town" (always one of my favorites), "Porgy," "Underneath the Harlem Moon," "He Brought Joy to My Soul," "Summertime"; I could go on listing and remembering with pleasure.

Eventually, there was *As Thousands Cheer*, [in] which Ethel sang first in Philadelphia, where I heard her and realized at once she had made a hit of vast proportions. (So, unfortunately, did the cast realize this fact—Marilyn Miller, Clifton Webb, and Helen Broderick.) So, fortunately, did Irving Berlin, the composer of the music. In Philadelphia, she had three songs. In New York, four. "Supper Time" was an absolute oddity for a musical revue, a tragic song about a Negro mother coming home to cook after her [husband] had been lynched. This was well contrasted with "Heat Wave," one of Ethel's most memorable successes, for it is well to remember she understands comedy as well as she understands tragedy.

There was more shilly-shallying after this, futile pictures, futile revues. I don't mean shilly-shallying on Ethel's part, but on the part of the managers and the playwrights. Finally came the unforgettable great first night of *Mamba's Daughters*. My wife and I both knew Ethel pretty well by this time, but when the final curtain fell, Fania said, "This wasn't Ethel, this was Hagar." There were, I believe, seventeen curtain calls for her alone. Later, when we went to her dressing room, Kit Cornell, Lillian Gish, Tallulah Bankhead, Judith Anderson, Helen Hayes, and Lynn Fontanne were there ahead of me on their knees to the new star.

Whatever may be said for or against the play, the performance of Ethel Waters in the role of Hagar calls only for the highest superlatives and has received them from all the critics. Rarely have I encountered such unanimity of opinion, such consistent enthusiasm. Seldom have I seen a first-night audience so excited, so moved, so carried away by "make-believe." The fact is that the audience and the critics were enjoying what is known as "great" acting, a phenomenon so rare that any generation is granted only a few examples of it, a phenomenon almost unheard-of on our contemporary stage. A great actress should not be confused with a celebrated actress. Examples of the latter are more common, for while it is not impossible for a great actress to achieve celebrity, it does not follow that a celebrated actress is always great. When I think of "great" performances I think of Ellen Terry as Portia, Rejane in *La Robe Rouge*, Mary Garden as Mélisande, Chaliapin as Boris, Sarah Bernhardt in *La Dame aux Camelias* . . . and now Ethel Waters as Hagar!

When Miss Waters leaves her dressing room to walk on the stage (the same dressing room and stage, by the way, employed by Maud Adams when she played Peter Pan) she leaves Ethel Waters behind her and steps into the very soul of Hagar. It is not an easy matter to communicate feeling to an audience in an inarticulate part, but Miss Waters succeeds in communicating that feeling, as only true artists can, the moment she appears in the courtroom scene at the beginning of the play. Some actresses would have stopped there. Not Miss Waters.

As the play progresses the feeling is intensified, the character grows in stature, until at the very end, just before the play is over, the tension of the emotion created becomes almost unbearable. In the final scene Miss Waters, so far as the effect she makes is concerned, might be playing the "Liebestod" of Isolde, or Juliet in the potion scene. No wonder the vast two-colored audience of the opening night rose to cheer her and who can ever forget her as she stood alone and magnificent on that stage as the curtain rose and fell, harassed by the enthusiasm, how she finally bowed her head and cried, the tears coursing down her cheeks!

I have only admiration for the rest of the cast: Georgette Harvey, Rosamond Johnson, Fredi Washington, Willie Bryant, and the others are all fine in their several rôles, and the direction of Guthrie McClintic could scarcely be improved. A word too should be spoken in praise of the excellent settings, the work of Perry Watkins, a new Negro scenic designer. The fact remains that in the presence of a star of such magnitude as Ethel Waters these matters sink into secondary importance.

What is to become of Miss Waters in the theatre? Few roles immediately suggest themselves as appropriate. Perhaps some playwright (maybe the Heywards themselves!) will be inspired by her genius to create a new part worthy of her. In the meantime we could always welcome her in her repertory of songs, for as a singer of popular ballads she stands at the top of another profession! I believe a revival for her of *Scarlet Sister Mary*, which Julia Peterkin hoped she would create in the original production, would be an excellent idea, but I cannot help feeling confident that in a Greek play, particularly in the *Medea*, Ethel Waters would more securely establish herself as the world actress of the first rank she indubitably is.

I rose early the next morning, eager to peruse the morning *Times*, which is the sole paper we take in. To my amazement, [Brooks] Atkinson had his doubts about Ethel's performance. The telephone soon began to ring and one after another of these voices—they were celebrated voices—complained about this review. Morris Ernst called and said he wanted to do something about it. "Ignore it," was my advice, "but I will write a short endorsement of Ethel's performance and we will get some of the stars to sign it." "Good," Morris replied, "and we will publish it as an advertisement in the *New York Times* tomorrow morning." I had no difficulty whatever in collecting signatures. Most of those who signed wanted to pay for a share of the cost of the advertisement. . . . The document appeared the next day in the *New York Times,* and later a magnified copy graced the lobby of the Empire Theatre:

AN OPEN LETTER ON BEHALF OF ETHEL WATERS

The undersigned feel that Ethel Waters's superb performance in *Mamba's Daughters* at the Empire Theatre is a profound emotional experience which any playgoer would be the poorer for missing. It seems indeed to be such a magnificent example of great acting, simple, deeply felt, moving on a plane of complete reality, that we are glad to pay for the privilege of saying so.

Judith Anderson	Helen Hall
Tallulah Bankhead	Oscar Hammerstein II
Norman Bel Geddes	Paul Kellog
Cass Canfield	Edwin Knopf
John Emery	Ben H. Lehman
Morris L. Ernst	Fania Marinoff
John Farrar	Aline MacMahon
Dorothy Gish	Burgess Meredith
Jules Glaezner	Stanley Reinhardt

Carl Van Vechten

The sequel, the unusual sequel, was that Atkinson later retracted his bad review, even apologized for it, in a subsequent Sunday article, also in the *Times*. He explained he had seen the play and the performance again and felt he had made a mistake on the first night.

Some years later, Ethel appeared in *Cabin in the Sky*, and made another deep impression, but although "Taking a Chance on Love" and "Cabin in the Sky" made an immediate success and she continued to keep them in her vocal repertory, the piece did not catch on, and her own success was considerably less than that she had achieved in Dorothy and Du Bose Heyward's drama.

After *Cabin*, for ten years or more she seemed to have been forgotten. Apparently nobody wanted her and when she did appear it was under the most drab auspices. Then came *Pinky* which at least offered her more of an opportunity than it did to anyone else in the cast.

One day she called me up and asked me if I had read *The Member of the Wedding* and what I thought about it in connection with her. At the time, the Theatre Guild planned to produce it. I had not considered this book as a possibility for the stage before, but I replied immediately, spontaneously, and instinctively, "The part in the book might have been written for you." This is not exactly true, but I knew that it would be, before the opening. As a matter of fact, the theatre version of Carson McCullers's moving story, when produced, became more successful than the novel.

The rest is history, so recent, it hardly needs retelling. The play and Ethel made a superlative success and they are still running to crowded houses and probably will continue to do so for many weeks to come.

Ethel is heard at her best, seated in a drawing room, surrounded by her friends. She has sung at our apartment voluntarily (we have never asked her to do so) many times, and before the elect. Once in the twilight at Luigi Lucioni's (he had painted her portrait) she sang for an hour, unaccompanied, seated in a chair. Tallulah Bankhead, wide-eyed and silent, sat at her feet. Once at our apartment, she sang for Fritzi Massary who admired her extravagantly. I said there was some talk of her appearing as Mrs. Alving in *Ghosts*. "Do you think she could do that?" I inquired of one of the great stars of the prewar German stage. "I think she could do anything," was the enthusiastic reply.

At a formal, and most exciting dinner for Ethel Waters, which I attended, Howard Lindsay, one of the speakers, asserted that Ethel was a genius. Nobody cared to contradict his verdict until Ethel, in her turn, got up to speak.

"I ain't no genius," she declared. "I can't feel anything on the stage I haven't felt in real life." Perhaps she can't. Can anyone? Can anyone write about anything he has not experienced or read about in some form or other? George Moore says somewhere that a woman cannot play Juliet until she has been beaten and made to wait in the rain. Ethel's life has been a hard one, but perhaps the Bon Dieu has a pragmatic intention in making it so. "Ethel," I can imagine Him saying to her, "I'm going to make you suffer, I'm going to make you suffer a lot, but this will make you understand others who suffer and, as a result, you will become a great actress." Acting is a combination of experience, imagination, instinct, and intelligence. I do not believe Ethel Waters is lacking in any of these qualities.

I have known a great many artists in various fields in my life. Three outstanding personalities in the theatre come to mind, Alicia Markova, the great ballerina, Mary Garden, the great opera singer, and Ethel Waters, the great actress. These three have devoted themselves unceasingly, exclusively, and intensively to the search for perfection. Nothing else has mattered. And the results have proved they were wise.

CLARA SMITH

Van Vechten prepared a paper about Clara Smith immediately following the publication in *Jazz Record* of his Bessie Smith memoir. He expanded the third section of his "Negro 'Blues' Singers" from *Vanity Fair*, March 1926, to include some later, more personal memories. A brief passage from the manuscript bibliography of Van Vechten's contributions to the James Weldon Johnson Memorial Collection of Negro Arts and Letters completes this composite essay. Neither has been published heretofore; indeed, the material exists only in a single draft and is unusually flat, although the information has some historical interest. Perhaps that overrides the limitations of the actual writing which often carries an uncomfortable condescension.

Several years earlier, in a letter to Walter White, Van Vechten had suggested that Clara Smith would make a success with white audiences: "Of all the Blues singers she is the one most fitted to carry this gospel into the alien world. She represents something that is fast going: the primitive old southern Negro, and when she sings 'Prescription for the Blues' or 'If you only know'd' she epitomizes the tragic moments in the love lives of those people. But she is expert in her delineation of comedy songs too. Personally, as you know, I consider her an important artist."

When we listen to Clara Smith we are vouchsafed another manifestation of the genius of the Negro for touching the heart through music. Like Bessie Smith . . . Clara is a crude purveyor of the pseudo-folksongs of her race. She employs, however, more nuances of expression, a greater range of vocal color, than the Empress. Her voice flutters agonizingly between tones. Music critics would say that she sings off the key; rather, she is singing quarter tones, and singing them for their full effect of a mystic kind of grief. Thus she is justifiably billed, by the Columbia Recording Company, as the World's Greatest Moaner. She appears to be more of an artist than Bessie, but I suspect that this apparent artistry is spontaneous and uncalculated.

Clara Smith lived in New York at the height of her fame, and consequently I saw her many times and got much better acquainted with her than I ever did with Bessie, who was *not* Clara's sister, although it is true that they appeared together at some time or other in a sister act. Clara lived in a big brick house belonging to her aunt, I believe, set back from the street in the shade of spreading trees on One hundred and twenty-ninth Street (or was it One hundred and thirtieth?) east of Fifth Avenue. To gain admittance you were obliged to walk up a flight of steps to a veranda and, once inside the entrance, you were escorted down a dark hall to the middle door which opened [into] Clara's apartment. I never visited the other floors in this house, but I recall this one very well. Beginning with the kitchen at the back, the next chamber was the bedroom, furnished with the barest necessities. There never seemed to be a carpet on the floor. In front of this was one containing a table and a few chairs, and it was here that Clara's company usually foregathered, for there were always neighbors running in and out, in addition to her business visitors and ofays like myself who paid attention to her because they liked her. The front parlor made up for the meagre furnishing of the rest of the apartment. It contained two complete "suites" (as they are called in One hundred twenty-fifth Street windows) of upholstered furniture, one in green, the other in red plush, probably about fourteen pieces in all. The room was not large, and these suites were packed in together so closely that it was not easy to make your way about in it to inspect the framed photographs of Clara and her forebears on the table or the not too skilfully executed oil paintings on the red-papered walls.

There must have been an upright piano in this room, too, but I do not remember Clara ever singing at home. In the first place an accompanist was lacking during my visits and in the second place Clara was not one to sing unless she were getting well paid for it. It was fun to talk to Clara, if perhaps not intellectually rewarding, and friends who went up with me to see her were always amused. Sometimes her husband, to whom she referred . . . affectionately as Tootie (I believe he was a baseball player on some minor Nègro league) put in a brief appearance. Once Clara invited me to buy him an overcoat—it was a cold night at the opposite monthly pole from the baseball season—but when I refused she retained her habitual good humor. At the same time Clara was making frequent recordings and appearances in [one-]week stands at Negro theatres, but nevertheless she always seemed to be short of money. On one occasion, I recall, when I visited her with several people in tow including Caroline Reagon, who had taken the Revue Nègre and Josephine Baker to Paris, and who was planning another Negro harlequinade, Clara was throwing a "rent party," a species of Harlem social commerce in which the guests paid money to attend, money which supposedly was presently employed to pacify the rental agent. In this particular instance, however, as the house in which Clara resided belonged to her aunt, the idea of a rent party seemed a trifle odd. It is possible the idea only occurred to Clara after I had telephoned from downtown that I was about to call on her with a few pleasant people. Jules Pascin, the celebrated Russian painter, present on this occasion, was enormously impressed with Clara's appearance and social manner.

Mrs. Reagon was impressed too and later, when she heard her sing, determined to star Clara in her new revue, and I am certain if this show had ever come off Clara would have made an appearance in it. Mrs. Reagon *did* arrange for a bachelor friend of hers who lived in a big studio in Washington Square to give a Sunday evening buffet supper, after which Clara entertained in the manner that was customary with opera singers at private parties in the Nineties, at any rate when the host could afford it. Clara sang a complete program of songs, perhaps fifteen, in groups of five or six divided from each other by short intermissions. For the most part the program was chosen by me from her phonograph records or from titles in her current repertory. I sat next to Ethel Barrymore during the concert and she frankly admitted she found Clara's singing afforded her emotional experience of a high order.

When she came on the stage at the Lincoln Theatre in Harlem, through folds of electric blue hangings at the back, she was wrapped in a black evening cloak bordered with white fur. Entertainers of this era, like entertainers of today, affected the chic, and Clara was habited in a fashionable hobble skirt, uniform of the speakeasy period.

She did not advance, but hesitated, turning her tortured face in profile. The pianist played the characteristic strain of the Blues. Clara sang:

> All day long I'm worried;
> All day long I'm blue;
> I'm so awfully lonesome,
> I don' know what to do;
> So I ask yo', doctor,
> See if yo' kin fin'

Somethin' in yo' satchel
To pacify my min'.

At this point her tones became poignantly pathetic: tears rolled down her cheeks; her plea carried the deepest chagrin:

Doctor!
Doctor!
Write me a prescription fo' duh Blues,
Duh mean ole Blues.

Her voice died away in a mourning wail of pain, as once again she buried her head in the curtains.

Clara's tones uncannily took on the color of the saxophone; again of the clarinet. Powerful or melancholy by turn, her voice wrenched the blood from her listeners' hearts. One learns from her that the Negro's cry to a cruel Cupid is as moving and elemental as is his cry to God, as expressed in the Spirituals. To hear her was a pleasure not unmixed with pain. She never sang "Sometimes I'm Happy."

Clara seems to have died of natural causes in Detroit, while on tour, around 1933, several years before Bessie. It was some time later, when I began to inquire about her, that I heard of her death. News of it did not, so far as I am aware, reach the Negro press and, indeed, to this very minute, I have been unable to establish the exact date. She was a remarkable figure.

Unfortunately, Clara is not as effective on the phonograph as Bessie. Nor was her choice of numbers as good. She was to be heard at her very best in a small room with a sympathetic audience. . . . But . . . her records are her monument and if you will play over "Nobody Knows Duh Way I Feel Dis Mornin," that theme song of the Splendid Drunken Twenties, or "If the first to introduce his native African dance to America; Josephine Baker,

BILLIE HOLIDAY

The memoir of Billie Holiday appeared in *Esquire* in December 1962 when the magazine invited Van Vechten to write a piece about the subjects its editors had chosen from among his photographs for a feature article. Van Vechten never liked the essay, saying afterward he would never again write anything on assignment. He had attempted a paper devoted to his whole career in photography which

Esquire rejected in favor of some short biographies, titled
"Portraits of the Artists." Nor did Van Vechten think much
of the magazine's selection of photographs: "A rather
peculiar list, but not unreasonable," he confided privately.
"They might have been happy businessmen's choices."

Although I had heard her sing many times at Café Society Downtown
(*Strange Fruit*), at Spivy's, at Carnegie Hall, and on records, I actually spent
only one night photographing Billie Holiday, but it was the whole of one
night and it seemed like a complete career. Gerry Major had arranged the
session of photography for the James Weldon Johnson Collection of Negro
Arts and Letters. Billie had been requested by Gerry to wear an evening
dress, but she appeared at my door at the appointed hour of eight in a plain
grey suit and facial expression equally depressing. The going was hard for
some time and I was nearly prepared to call off the sitting as a failure. My
assistant, Saul Mauriber, was even more convinced we were getting nowhere
when suddenly I had the brilliant inspiration to show her an extraordinary
photograph I had taken of the fantastic Bessie Smith in the mood of the
Blues, one of my greatest photographs and certainly the only really revealing
photograph that the "Empress of the Blues" had ever had taken. Looking at
this photograph, Billie immediately burst into tears, explaining that Bessie
had been a good friend to her mother and her *own* inspiration when she
began to sing. From that moment on, she was putty in my hands. The
portrait of Billie singing . . . was made directly after she had seen Bessie
Smith's picture. Thereafter she removed the suit and submitted to Saul's
improvisations. Lacking a dress for her, he draped a piece of material on her
in an arrangement more suitable for a concert appearance. About midnight,
she assured me she had to go home briefly; naturally I assumed this journey
was in search of marijuana, cocaine, heroin, or some other sudden form of
inspiration or intoxication. To insure her reappearance I requested Saul to
accompany her to Harlem. They returned an hour later with Mister, her
boxer. She was now on a different plane, all energy, sympathy, cooperation,
and interest. We photographed her for two hours more, in assorted positions
and locations, even on the floor with Mister. After we were through with
Mister, and Billie continued to expand before the lens, the neglected dog
roamed through the apartment chewing cushions or stuffed pseudo-mammals
into unrecognizable bits. Eventually we collected Mister, who, now that he
had Billie's complete attention, became docile and behaved like a gentleman.
Once ensconced in the salon, she related in great detail the sad, bittersweet
story of her tempestuous life. It was a heartbreaking story, one no one could
invent, and was told simply, but with a good deal of feeling and, on occasion,
of dramatic intensity. Somewhere during the course of this recital, Fania,
who usually disappears when I take photographs, came in, semidressed,

averring she could not sleep with the sound of voices so prominent in her ears. In a short time Fania, like the rest of us, was in tears, and suddenly, also like the rest of us, found herself as attached to Billie as if she had known her intimately for years. At four o'clock, Billie's then husband, a Mr. Levy, appeared and Scheherazade's story went on until five, when Billie and Mr. Levy took their departure from a tearful group. We never saw her again, but not one of us will ever forget her. Without exaggeration, it could be called a memorable evening.

RICHMOND BARTHÉ

Van Vechten's observations about Richmond Barthé are drawn from two catalog notes, one for an exhibition of sculpture in 1939, and the other for an exhibition in 1947. In between, the plans to have Barthé design and execute the James Weldon Johnson Memorial were born and subsequently died. An account of Barthé's involvement with the project occurs in Van Vechten's papers about it, included in the group of essays about James Weldon Johnson in this collection.

I have never seen works of art which call for less explanation or description than the sculptured figures and heads of Richmond Barthé. They sing and speak and dance for themselves. For this and another reason it is not easy to write about Barthé s work. The other reason is, I can say from experience and acquaintanceship of long standing with his creations, that Barthé is unpredictable. You never know what he will do next.

He studied drawing at the Art Institute in Chicago, a course which fortunately included anatomy: subsequently he became a sculptor and seldom draws at all nowadays. He quickly learned to make his first sketches in clay. His early pieces were neither suggestive of the American Negro, nor of the African. Why should they be? He is neither African nor insincere and his first knowledge of art did not come to him through Negro instructors. The Negro was a secondary inspiration, deeper perhaps than the influences which inspired his beginnings because it is based on a profound love of his race. This later inspiration, then, gives his work strength and offers him a convenient background on which to lean. Now he desires to visit Africa, to learn at first hand the mysteries of its treasures and its people, who share his ancestors.

It is not necessary to know much about technique to understand that Barthé does not stylize. Surfaces, indeed, seem to interest him very little.

What he is actually seeking are the spiritual values inherent in moving figures. He says if you find these the surfaces will take care of themselves. His enthusiasm and vitality are boundless and he dashes about among his models and his images with an immense amount of energy, creating living works of art, with equal facility and success, out of stevedores, bootblacks, and Gypsy Rose Lees, sometimes with strength and passion and sorrow, as with *The Negro Mother*, sometimes with the grace and a frank admiration for African beauty, as with the *Feral Benga*, and finally, with complete mastery of a new (to him) medium, in the amazingly vital head of Jimmie Daniels.

Although this was his first carving in marble, it can in no respect be regarded as an experiment. It seems to me that his first flight in this direction was as skilfully planned and executed as Lindbergh's flight to Paris. I am still unable to explain to myself what he has done with this head to give it so much life and charm. I stand before it a little bewildered, completely admiring, and wonder who else, save Donatello himself, would be capable of giving us such a degree of perfection.

The theatre, as represented by the drama and dance, has always been one of Richmond Barthé s major interests and naturally he turned to it for subjects early in his career as a sculptor. Harald Kreutzberg and Rose McClendon, friends of the artist, were perhaps the original inspiration for the idea of the little group now on exhibition in this gallery. It is probable, too, that the dancer and the actress posed, and more than once, for the portraits which represent them.

Latterly, however, the sculptor has altered his technique in this matter. He prefers to study his subjects from a chair in the orchestra, during a performance. He went again and again to see John Gielgud, Katharine Cornell, and Muriel Smith in *Hamlet, Romeo and Juliet,* and *Carmen,* and gradually acquired a deep sympathy for the insides of the characters they were portraying. An actor in a studio is quite likely to be dead, but on the stage he lives, the success of his roles depending on his talent for expression. So it was on the stage itself that Barthé determined to look for his inspiration and on the stage he found it.

Sometimes he has invited his model in at the end for a final sitting "for corrections," but this can be dangerous, he has discovered, because he can be misled, by the appearance of the actual person, into criticizing a detail already successfully expressed in clay, which he had really seen happen in the theatre.

There is another interesting fact to record about these heads and figures. One or two of them have been orders, but for the most part they are the artist's own choice of subjects. In other words, he has selected from his theatregoing the actors and dancers he has preferred to preserve in marble or bronze. So there is nothing accidental or tentative about the fact that he has recreated them in clay. They are all distinguished figures and he has awarded them his warmest and most sympathetic attention. He will be delighted to learn that he has made them live again in the eyes of the spectator.

MARIAN ANDERSON

Barry Hymans, representing Sol Hurok, asked Van Vechten if he would write a piece about Marian Anderson for a new souvenir program in 1947. He responded with pleasure, adding that he would give the check in payment for his work "to the James Weldon Johnson Memorial Collection of Negro Arts and Letters, which I founded at Yale University. Naturally, I wish the cheque were larger than the amount you suggested." (The budgetary allowance offered $75 for the piece.) To it I have appended Van Vechten's review of Marian Anderson's autobiography, *My Lord, What a Morning!*, which he called "Soft Voice of Feeling." It appeared in *Saturday Review*, 3 November 1956.

I have just come from the Lewisohn Stadium where Marian Anderson, resplendent and noble in white, a cluster of crimson roses at her belt, sang and communicated with an audience of 20,000, sang indeed more magically than I have ever heard her sing before, projecting Massenet's "Ne Me Refuse Pas" from the opera *Hérodiade* into the vast spaces in front of her with a wealth of tone and a fiery intensity that exhibited this singer as a great dramatic artist. She closed the program with a group of Negro Spirituals rendered to piano accompaniment. At the end of the printed list the vast audience as a whole remained to cheer until she had added five more numbers. I was sitting in the front row and I observed that Leonard Bernstein, the conductor of the evening, stood in the wings to listen until she had sung the last note of Schubert's "Ave Maria," her goodnight. It is a rare singer who is able to evoke such extraordinary behavior on the part of a conductor!

My memories of Marian Anderson, which are surprisingly consistent, go back to her beginnings. I was introduced to her voice, I believe, before she had made any stage appearances. Walter and Gladys White had invited me to hear a young girl sing in their Edgecomb Avenue apartment and that is where I met Miss Anderson. She sang on that occasion, I remember, with no false modesty, but with no bravado either, the air from *Samson et Dalila:* "Mon Coeur s'Ouvre à ta Voix." This air demands of its interpreter a sensuous quality of sound which has never been this contralto's stock in trade, but the resonant tones of her noble organ made a profound impression on me. What I noticed more than anything else about her was a kind of dedication of spirit.

It was in the New York Town Hall that I heard her next on the occasion of her return to America after her triumphs in Vienna and Paris. As the audience filed into the theatre they may have remarked an unusual circumstance: the curtains were drawn to conceal the stage. Later, when they were opened, Miss Anderson was discovered standing in the center of the stage near the piano. At the first intermission the singer explained that she had twisted her ankle on one of the stairways of the boat which had brought her back to America. As her foot was in a cast she could not move freely. She had, however, been unwilling to postpone this first American concert, so long looked forward to, and had devised this unconventional method of presenting herself. I was impressed by her singing on this occasion, particularly by her rendering of the German *lieder*, but I was even more impressed by this demonstration of her loyalty to her art and to her public.

Some years later (I had heard her sing many times in the interim) she had made an appointment a few days ahead to be photographed by me in my apartment. The appointment was for midnight, as she was singing in Hartford the afternoon of the day in question and must give herself time for her return to New York. When the night arrived a tremendous blizzard blew up, the worst storm, indeed, of that particular winter. I waited by the telephone expecting a call from Miss Anderson that she would be unable to keep the appointment. The telephone bell did not ring. She was at the front door at one o'clock with a bag containing certain dresses I had asked her to bring. I was aghast at the trouble I had caused her. "Why didn't you wait for an easier time?" I asked her. "In my life," she responded, "there are no easy times. I am always busy. One hour or one day is like the next." Again I was compelled to award her character a vast degree of admiration. There certainly exist no difficulties that an indomitable spirit like this cannot surmount.

During the late war, one of my duties with the American Theatre Wing was to arrange for a weekly entertainer to appear at the Service Women's Tea Dance held every Sunday afternoon in the Grill Room of the Hotel Roosevelt. The young people in uniform of both sexes who attended these dances were not overly sophisticated: many of them had never been inside a theatre or a concert hall as their homes had been far away from large cities. Nevertheless, early in my experience with this constantly shifting group I discovered it was never deceived by spurious talent, and that it always appreciated the best. Time after time this was proven by such great artists as Alicia Markova and Josef Hofmann. There was something compelling about a great personality which seemed to hold the young people spellbound. Even I, however, was unprepared for the tremendous effect Marian Anderson made on these boys and girls. She sang one group of songs, about twenty minutes altogether, but the songs, save for one Spiritual, were in French or German. She sang "Die Forelle," "Der Tod und Das Mädchen," and the "Ave Maria" of Schubert, and these young people in uniform (mind you, the place was packed) received her with a reverent attention which must have seemed unusual, even to her. I was accustomed to the magic spell she wove around her listeners, but never, I believe, until then, had I found myself so fully aware of it. They listened as if they were part of the music; indeed, part of her! They applauded as if they were handing her their young hearts. I am sure this artist felt a special quality in their warm response; in turn, I was aware of a special quality in her singing.

I also recall with a kind of warm nostalgia the supper Mr. Hurok gave her at Sherry's in honor of the tenth year of their association. I recall how, robed in gold, she sat nobly enthroned in the center of the dais which also held Paul Robeson and many other notables. I recall with what grace and humor she accepted what must have been to her the surprising toast of the Don Cossacks. On this occasion she did not sing, but she spoke, so simply from the heart, so sensitively, that everyone present must have been deeply moved.

Many writers have tried to describe Marian Anderson's personality and art, but any writer who tries to do this anew must feel a certain hesitancy in making the attempt: many a listener has come away from one of her recitals uncertain whether he has enjoyed an aesthetic or a religious experience, so completely fused are the two ideals in this great artist's own nature. When she sings she gives everything she has to God and He in His generosity gives it back to all the listeners within hearing. Her presence itself is compelling. Seemingly, without making any conscious effort, she commands complete attention. Seldom, indeed, has such simplicity of manner, such peaceful bearing, been accompanied by so much power and glory.

It has always been a mystery to me how a singer with such deep contralto tones can also be mistress of one of the lightest of organs; how she can sing Scarlatti's "Le Violette," or Jenny Lind's fabulous "Echo Song," or a folksong like "Yarmouth Fair," and follow it with "Der Erlkönig" or "They Crucified My Lord," or the magical "Amuri, Amuri" in which a sleepy Sicilian carter, driving home, walks by the side of his horse, muttering of the unhappiness of love. Unless you have heard Marian Anderson sing this song there is a subtle side of her art of which you are still unaware.

I have mentioned "The Crucifixion" and it is perhaps to the Spirituals that Miss Anderson devotes her best talents. She has said, "I do a good deal of praying," and surely a good deal of it is done in the concert hall, praying and preaching too. She communicated to these religious songs something of the rarity of her own poetic vision. There is nothing superficial about this singer's attack; she gives all she has to any song she elects to sing; but to the Spirituals she can give more than to any of the others because she can give her racial integrity and warmth as well as her religious and aesthetic feeling. It is a pleasure to be able to write that there are not many artists alive today who come so near as she does to the realization of the heart of a song by Schubert, but perhaps the very reason for this is because she has identified herself so completely with the Spirituals that she can approach art songs with a similarly true devotion. It is possible, in fact, that Marian Anderson's innermost secret is that she lives as she sings. Her respect for her art is no greater than her respect for her life.

The principal facts about the life and career of the author and subject of *My Lord, What a Morning!* are nearly as celebrated as those of Cinderella. Marian Anderson was born in Philadelphia of working-class parents. It was early discovered that she possessed an unusual voice, and her family, with some help from outside, was able to provide for her first tuition. Her mother was sensible and religious, aware of spiritual values. She sympathized with her daughter's ambitions and stood firmly behind her at all times. Miss Anderson's successful ascent to the throne of fame was gradual and not without hard bumps. She sang to no great effect until she won a contest which gave her the opportunity to appear at the Lewisohn Stadium in New York City. Even after this important debut her position in American musical life remained insecure. She went abroad to study and sing; Toscanini announced, "A voice like yours is heard only once in a hundred years"; and she became known even in obscure corners of the globe. The rostrum of Constitution Hall in Washington was denied her by the DAR. Mrs. Roosevelt immediately resigned from the bigoted organization and invited Miss Anderson to sing before the king and queen of England at the White House. She continued to grow in fame and popularity and sang in most parts of the world, including Asia and the Soviet Union. Eventually, she made her debut in opera at the Metropolitan Opera House as Ulrica in *Ballo in Maschera*, with a brilliant cast and Mitropoulos as conductor. She is, I would say, at the present day the world's most celebrated singer.

Miss Anderson possessed a superb voice, powerful and warm if not flexible, in the beginning; but when I first heard her (at Walter White's behest, in Harlem) she was not yet fully prepared for the concert stage. Further, she sang the type of song, "Mon Coeur s'Ouvre à ta Voix," in which she has never become expert. She is well advised to prefer Schubert and the Spirituals of her race, in which, on the whole, she excels, although William

Warfield's German is more accurate and Lotte Lehmann has perhaps more German feeling for the *lieder*, and some, who sing the Spirituals, derive their inspiration more directly from the soil. No one, however, interprets any music with more nobility or intensity of feeling.

Miss Anderson has worked hard with several teachers to fulfil her ambition and, except for a period when her voice was at its prime, she has continued to study. All voices, particularly the occasionally refractory contralto voice, demand this expert attention. She devotes a great deal more space to teachers and accompanists than is usual in autobiographies by singers, who often imply that they sprang into being with their wings spread wide and their voices soaring—which is true, so far as I can recall, of but two modern sopranos, Adelina Patti and Nellie Melba. She acknowledges many times her obligation to her manager, Sol Hurok.

Miss Anderson's manner in this autobiography is modest and unassuming. Sometimes she permits the facts to speak for themselves. Occasionally she says far too little about important incidents. It is a well-written book, the prose suggesting Miss Anderson in conversation. For the most part it expresses what the lady attempts to express. There is no indication that there has been a middleman or ghost-writer, but I presume she had advice in its preparation now and again.

There is a chapter on how she studies her repertory and arranges her programs; and there is a chapter on clothes, always an important feature with audiences at concerts by lady singers, but one too infrequently discussed in a book. Concert dresses are usually ageless and can be worn in any city where they have not been viewed before, but assuredly cannot be seen twice in one place, a catastrophe that any lady in the audience would discover at once. To prevent such an unpleasant accident the singer keeps a book detailing what she wore in Chicago, San Francisco, etc., on various dates. When Miss Anderson visits a hall for the first time she may discover that, as the gown she has announced to some journalist she will wear clashes with the color of the hall, she wishes to change it. Sometimes this creates ill-feeling, but it is unavoidable.

Miss Anderson, like other Negroes, has endured experiences in which white people have behaved in a shameful, shameless, and even inhuman manner. She attributes this to lack of education or the proper experience (she is tactful enough not to speak of lack of breeding). In her book Miss Anderson is not bitter about this, but she lets it be known on every page that she is proud of being a Negro.

Marian Anderson lives up to the words of God, the deep religious feelings of her mother, and her own instinctive beliefs. She regards herself first of all as an American, then as an American Negro. She is, I believe, a great singer, but more than that, a great woman.

The brief memoirs of Nora Holt and Josephine Baker, both previously unpublished, appear in the manuscript bibliography for the Johnson Collection at Yale, while the short pieces about Henry Armstrong and Bricktop have been published in the *Esquire* article on photographic subjects, "Portraits of the Artists," in December 1962.

NORA HOLT

Although Van Vechten knew the other three only briefly, Nora Holt was an intimate friend from the time of their meeting in 1926 until Van Vechten's death in 1964. An elegant and witty woman, Nora Holt was the first black person in America to earn a master's degree in music, through the Chicago Musical College. Subsequently, she became the first music critic for the *Chicago Defender* and, two years later, established the National Association of Negro Musicians. When Van Vechten first met her, she was a nightclub singer with a voice, perhaps, like that of the currently popular Cleo Laine, ranging from "deepest bass to shrillest piping," according to her admirers. Many years later, Nora Holt became New York's dowager music critic, writing a regular column for the *Amsterdam News* and conducting a radio program. Not only did she serve as the model for Lasca Sartoris in *Nigger Heaven*, she also supplied more than one smile in the novel, according to Van Vechten's notes. Sniffing behind her ear, he queried, "Coty?" "No," Nora Holt replied, "body."

She signs Nora Douglas, her own name, I think. Nora was originally Lena and she is still known as Lena by Cyrus McCormick and other Chicagoans. She was married several times and her penultimate husband was a George Holt of Chicago; she afterward married Moe Ray, long-time valet for Charles Schwab, who had the restaurant concession at the Bethlehem Steel Works.

A fabulously amusing and talented person who deserves a biography of her own, she played the piano divinely and was a fine artist as an interpretative singer. Extremely chic, she had a long and notable career, beginning in the West and later singing in fashionable nightclubs and houses in New York, London, Paris, and even Monte Carlo and Shanghai. A social favorite and known to many of both races, [she is] at present (1941) operating a beauty parlor in Los Angeles.

JOSEPHINE BAKER

Caroline Dudley, now Mrs. Joseph Deltiel, planned for a long time to take a Negro show to Paris. Everywhere she searched for ideas and performers. Her first idea for a star was Gertrude Saunders who followed Florence Mills in *Shuffle Along.* She wouldn't go, so Miss Dudley looked up Ethel Waters. Never having seen her she went to a nightclub to have a peep and discovered Miss Baker in the chorus instead. The night the *Revue Nègre* opened at the chic Champs-Élysées Théâtre in Paris in 1925, she became the sensation of the French capital. She was such a sensation, indeed, that she broke her contract with Miss Dudley to go to a variety theatre in Berlin, returning to Paris to star at the Folies Bergère. She never lost her popularity in Paris and, aside from performing at the best music halls, has sung in a revival of Offenbach's *La Creole* and appeared in many moving pictures. In July 1927 she married the Conte Pepito Abatino. Later both the count and the marriage were labelled bogus but in 1937 she actually did marry Jean Lion, wealthy French manufacturer and amateur aviator. In 1936 she visited America for an appearance in the *Follies* at the Winter Garden, where she was not successful. Briefly, too, she appeared in a New York nightclub that season. She returned to Europe where she has undertaken many tours and to Paris which always loves her. Her present whereabouts (1941) are unknown. Miss Baker has a beautiful body, a grotesque sense of comedy, a small but pleasant voice which she uses well, and is an excellent actress. She also has sex appeal and personality. Her only rival on the Paris revue stage during the past fifteen years has been the aging Mistinguette.

HENRY ARMSTRONG

I was unacquainted with Henry Armstrong personally, although I had seen him in the ring and had observed well his lightning delivery of punches, his magical and mysterious feints, his amazing footwork, so like that of a dancer. As a matter of fact, his performance resembled that of the *best* dancer, Erik Bruhn. Langston Hughes knew his companion and associate, who called himself Harry Armstrong, although actually he was not a relative of the pugilist, so I asked Langston if he could invite Henry to pose for me through his pseudo-brother. Langston could and did. The "brother" came to my apartment with Henry and assisted him materially in dressing. I have photographed other prizefighters and other kinds of athletes—Gene Tunney, Joe Louis, Sandor Szabo, the Hungarian wrestler—but none of the others was quite as adept at suddenly dashing into striking action, no one else was as picturesque and agile. In brief, Armstrong's attitudes were the epitome of the art of the prizefighter, expressing, without an opponent, all that was needful to recreate great moments in the ring. Indeed, the finished photographs made it reasonable to credit that, at the time, Henry was champion in two classes.

BRICKTOP

I cannot recall exactly the day when I first met Bricktop (the red-haired appellation of Ada Smith, later Madame du Conge), but it must have been in the late Twenties. I became interested in her when it was reported to me that she had journeyed to Le Havre to meet the Negro Gold Star Mothers, after the Great War, when they were given an opportunity to visit the spots where their sons had fought and died and were buried. Accompanying them to Paris, she spoke French for them and found places for them to sleep. This story endeared her to me to such an extent that when Fania and I were in Paris in the late Twenties, we sought her out at her nightclub in Montmartre. Mabel Mercer was her leading singer at the time, a Mabel in her thirties, fresh from England, a very dear Mabel whose singing I have enjoyed so much in New York, especially her interpretation of "Sunday in Savannah." Louis Cole, whom I had known in New York, was a dancer at the club. I photographed Brick in Paris in 1934 and we wandered pretty much all over Montmartre to discover appropriate locations.

CHESTER HIMES

Van Vechten first met Chester Himes through Richard Wright, the author of *Native Son* and *Black Boy*, in the mid-Forties and was instrumental in arranging for Alfred A. Knopf to publish some of his work, notably the novel, *Lonely Crusade*. His interest had begun, however, with the manuscript of an earlier novel, "Yesterday Will Make You Cry," which Himes had based on his life in prison. Van Vechten always regretted that it was so radically changed

and cut for publication as *Cast the First Stone* because, he
believed, in its original form the novel would have insured
a permanent, early critical success for Himes.

"Red Fires for Chester" is a preface, heretofore unpublished, for a collection of early fiction. I have deleted a
long passage in which Van Vechten recounted a brief
plot line for each of the stories, meaningless without the
full text at hand. The manuscript is dated 27 July 1954.

Chester Himes differs from other top-drawer Negro writers in several important particulars. He is more versatile than some, more unpredictable than others, and more prolific than most. He can be extremely chauvinistic and he can be completely open-minded. He does not find all Negroes worthy of inclusive admiration (or all white persons either) and yet he can indulge in deliberate propaganda as enthusiastically as the next one when his subject demands it, or even admits it. His greatest novel (and few writers of any race have written a better in modern times), *Lonely Crusade*, failed because it annoyed both races and neither was brave enough to accept the criticism it implied. Many Negroes were actually shocked by this outspoken book and Negro authors, for the most part, disliked it cordially. Nevertheless, I believe it to be a masterpiece.

Chester Himes writes equally well about his own race or the other; he writes what he happens to know or feel about either. He does not pull his punches. I would say he is as uninhibited as any writer could be. On occasion, he has even shown a tendency to dissect himself on the operating table.

My People—My People, on the pages of which follow this preface, is a book of short stories, none of them new or unpublished (though, speaking personally, I have not seen one of them in print before), all probably written with the intention of beguiling the dollar (by no means an unworthy ambition for a writer). They are limited, for the better part, to the lowest spheres of Negro life, and the various subjects are typical of that life. But "upper class" Negroes make brief appearances and even white people stroll in frequently—sometimes they are responsible, despite the shadowy forms in which they are encountered, for a story's very existence. Notwithstanding, in every case, the fable is about a Negro, or Negroes. . . .

Most of these stories deal with the sorriest kind of Negro life with which the author obviously is well acquainted. They do not exhibit Mr. Himes at his best, or his most brilliant, but they do expose us to a view of a new, and fascinating, phase of his extraordinary talent. But let us permit him to speak for himself:

The title, My People—My People, might be what the monkey said when a big shiny Cadillac full of laughing black folks ran over him and cut off his tail. My people—

my People, said in two tones of voice, on two levels: the first with commiseration and vexation, both at losing his tail and his people's thoughtlessness; the second with a note of pride at seeing his folks riding in a big shiny car, enjoying themselves and making progress. I've often said the same thing myself, in the same tone and for the same reasons.

It is some consolation to realize that our world is changing rapidly, the Negro world along with the rest.

ALVIN AILEY

"Eloquent Alvin Ailey" must be in point of time Van Vechten's last work to deal with a black artist and his last to deal with the dance. He saw Ailey first in *House of Flowers*, the Harold Arlen-Truman Capote musical play, in 1955, photographed him extensively during the ensuing years, saw him occasionally as a guest at parties chez Van Vechten, 146 Central Park West, and wrote about him for *Dance 62* in January 1963.

The first important Negro dancing that I remember is George Walker's extravagantly elegant performance of the cakewalk, pranced with his equally talented wife, Aida Overton Walker, as partner; a performance derived from spectacular muscular control that, by comparison, makes other, more recent, exhibitions of this back-straining folk dance seem weak-jointed and flabby. George Walker could strut to the queen's taste, and eventually, with his celebrated vis-à-vis, Bert Williams, he did just that at a command performance at Windsor Castle before the noble eyes of her Royal Majesty Queen Victoria, Empress of the Indies.

The next great Negro dancer I recall is Bill Robinson, the superb Bojangles, one of the few executors of any race who employed his entire body in his act. He tapped not only with his nimble feet, but also enlisted, with electrifying results, the aid of both hands, both expressive eyes, his mobile torso, and even his hat, which appeared to have a life of its own, in his brilliant exhibition.

After these major interpreters, Negro dancers arrived in profusion: Katherine Dunham, more a creator than a performer; Pearl Primus, who first developed a fine style all her own, moving expertly, with great precision to Negro folk tunes, and who later became adept in authentic African gyrations; Janet Collins, one of the earliest to create viable emotional movement for the Spirituals, later enjoyed ending a program with a vivid impression of a tipsy New Orleans belle in red calico ruffles, returning from a Mardi Gras ball, and who eventually transformed—through her transcendent grace and magnetic personality—the ballet in the second act of *Aida* into a work of art on the vast stage of the Metropolitan Opera House. Avon Long was irresistible in his own sharply etched, unique manner; Asadata Dafora was probably the first to introduce his native African dance to America; Josephine Baker, in her fantastic and capricious performances, aroused the jaded French to the highest degree of enthusiasm they had shown to any foreigner since the retirement of Mary Garden.

Arthur Mitchell has become an important artist with the New York City Ballet, and his partners are the most beloved of the white ballerinas. Mary Hinkson and Matt Turney are two of the most highly regarded dancers of the Martha Graham Company. Mary Hinkson has also danced with Arthur Mitchell and the New York City Ballet in *The Figure in the Carpet* and with Alvin Ailey in Harry Belafonte's *Sing, Man, Sing.*

I have seen the beguine danced to perfection at the Bal Colonial in Paris, and I have witnessed spectacular calypso dancing on the quai of Port of Spain, Trinidad, where Geoffrey Holder became acquainted with mystical voodoo rituals and the natural beauty of the West Indian folk dance.

Into the midst of this luxuriant medley Alvin Ailey, with his beautiful partner Carmen de Lavallade (herself an unusually gifted dancer) plunged into *House of Flowers* like two young animals. The effect was like that of a happy explosion. Such really desperate energy has rarely been evoked in a light musical.

Alvin Ailey has all the attributes of a great dancer: he is young, beautiful, strong, with a perfect body and with the technique of dance well welded into his system. He knows how to approach practically all dance problems, except perhaps those of the classical ballet, and I daresay he could easily learn to perform these—given desire, time, and a period of study with the professional experience of George Balanchine. He can lift, leap, crawl, and slide, even glide, to make your heart beat faster. His prodigious strength makes it possible for him to execute consecutive movements without pause in perfect rhythm. Great strength is the basis of all great dancing, for a dancer must be tireless in the face of any difficulty. Ailey is a gifted actor, too, with real atmosphere in any costume he may assume.

Since her first appearance with him, Carmen de Lavallade has danced with him on many occasions, and they were seen together in their unforgettable brilliance in his lowdown *Roots of the Blues*, an experience—almost a career—for any beholder in its compelling realization of John Sellers's wailing melodies, illuminated by towering ladders in the background.

Alvin Ailey choreographs all the numbers he dances with skill, invention, a good deal of imagination, and variety. In the *Hermit Songs* of Samuel Barber, he employs a deeper, more passionate emotion than he used in *Roots of the Blues* in his spontaneous and eloquent movement. He should further be inspected in *Revelations*, a dramatic setting of some familiar

Spirituals, and in *Gillespiana*, danced to music by the celebrated cornetist.

Some of us remember, many of us will never forget, a tender, introspective piece of Ailey's called *Ode and Homage*, in which he danced with a kind of solemn mournfulness. This was a tribute to his teacher, Lester Horton, also the instructor of Janet Collins and Carmen de Lavallade. It was performed to music by Peggy Glanville-Hicks and was given only once in March of 1958. It can be said truthfully that it deserves a revival.

Alvin Ailey danced in *Jamaica* with Lena Horne's company, at Jacob's Pillow, at the Lewisohn Stadium, and in the picture version of *Carmen Jones*. He also acted successfully in plays. As a matter of fact, he is unusually successful in whatever he attempts to do.

GEORGE WALKER

> Carl Van Vechten first saw George Walker and Bert
> Williams in Chicago at the turn of the century. His descrip-
> tion of George Walker's celebrated cakewalk was part of
> his keynote speech at the Fifth Annual Capezio Award
> Luncheon in March 1956. The speech was printed as
> "Terpsichorean Souvenirs" in *Dance Magazine*, January
> 1957.

. . . the really great George Walker (of the team of Williams and Walker) . . . performed the cakewalk, actually a folk dance, with his wife Aida Overton Walker. This assuredly is one of the great memories of the theatre. The line, the grace, the assured ecstasy of these dancers, who bent over backward until their heads almost touched the floor, a feat demanding an incredible amount of strength, their enthusiastic prancing, almost in slow motion, have never been equalled in this particular revel, let alone surpassed. The cakewalk has been revived by several modern performers and choreographers, but never successfully except in *Shuffle Along* (the song was "I'm Just Wild About Harry"), and even there it was only a faint copy of the great Walker's thrilling performance. Most of the subsequent and current representations of the cakewalk were and are as authentic as Mae West would be in *Les Sylphides*.

BERT WILLIAMS

> Van Vechten first wrote about Bert Williams in the
> *New York Press*, 23 December 1913, when the entertainer
> was appearing at the Palace; he wrote about him last for

The Reviewer in October 1922, shortly before Williams's death. Bert Williams was, in part at least, responsible for Van Vechten's initial enthusiasm for the Negro as an artist. As a boy in Chicago, he had been left "trembling between hysterical laughter and sudden tears." Van Vechten never outgrew that response, and declared, moreover, long afterward in conversation, that the ability to simultaneously command such contrary emotions explained the unique genius he found in Negro arts and letters.

The return of Bert Williams to the Palace Theatre yesterday afternoon brought out a crowd that packed the music hall to its doors. Williams was warmly greeted when he came on and was not permitted to leave the stage until he had added several songs to the list he had prepared, including, of course, "Nobody" and "In the Evening" followed by the now famous pantomime of the poker game.

But there were several new songs, the best of which, "You Can't Get Away from It," dealt with the prevailing dance craze. It was followed by one of the most excruciatingly funny pantomimes Williams has ever devised, in which he circled an imaginary partner through a tango and a turkey trot.

There was another song in which he described how he would carve up a poker party with a razor unless the game were played according to him and not by Hoyle. Between songs, of course, he told stories.

The death of Bert Williams removes one of its most interesting figures from the American stage. When Duse saw this Negro, twenty years or so ago, she exclaimed at once that he was the greatest of American actors. So felt many of us, who attended the Williams and Walker gaieties in those old days. His talent for pantomime was especially notable. But the position of the Negro in America restricted his ambition and put definite limits to his career. On the American stage, the Negro is permitted to be an entertainer; he is welcomed as such. But until Eugene O'Neill wrote *The Emperor Jones* and gave Charles Gilpin his chance, little encouragement has been offered to the Negro who undertook serious work. All Negroes have good voices; most of them have expressive bodies as well. They are particularly well fitted by nature to excel in this branch of interpretative art, much better fitted, probably, than the so-called white Americans. Williams, however, having achieved a certain kind of fame, once Walker was dead and the firm dissolved, after a few seasons in the music halls, drifted quite easily into Ziegfeld's *Follies*, where his field of action was prescribed from the beginning, and where no opportunity was offered for artistic growth of any kind. From that moment, although he repeated a few of his best-known pantomimic tricks, such as his famous poker game, as an artist he died. He had become, instead, an institution, a slowly decaying institution. In Germany or Russia he might have become a great actor, but in America we order things differently.

Ethel Waters singing "Underneath the Harlem Moon," 1933

William Christopher Handy, 1932 *(Courtesy Collection of American Literature, Yale University Library)*

193

Langston Hughes, 1936

Zora Neale Hurston, 1934

Henry Armstrong, 1937 *(Courtesy Paul Padgette)*

Nora Holt, 1937 *(Courtesy Collection of American Literature, Yale University Library)*

Bessie Smith, 1936.

Bill "Bojangles" Robinson, 1941 *(Courtesy Paul Padgette)*

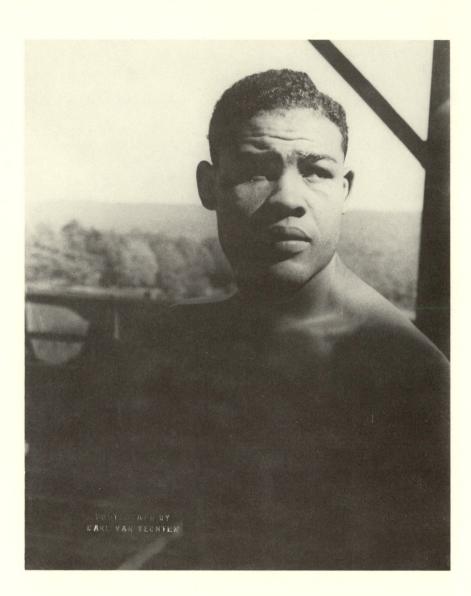

Joe Louis, 1941

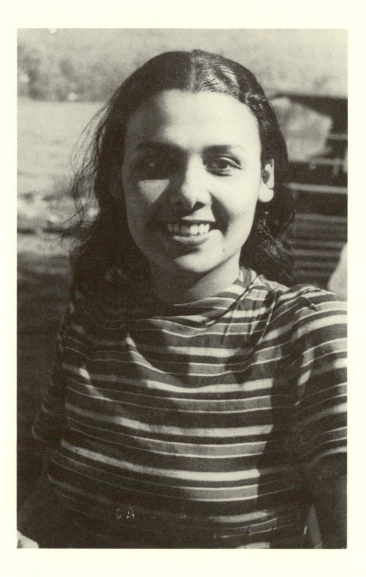

Lena Horne, 1941

Marian Anderson, 1940 *(Courtesy Collection of American Literature, Yale University Library)*

Pearl Bailey in *St. Louis Woman,* 1946

Billie Holiday, 1949

Harry Belafonte in *John Muray Anderson's Almanac*, 1954

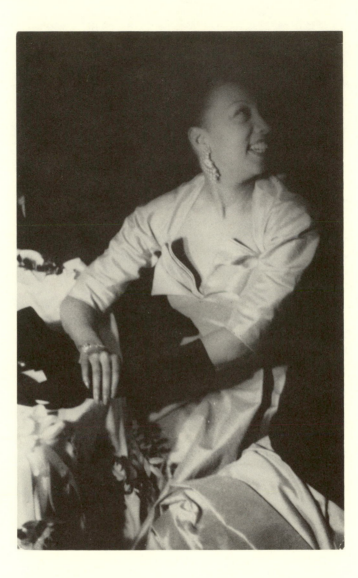

Josephine Baker on "Josephine Baker Day" in Harlem, 20 May 1951

Dizzy Gillespie, 1955

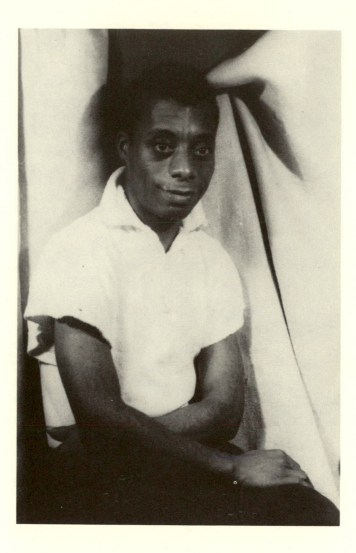

James Baldwin, 1955

LeRoi Jones, 1962

Alvin Ailey, 1955

Ruby Dee and Ossie Davis, 1961

Chester Himes, 1962

Mahalia Jackson, 1962

Bobby Short, 1962

Mabel Mercer, 1963

5

Ceremonies and Saltations

NASSAU OUT OF SEASON

"Nassau Out of Season" is not Carl Van Vechten's title.
In 1917, he sketched out two essays in a journal during a
trip to the Bahamas with his wife, the actress Fania Marinoff.
She had gone there to appear in a film version — apparently
the first location movie — of George Barr McCutcheon's
Nedra. "On Visiting Fashionable Places Out of Season"
appeared initially in *The Reviewer* in January 1923 and, later,
in *Excavations* (Knopf, 1926). "The Holy Jumpers" first appeared in *In the Garret* (Knopf, 1919), shortly after the
Nassau holiday and, heavily revised to delete Van Vechten's
attempt at black dialect, later in *Sacred and Profane
Memories* (Knopf, 1932), his last book. As both essays dealt
primarily though not exclusively with Negro subject
matter, I have included them here freely combined into a single
paper. I have deleted material irrelevant to the concerns
of this collection and material Van Vechten repeated.
(He was a frequent self-plagiarist, as other papers in this
anthology attest.) In both instances, I have used the later
versions, without editing any stylistic idiosyncrasies. Here,
and elsewhere, I have indicated the deletion of material,
regardless of its length, with a conventional elipsis. In the
seventh section of this composite essay, however, describing the ritual of the "Holy Jumpers," Van Vechten incorporated the elipsis as well as the dash to suggest the
ebb and flow of activity. In this passage I have made no
omissions; the elipses are categorically literary rather than
editorial.

One autumn during the long war years my wife was engaged to make a
moving picture in the Bahama Islands and I seized the opportunity to accompany her. Our destination was Nassau on the island of New Providence,
a town which boasts a season in February and March, when it is utilized as
a sort of annex to Palm Beach. If the idle rich tire of Florida, an excursion to
Nassau is suggested, and the suggestion, occasionally, is acted upon.

September is *not* the season. The weather is uncomfortably warm; in the
sun the temperature often registers 115° Fahrenheit. There are three thousand
or more islands in the Bahama group, many of which are minute and unin-
habited. The total population reaches fifty-eight thousand, of which fifty

thousand must be black or mulatto. Nassau, the largest city and the seat of the Governor and Parliament, has a population of ten thousand or more. Here, there are two large hotels and several smaller ones and, during the brief period of invasion from the continent, everybody takes in boarders, but there is little hospitality of this kind offered in the summer or early fall. The two superior hotels are then closed tight; the only sign of life about them is the stir made in the upkeep of their elaborate gardens. Even the minor hotels are reticent about remaining open and the stray visitor to Nassau will be hard put to discover a place to eat and sleep.

Early one morning, as the dawn softly broke through the pink-flushed cloud banks, we entered the beautiful harbour. As prismatic as a black opal, streaks of emerald, amethyst, and the most vivid indigo succeeded each other in the transparent water. In the depths, over the clean white sand, one could see the quivering sea-garden alive with brightly coloured fish; here a sea-wasp, a filmy, inverted globe ready to sting the swimmer, and there the white belly of a hungry shark. The coast showed a low line of hills on which squatted pink and yellow plaster houses with green blinds. Everywhere the fronds of palm trees waved. We landed near the public park, crowded with Negroes, more fully clothed, was my first impression, than seemed essential or even proper in the tropics, and shaded from the sun by spreading straw hats. There were a few white men in the group. Now the low plaster houses shone very pink, yellow, and green in the hot sunlight. In this clear atmosphere, the white shell roads sparkled like silver snakes while the black natives seemed carved of ebony.

After much searching and more discouragement, we finally settled in the half-closed Hotel Nassau, from the balcony of which I might gaze across at two pink stucco houses, mysterious, shuttered villas, suggesting a suitable setting for a tale by Arthur Machen. Between these cottages lay a garden, with a banana-tree and a palm, beyond which a view of the indigo harbour opened, the masts of the schooners, rising in a design of parallel vertical lines, the sails, half-unfurled, bellying in the soft breeze. Further on, wide stretches of water shone vivid emerald-green or sapphire, creating with the indigo the iridescent colouring of the darkest black opals; and yet beyond extended the low green line of Hog Island, over which, in rough weather, the surf of the ocean broke. . . . It was a mile across the harbour to Hog Island, and then only a narrow strip of land separated me from sea-bathing, a strip of land wildly entangled with oranges, almonds, eaten green, and guavas which, when cut and placed in bowls, form a colour combination suggestive of a Japanese print, a delicate salmon-pink enclosed in a rind of yellow-green.

The bathing accommodations on Hog Island were primitive, for, during the season, the Hotel Colonial offered its own bath-house to visitors from Palm Beach. The bathing itself, however, was of a variety seldom vouchsafed to mortals. Here Venus might have risen radiantly, her nether portions magnified in the transparent water. The beach was clean, shining, shimmering sand; the water was warm and the depth sloped gradually. The favoured spot lay in the curve of a bay where, even when the ocean was rough, the water remained limpidly smooth. Those who desired surf bathing might satisfy this craving farther up the shore where the breakers rolled in with great intensity. Out of season, at any rate, there was no bar against bathing nude, and many of the Negroes came here for that purpose, although the majority of the blacks took advantage of the more accessible beaches on the shores of New Providence, those gracious dominions known as Prospect or Labourchère, a mile or two west of Nassau.

Wonderful in their lithe nudity, these Negroes, gleaming in their bronze perfection: I never could sufficiently admire their swimming prowess. Their stay under water seemingly could be prolonged indeterminately. Water, it appeared, was as elemental to their natures as the air they were more accustomed to breathe. Assuredly, they were amphibious. Their dressing was accomplished without the aid of towels, their bodies drying quickly in the sun, their thick metallic skins apparently immune to sunburn. At the beaches where clothing was required, they did not employ bathing garments; such as they were, they wore their street clothes, consisting, usually, only of a shirt and a pair of ragged trousers, and these, too, dried rapidly after emergence. Like Negroes everywhere, they sang a great deal, but I heard no folksongs. Rather they sang Tipperary, or Goodbye, boys, I'm going to be married tomorrow. I was amazed to hear one youth—he could have been no more than twelve—lustily whistling the Marseillaise, with especial emphasis on those stirring phrases which underline the works, Aux armes, citoyens!

Aside from the pleasure afforded by the sea, the stranger will derive entertainment from walking through the streets of Nassau, past the sidewalk vendors of fruits, with their baskets of yellow and gold and green balls, past the cock-sellers, lightly balancing flat baskets of fowl on their heads, past the charming houses, hung with Bougainvillaea, the owners of which are protected from the sun by dropped jalousies, past the churches, of which there are so many, set deep in fragrance and shadow. Negroes everywhere, all walking with the peculiar slouch and talking with the peculiar drawl indigenous to the British West Indies. There are quarters devoted to them, Grant's Town, Fox Hill, and Free Town, and there you may see street after street of picturesque huts, some of them with thatched roofs, but the Negroes live anywhere they please—and can afford to—in Nassau, and clerk in all the shops. There are a few mulattoes dubbed Conchy Joes, because their colour is akin to that of the conch shell, but blacker blood predominates. . . .

Outside, the Negro women pedlars, their heads bound with red and yellow bandannas, over which they wore straw hats of huge dimensions, sat at the corners of the streets, vending fried fish, baked breads, small fruits, alligator pears, guavas, green peppers, and peanuts. Other Negro women, casually balancing great burdens on their heads, and men, balancing flat baskets containing three or four live, white cocks, their feet securely tied, passed. Two-seated vehicles, and donkey-carts, driven by Negroes, rolled slowly along the glistening shell roads. By Street, the main thoroughfare, was lined with haberdashers, shoe- and grocery-marts. The islanders boasted quaint names. French cognomens had crept in from the outer keys. I encountered a Negro who called himself Irving l'Homme. Other common Negro names were Jean-Baptiste, or even John-Baptist, Cecil, Cyril, Reginald, Percival, Harry, Veronica, Muriel, Evelyn, and Mildred. The keeper of a pub had caused his full name, Timothy Darling Orlando Garrick Elder, to be painted on the sign over his door.

In the evening of the first day, besought by a Negro to take a drive in one of the phaetons which are the conventional conveyances of the island, we passed through Grant's Town, the huts of which, set among banana, palm, and silk-cotton trees, were dimly lighted. Then we followed long stretches of dwarf, plaster walls, like the walls in Tuscany, until at last we came to a structure built in the form of a tabernacle, the thatched roof of cocoa-palm leaves upheld by posts. The sides were open. The ground was strewn with dried palm branches. On a platform at one end of the building, a preacher exhorted his brethren. Behind him sat a group of elders and deaconesses, the pillars of his church, while below extended row after row of black faces framed in gigantic straw hats. Still other worshippers stood outside. Our driver informed us that this was a meeting of the evangelical sect known as the Holy Jumpers. Descending from our ancient vehicle we found seats in the tabernacle.

Your time has come! the preacher was shouting. You've got to come to Jesus if you want to come at all. He suffered for you and you've got to suffer for Him! Climb in the chariot! Hustle up the golden stairs! Kick those devils down! Shove 'em off! Don't let none of 'em come near you! Don't you hear Him calling you all? Oh, God, give these people into the keeping of Jesus!

Hallelujah, amen! Glory to God! Yess'r! Preach it! were shrieked from the benches.

The preacher's effects were varied with the nicety of a Mozart overture. There were descents into adagio and pianissimo, rapid crescendoes and fortissimos. Slowly, slowly, the assemblage was worked upon and as the speaker progressed in his exhortation he was more and more frequently interrupted by shrill, distorted cries.

Is there a sinner among you? Let him stand forth! If there is one without sin down there I don't know who he is! Come, brothers, before it is too late. Repent! Repent! The time of Jesus' glory is at hand.

O God, take a poor sinner! wailed a treble voice.

Hallelujah! Amen!

O Jesus! Lamb!

Glory to God!

Some one on the platform started the hymn, Oh, what a wonderful life! and soon the voices all joined in, growing more and more resonant, richer and richer in spirit and feeling. Now a contralto dominated, now a high tenor, now a bass, but what harmony, what volume of tone, what an attack! After a time another hymn followed and then another and finally, without a break in the singing, the tremendous and awful Hiding in the blood of Jesus, a variation perhaps of Washed in the blood of the Lamb. Now the congregation swayed to the pronounced rhythm it was creating. From side to side the lines of huge straw hats swayed. Back—and forth. . . . Back— and forth. The rhythm dominated us, ruled us, tyrannized over us. The very pillars of the tabernacle became unsteady. A young black woman rose and whirled up the aisle, tossing her arms about jerkily. O God, take me! she cried as she fell in a heap at the foot of the platform. There she lay shrieking, her face hideous, her body contorted and writhing in convulsive shudders. Heads here and there wagged swiftly out of rhythm. Moans and hoarse cries mingled with the terrible, inexorable singing. . . . Back—and forth. . . . Hiding in the blood of Jesus. A young girl fell flat on her back in the centre aisle. She was near enough to me so that I could see the circle of foam forming around her lips. Her teeth were clenched, her fists set tight, her arms and legs executed unreasonable gestures. Now a deaconess from the platform was bending over her. The Lord is coming to you! she shouted. Take him in! Hear me, take Him in! Get rid of your devils! Shake 'em out! Open your mouth and receive the Lord! . . . The initiate continued to shriek and struggle. Inarticulate, meaningless sounds emerged from between her clenched teeth. The foam reformed around her lips. The nerves in her epileptic ankles seemed to be raw. . . . The congregation swayed. Hiding in the blood of Jesus! Back—and forth. . . . Back—and forth. The deaconess grew con- fidential. You got to come, she almost whispered. You got to come. You don't want to be a wicked sinner any longer do you? Come! Come! Come! Come! Come! Come to the Lord! Open your mouth and take Him in. . . . Ai! Ai! shrieked the poor sinner. . . . Hiding in the blood of Jesus! Back— and forth. Back—and forth. Back—and forth. . . . Here He is. He's coming! He's coming! . . . The stooping woman herself became hysterical. Her eyes rolled with excitement. Supreme pleasure was in her voice. The crisis was approaching. It seemed as if the girl lying prone was in a frenzy of delight. Every muscle twitched, her nerves seemed to be raw, her finger-nails dug into her palms. Uncontrollable and mystic cries, unformed obscenities struggled from her lips . . . and then at last a dull moaning and she lay still.

How closely the ecstasy of Negro sanctity approaches sorcery. If he had seen the Holy Jumpers, would Huysmans have altered his famous description of the Black Mass? According to Rémy de Gourmont, the author of *A Rebours* would have welcomed such first-hand experience. Le messe noire est purement imaginaire, writes the French critic in the third series of Promenades Litteraires. "C'est moi qui cherchai les détails sur cette cérémonie fantastique. Je n'en trouvai pas, car il n'y en a pas. Finalement, Huysmans arrangea en messe noire la célèbre scène de conjuration contre La Vallière pour laquelle Montsepan avait prêté son corps aux obscènes simagrées d'un sorcier infâme."[1]

Next day at breakfast, black Priscilla at the hotel expressed her opinion.

I'm a Baptist, she said, I don't hold by those jumpers. The females jump and the males jump after 'em.

One night, on request, the natives arranged a "fire dance." This is a ceremony celebrated in secrecy during the season, when, according to report, the bucks and their doxies dance naked in some secluded nook in the forest, if a sufficient purse has been collected to make it worth their while. In the summer the young girls and boys prance for enjoyment before a bonfire, kindled for illumination rather than heat. They were quite willing to permit the spectacle to be observed, but the gate-receipts apparently were not adequate to encourage disrobing. The music was furnished by a drum, made by fitting a skin over the head of an empty cask, and beaten with extraordinary rhythmic effect, and by the clapping of hands and singing of the group of native spectators. When the skin of the drum became loosened, it was held over the fire to dry taut again. The words of the songs were often indistinguishable; sometimes, indeed, they consisted merely of harsh cries. I can perhaps best designate their nature by appending a rude sample:

> He's gwine roun' dah circle!
> Tum ti tum tum, tum tum tum!
> He's gwine roun' dah circle!
> Tum ti tum tum, tum tum, tum!

Monotonously, this primitive jingle was reiterated, until the dancers tired. The tunes did not vary greatly in effect, not at all in time, and they bore some esoteric, inexplicable relation to Russian folksong. As in so many of the Russian dances, one dancer performed at a time, indicating his successor by a nudge in his or her direction. There was not much variety in this exhibition, obviously, in its inception, symbolic of manifestations of sex. The movements included wild leaps, whirls, contortions of the body, girandoles, ocasionally suggesting the barbaric Polovtsian dances in Prince Igor. Almost invariably, the arms were held close to the sides, sometimes with the forearm horizontal to the body, but seldom higher. A man advanced slowly, one leg dragging behind the other, with a curious suggestion of lameness. One of the girls, a savage creature, with a mass of untutored hair, danced with a peculiar clawing motion of the hands. In one of her figures she stooped almost to the earth, continuing her odd rhythmic clawing as she shuffled around the circle of hand-clapping, shouting hysterics. Her thin arms and legs, her angular, awkward grace, if not her wild gestures, brought to mind the marionettes which are employed in Ceylonese shadow shows. When the crowd, exicted, bent forward, encroaching too much on the central space, one of the boys snatched a fiery brand from the bonfire and with a swift sweep of his arm singed the bare feet of the eager spectators. They spread back with alacrity.

I passed an hour or two in the court house, listening to the English magistrate while he sentenced black boys to hard labour for minor offenses, but, naturally enough, interest anywhere centres after a time—and I spent three weeks in Nassau—upon something other than a round of street and court scenes and Negro dances. I sought diversion in reading. . . . Out of season, indeed, Nassau is the most uninhabitable, unsocial town I have ever visited and yet, so perverse is my nature, I am sure that I would prefer it to Nassau in season.

1. "The black mass is purely imaginary. It is I who sought the details of that fantastic ceremony. I did not find them because they are not to be found. Ultimately, Huysmans arranged as a black mass a celebrated conjuration scene against La Vallière for which Montespan loaned her body to the obscene devilish incantations of the infamous sorcerer." (Editor's translation)

THE LINDY HOP

On occasion, Carl Van Vechten inserted discursive
observations in his novels. In *Parties* these miniature essays
punctuate the frenetic drinking bouts and passionless
sexual forays of his "Splendid Drunken Twenties." Published

in 1930, *Parties* was condemned as "sniggering," "taste-
less," "cheap," "vulgar, inane, and rotten," "specious,"
"dull" — by various reviewers. Only George Dangerfield, in
Bookman (September 1930), likened it to an earlier indictment of the society it reflected, *The Feast of Trimalchio* by
Petronius. Half a century later, it is perhaps the clearest
view of that extraordinary decade and its downfall. Van
Vechten thought *Parties* was his best book.

His account of the Lindy Hop — one of those miniature
essays in *Parties* — was first excerpted in a triple issue of
Dance Index (September-October-November 1942) devoted
in its entirety to Van Vechten's dance writings, and later
included in Paul Padgette's anthology, *The Dance Writings
of Carl Van Vechten* (Dance Horizons, 1975). More recently,
Avon Books has reissued the novel in paperback. In the
following passage, which opens the fourteenth chapter,
the Gräfin Adele von Pulmernl und Stilzernl, an aging
German noblewoman, visits a Harlem ballroom in the
company of some friends.

Every decade or so some Negro creates or discovers or stumbles upon a
new dance step which so completely strikes the fancy of his race that it
spreads like water poured on blotting paper. Such dances are usually performed at first inside and outside of lowly cabins, on levees, or, in the big
cities, on street-corners. Presently, quite automatically, they invade the
more modest nightclubs where they are observed with interest by visiting
entertainers who, sometimes with important modifications, carry them to
a higher low world. This process may require a period of two years or longer
for its development. At just about this point the director of a Broadway
revue in rehearsal, a hoofer, or even a Negro who puts on "routines" in
the big musical shows, deciding that the dance is ready for white consumption, introduces it, frequently with the announcement that he has invented
it. Nearly all the dancing now to be seen in our musical shows is of Negro
origin, but both critics and public are so ignorant of this fact that the production of a new Negro revue is an excuse for the revival of the hoary old
lament that it is a pity the Negro can't create anything for himself, that he is
obliged to imitate the white man's revues. This, in brief, has been the history
of the Cake-Walk, the Bunny Hug, the Turkey Trot, the Charleston, and
the Black Bottom. It will probably be the history of the Lindy Hop.

The Lindy Hop made its first official appearance in Harlem at a Negro
Dance Marathon staged at Manhattan Casino some time in 1928. Executed
with brilliant virtuosity by a pair of competitors in this exhibition, it was
considered at the time a little too difficult to stand much chance of achieving
popular success. The dance grew rapidly in favour, however, until a year

later it was possible to observe an entire ball-room filled with couples de-
voting themselves to its celebration.

The Lindy Hop consists in a certain dislocation of the rhythm of the fox-
trot, followed by leaps and quivers, hops and jumps, eccentric flinging about
of arms and legs, and contortions of the torso only fittingly to be described
by the word epileptic. After the fundamental steps of the dance have been
published, the performers may consider themselves at liberty to improvise,
embroidering the traditional measures with startling variations, as a colora-
tura singer of the early nineteenth century would endow the score of a
Bellini opera with roulades, runs, and shakes.

To observe the Lindy Hop being performed at first induces gooseflesh,
and second, intense excitement, akin to religious mania, for the dance is
not of sexual derivation, nor does it incline its hierophants towards pleasures
of the flesh. Rather it is the celebration of a rite in which glorification of self
plays the principal part, a kind of terpsichorean megalomania. It is danced,
to be sure, by couples, but the individuals who compose these couples barely
touch each other during its performance, and each may dance alone, if he
feels the urge. It is Dionysian, if you like, a dance to do honour to wine-
drinking, but it is not erotic. Of all the dances yet originated by the American
Negro, this the most nearly approaches the sensation of religious ecstasy. It
could be danced, quite reasonably and without alteration of tempo, to many
passages in the Sacre de Printemps of Stravinsky, and the Lindy Hop would
be as appropriate for the music, which depicts in tone the representation of
certain pagan rites, as the music would be appropriate for the Lindy Hop.

The Gräfin, after ascending a long flight of marble stairs, gasped her
astonishment as she entered the great hall with its ample dance-floor enclosed
on three sides by a brass railing behind which tables and chairs were provided for spectators and those who desired light refreshment. The fourth
side of the floor was occupied by a long platform on which sat two bands
of musicians which alternated in providing stimulation for the feet of the
dancers. The floor at the moment was filled with Negroes, dancing as the
Gräfin felt everybody should dance. She had frequently before watched
Negro dancing with delight, but all the dancing she had hitherto seen was
professional, or sexual, or merely the casual expression of a lazy rhythm.
This dancing was exalted, uplifting, dangerously exciting to the mere observer. It was evident that the performers felt its spirit even more keenly.
The band, too, had fallen under the magic spell, playing a wild tune, in
which saxophones, drums, and banjos vied one with the other to create
new effects in rhythm, in harmony, or in the decoration of the melody.

Leaning a little on King Swan and Roy, the Gräfin pressed forward to the
ringside table that had been reserved for her, and presently she pushed aside
a proffered beverage to devote her attention to the miracle of movement
spread before her. She was, she was fully aware, not sitting in a night-club
with its fusty, artificial atmosphere and its greedy entertainers, but in a

dance-hall of the people, as she might have sat in a hall used for similar purposes in Neuilly or Naples or Innsbruck, but with what a difference! For here every individual effort was devoted towards the expression of electricity and living movement. Each dancer gave as serious an attention to his beautiful vocation as if he were in training for some great good game, and the colour of the participants, too, added attraction to the spectacle. This lithe African beauty, shading from light tan, through golden bronze, to blue-black, these boys and girls with woolly hair, these boys and girls with hair ironed out and burnished, themselves imparted to their savage pastime a personal fascination which was a rich ingredient in its quality.

It is kolossal, kolossal, cried the Gräfin, enraptured, clapping her hands together in her enthusiasm.

King Swan nodded his luke-warm approval, while Roy apparently was utterly unaware of the madness by which he was surrounded. Every now and again he helped himself to a draught from the flask which he had brought with him.

The dancing on the floor was perpetual, for one of the two bands was always playing. Wilder and wilder the couples became in their abandon, individuals separating one from the other to indulge in breath-taking displays of virtuosity and improvisation, and then joining again in double daring, until the scene resembled, to the spectator, an infinitely arranged chaos, and, to the participants, became that perfect expression of self so often denied human beings. Just when the tension for observer and dancer alike was becoming unbearable, the band would modulate the rhythm into that of a slow waltz, and violent energy was succeeded by lazy languor.

6

Advertisements and Accolades

However ephemeral the materials in this chapter may be, they have a genuine value in any assessment of Van Vechten's contributions to black arts and letters. His note in a Harlem high school yearbook is, in its own way, as meaningful as the announcement of a $200 cash prize he established in *Opportunity*. Both of them are included too.

TWELVE ENDORSEMENTS

Sometimes at the request of a publisher or writer and sometimes of his own volition, Carl Van Vechten supplied endorsements for books. Several of these, devoted to the work of black writers, are in Van Vechten's scrapbooks along with others written for works by white writers dealing with black subject matter or black performers. Occasionally, he feigned enthusiasm in reviews of books he cared little about simply to draw attention to black achievements. Of the following selection — collected chronologically — all but one of the advertising blurbs appeared in the *New York Times*; some appeared in additional publicity releases as well. Van Vechten's endorsement for Chester Himes's *Cotton Comes to Harlem* never appeared in print in its entirety. This version comes from a letter Van Vechten wrote to Himes, advising him it had been sent to the publisher. The passage from "Unsung Americans Sung" is excerpted from a review of W. C. Handy's book of that title. It was printed in *Responsibility* in the fall issue of 1944. The passage from "Soul of a People Lifted in Song" is excerpted from a review of *My Songs* by Roland Hayes. It appeared in *New York Herald Tribune Books*, 21 November 1948.

THE FIRE IN THE FLINT, by Walter White, 1924

This bitter and sensational arraignment of a pseudo-civilization, written by a Negro, would arouse the latent sense of injustice even in the soul of a United States senator. *The Fire in the Flint* is a story of a lynching, but it is worthy of note that the author has been fair enough to make a white man the most charming character in his book, while the hero is betrayed by one of his own race. The plot is most ingeniously articulated, the characters well drawn. In certain nervous passages the novel achieves a power, through the use of a curiously subtle variety of restraint that almost lifts it into the realm of art. I defy anyone to read it without emotion.

PASSING, by Nella Larsen, 1929

A strangely provocative story, superbly told. The sensational implications of *Passing* should make this book one of the most widely discussed on the spring list.

SWEET MAN, by Gilmore Millen, 1930

This powerful novel . . . flames like a great lithograph printed in red and black and gold. If it is daring and even sensational, I think I am safe in believing that it is also true.

THE WAYS OF WHITE FOLKS, by Langston Hughes, 1933

Having written and published several volumes of poetry with great success and having created a novel which has been generally accepted as the best novel yet to be composed by an American Negro, and, leaving racial considerations aside, a fine novel on its own account, Langston Hughes has now turned his attention to the short story and in this difficult form, at his best, immediately challenges comparison with such masters of the art as Katherine Mansfield and Chekhov.

These stories represent a departure in technique. They are stories of the relations between white and colored people described from the Negro point of view. With stories of white and colored people from the white point of view we are well acquainted, but perhaps the Negro point of view has never before been so adequately represented. Langston Hughes has known white people intimately in both the capacities of servant and friend and his acquaintance with his own race is equally wide; his tales, therefore, are not to be regarded as fanciful embodiments of wish fulfillments.

Of the stories in this volume I recommend "A Good Job Gone," "Cora Unashamed," and "Little Dog" to anyone who happens to be looking for masterpieces. I must admit, however, that I read the book in manuscript through at one sitting with that sensation of rising excitement that is the usual accompaniment to the recognition of important art.

NEGRO AMERICANS, WHAT NOW?, by James Weldon Johnson, 1934

Offers proof on every page that its author is one of the greatest masters of English prose. . . . This book may make history; at any rate it *is* history.

JONAH'S GOURD VINE, by Zora Neale Hurston, 1939

As fiction, as sociology, as folklore, this book seems to me to be so extraordinary that I can only recommend it with unrestrained enthusiasm. It should serve to place Miss Hurston at once in the very front rank of those (white or colored) who write about the Negro. Accept my heartiest congratulations!

UNSUNG AMERICANS SUNG, edited by W. C. Handy, 1944

Unsung Americans Sung, through its vocal biographies of Negro individuals of importance, sings the history of the Race. . . . This is a book to open at random or to study at leisure. It can be used to advantage in any of the schools and any group will find it of assistance in profitably exploiting the long hours of a winter evening. It will serve as a living reminder of the many celebrated and distinguished figures of which the Race can boast.

ON THESE I STAND, by Countée Cullen, 1947

Admirers of this Negro lyric poet's work, of which there are a great many, will find all their favorites, while strangers to his genius could ask for no better introduction.

LONELY CRUSADE, by Chester Himes, 1947

This novel boasts such power of expression and such subtlety of treatment, the author possesses so sensitive a command of character and incident, and the culmination is so reasonably magnificent, that I, for one, am not afraid to call this book GREAT.

MY SONGS, by Roland Hayes, 1948

If there are any persons at large who are still unfamiliar with the name of Roland Hayes, the title of this book may prove misleading to them, for the songs in this book are not original compositions, but arrangements of the religious songs of the Negro race, the songs created spontaneously by the slaves. If, on the other hand, these songs are not the exclusive property of this tenor, it may be stated categorically that it was he who, almost single-voiced, introduced them to the concertgoing public. . . .

In the introduction, Mr. Hayes speaks of his education in music and tells us how it was through a meeting with Africans and an acquaintance with African music that he was gradually led back into a perception of the beauty and importance of the Aframerican folksongs. Throughout the book the various prefaces to the songs bear witness to the religious spirit and, indeed, to the ecstasy of the arranger and editor. In fact the book may be, and doubtless will be, regarded as a souvenir and reminder of the art of Roland Hayes by those who purchase it. As such it completely fulfills its purpose.

SERAPH ON THE SUWANEE, by Zora Neale Hurston, 1948

A superb creation—perhaps a masterpiece. . . . This is one of the most original books I have ever encountered.

COTTON COMES TO HARLEM, by Chester Himes, 1955

Chester Himes's Harlem detective stories have been popular in Paris for years, and Jean Cocteau has praised them highly. One or two have appeared in paper in America, but they have not been advertised or reviewed. So they have not met with popular success. Now he has written his best one, *Cotton Comes to Harlem*. It is published in boards in America, and I recommend it without reservation to anyone who wants to read a good English prose style with chills, thrills, and goose pimples.

THE SABBATH GLEE CLUB OF RICHMOND

"Pastiches et Pistaches" was a collection of short pieces on a great variety of subjects that appeared in several successive issues of *The Reviewer*, the literary quarterly published in Richmond, Virginia. Its editor, Emily Clark, regularly solicited contributions—without paying for them—from many successful writers of the period: H. L. Mencken, James Branch Cabell (who helped her get out the first issues), Joseph Hergesheimer, and others. Van Vechten's last

Installment of "Pastiches et Pistaches" included his
encomiastic response to Richmond's Sabbath Glee Club.
It appeared in the January 1924 issue of *The Reviewer.*

When Joseph Hergesheimer and I recently visited Richmond, Miss Julia
Sully arranged that we should hear The Sabbath Glee Club. This Negro
organization, under the capable direction of Joseph Matthews, who, I
believe, is a night-watchman in one of the Richmond banks, has been in
existence for ten years. These men came together for the purpose of per-
petuating the Negro Spirituals, the only folksongs America has produced,
in the only manner that they can be effectually perpetuated. They cannot
be accurately set down in musical notation for the simple reason that they
were created in a scale more inclusive than the tempered scale which the
vogue of the piano has dictated. They were also created to be sung unaccompanied, but I believe their harmonization to be entirely traditional
with Negro singers, a matter of interpretation in which they differ from the
folksongs of other races.

The Sabbath Glee Club has an astonishingly large repertory of these
Spirituals, including "No Hidin' Place," "Toll the Bell," "I Want to Be
Ready," "Every Time I Feel the Spirit," "Roll, Jordan, Roll," "Go Down,
Moses," and, of course, the familiar "Swing Low, Sweet Chariot." The
interpretation is reverent—one is, indeed, reminded of the old spirit at
Oberammergau—and musically thrilling. I could wish, at times, for something more of the true Negro temperament, a little more hysteria, a little
more care to reproduce the original dialect of the songs. It is important to
get such things right before they become a lost art.

I told these men, after listening for an hour to their marvellous singing,
that I considered their organization more important than any symphony
society in the country. I meant exactly what I said. These Negroes not only
are performing a service of vast value to the musical historical; they have
also created an institution capable of giving the greatest amount of musical
pleasure. Several of the Negro schools in the South have built up choirs for
the purpose of keeping the Spirituals alive, but none of these choirs that I
have heard touches so nearly the essence of these songs as the Sabbath Glee
Club, the members of which are all laboring Negroes.

I was amazed to discover that the white population in Richmond exhibits
only a meagre interest in these singers. Until four years ago, when Matthews
enlisted the sympathy of Miss Sully, the group had been kept together only
by the enthusiasm of its members. Even today this club has no hall in which
to work, to practice and learn the music; the thirty men are forced to meet
in each other's parlours. The club has not even a hall to sing in. Ruth Draper
recently listened to them in the auditorium of the Negro YMCA, and Hergesheimer and I heard them in the same place, a room too modest in size to

support the resonance of so many voices. It would be unfortunate if the future endowment of this organization should be supplied by northerners, more unfortunate still if a continued lack of support should cause the Negroes to become disheartened and disband. I do not think the latter eventuality is likely to occur; a healthy opposing sign is the fact that several young men have lately joined the group. The first is more likely to happen unless the people of Richmond begin to realize the value of these singers to their community.

If the Sabbath Glee Club were provided with a hall for rehearsals and performances and its existence were suitably advertised, I prophesy that visitors would come to Richmond from all parts of the country to hear them, just as Europe has its pilgrims to Bayreuth and Oberammergau. If these singers never travelled—and I should be opposed to touring as tending to rub off the naïveté and simplicity so important to the true delivery of this kind of music—and gave a concert once a month in a place suitable for such an entertainment, I think, within a short period, that these concerts would be attended not only by Southerners but by music lovers from every part of the North and West.

TWO OPEN LETTERS

Van Vechten's open letters in *Opportunity*, in January and July 1927, demonstrate the dimensions of his involvement with the Harlem Renaissance. Ironically, Langston Hughes— whom Benjamin Brawley wrongly believed to have been influenced by Van Vechten—won honorable mention in the contest Van Vechten proposed.

For some time my admiration for *Opportunity* has been steadily increasing. It seems to me that this magazine has made such strides that it is no longer fair to merely say that it is better than any other Negro periodical. As a matter of fact it may now be favorably compared with any magazine of a similar character published in these United States.

I have been trying to think of a way to show my appreciation of your editorship and at the same time to encourage young writers to continue to give their best to *Opportunity*. I have hit on a plan which I hope will meet with your approval.

Simply, it is this: I offer a prize of $200 for the best *signed* contribution published in *Opportunity* during the year 1927. It may be a poem, a play, an essay, a story. The judges may give the award to literary merit or to research work of importance. I wish to allot them the greatest amount of latitude in this respect. The judges should arrive at their decision not later than December 10, 1927, in time to announce it in the January 1928 number.

The manner of arriving at a decision follows: Each of the three judges will keep a scorecard as he reads his copy of *Opportunity* each month. At the close of the year he will make from this card a list of what he considers the twelve best compositions, in the order of his preference. Then the judges will meet to compare lists. The award will be made to the contribution which stands highest on the most lists. The standard of *Opportunity* is sufficiently high to make it conceivable that the judges' lists may differ, one from the other, in toto. In that case the judges will arrive at a decision in conference.

Carl Van Vechten

My dear Mr. Brawley,

I have read with interest your paper entitled "The Negro Literary Renaissance," in the *Southern Workman*. Your opinions are your own, and although I do not share them you are entitled to them. I think, however, that in such a paper, written by a college professor, one might expect a meticulous niceness in regard to matters of fact. You write: "When Mr. Hughes came under the influence of Mr. Carl Van Vechten and *The Weary Blues* was given to the world," etc. "The Weary Blues" had won a prize before I had read a poem by Mr. Hughes or knew him personally. The volume, of which this was the title poem, was brought to me complete before Mr. Hughes and I had ever exchanged two sentences. I am unaware, even to this day, although we are the warmest friends and see each other frequently, that I have had the slightest influence on Mr. Hughes in any direction. The influence, if one exists, flows from the other side, as anyone might see who read my first paper on the Blues, published in *Vanity Fair* for August 1925, a full year before *Nigger Heaven* appeared, before, indeed, a line of it had been written. In the paper I quoted freely Mr. Hughes's opinions on the subject of Negro folksongs, opinions which to my knowledge have not changed in the slightest.

I might say a word or two apropos of the quotableness of Countée Cullen. Suffice to say that the fact is that he is quoted more frequently, with two or three exceptions, than any other American poet. I myself quoted four lines as a superscription to *Nigger Heaven*, and two other lines later in the book; I think the concluding lines of his beautiful sonnet, "Yet Do I Marvel," I have seen printed more often (in periodicals in other languages than English, moreover) than any other two lines by any contemporary poet.

I beg to remain yours very sincerely,

Carl Van Vechten

AN AFTER-DINNER SPEECH FOR THE
JAMES WELDON JOHNSON LITERARY GUILD

> In recognition of his founding of the James Weldon
> Johnson Memorial Collection of Negro Arts and Letters,
> Carl Van Vechten was guest of honor at a dinner given by
> the James Weldon Johnson Literary Guild in November
> 1942 in a Chinatown restaurant. Until then, Van Vechten
> had avoided speech-making, as he explains in this type-
> script of his remarks that evening. It suggests, however,
> that he fully enjoyed himself during the chore. The speech,
> which exists in two drafts at Yale, has not been published
> before. I have deleted a long list of names designed to
> acknowledge guests present as well as absent. With few
> exceptions, the figures about whom he had written for
> nearly twenty years were present, and he paid homage to
> those who were not. Among others, Alain Locke, Fannie
> Hurst, and Lin Yutang spoke, representing broadly the
> races; Walter White delivered some extemporaneous
> remarks at the last minute, having hurried back to New
> York from Washington, D.C., for the occasion; some of the
> guests entertained, and Langston Hughes — absent that
> night because he was in California — wrote a poem in Van
> Vechten's honor that Canada Lee, the black actor, recited.

But for an accident you might have been spared the necessity of listening
to this address from me tonight. Being fairly confirmed in the belief that it
was distinctly not my métier, I have hitherto consistently refused to speak
on public occasions. About a month ago, however, I attended an overflow-
ing meeting which had gathered to discuss the dance project of Mr. Wilson
Williams. I was listening in a carefree manner to Felicia Sorel's account of
what Mr. Williams's dancers intended to do when quite abruptly, or so it
seemed to me, she closed with the words, "And now we will hear from Mr.
Van Vechten."

I was taken completely by surprise. In the half second or so I gave to
reflection I convinced myself that any excuse I gave, in the circumstances,
would sound rather lame. So I began to speak and soon discovered, to my
great astonishment, that I liked to talk to people without danger of being
interrupted. I was even pleased with the sound of my voice. In other words,
a new, if belated, public speaker was born.

And so I am delighted to thank Miss Roberta Bosley and the members of
the James Weldon Johnson Literary Guild for the opportunity of speaking
tonight. It is an honor and a pleasure to be standing in the center of so many
of our old Harlem friends, many of whom Fania and I have known for nearly
twenty years. . . .

It is most appropriate, too, that some of my Chinese friends should be here tonight in this Chinese setting. I welcome them heartily.

I am happy to see so many of my ofay friends passing tonight. If they would keep up the practice they would find their lives . . . richer, their knowledge of human nature deeper, their sympathies broader.

Many of you doubtless came here tonight under the impression that this dinner was being given in my honor. That is only incidentally true. I am the symbolic excuse for this occasion, the true purpose of which is to celebrate the James Weldon Johnson Collection of Negro Arts and Letters which I founded at the Yale University Library. It was my original intention to endow this collection with all the Negro material in my possession and that, I believed, would be an end to the matter. I had no idea that the librarian at Yale and the Negro world in general would encourage me to continue soliciting gifts for the collection until what began as a JOB has grown into what I might call a career. At least the major part of every waking day is occupied by me in enlarging the collection, writing letters of solicitation and thanks, buying new material, and examining and explaining the masses of material sent to me by others.

Nearly all the Negroes of my acquaintance, a great many whom I don't know, have been helpful in collecting this material: books, pamphlets, phonograph records, photographs, and especially letters and manuscripts, have poured in on us, and continue to pour in on us, until I am certain that the time will not be far distant when this collection will be the most valuable in its field extant.

It is unfortunate that Mr. Knollenberg, the librarian at Yale who has given this collection his widest enthusiasm since its inception, cannot be here to talk to you tonight. He is engaged in important duties with the government relating to the carrying on of the war. I can say for him, however, that he has shown in every way that the collection is the apple of his eye and the treasure of his library. He leaves no stone unturned to make it more complex. His assistants, Mr. Babb and Mr. Wing, appear to share his enthusiasm.

As I have intimated, in the work behind me I have received able assistance from a great number of persons, but it would be ungrateful if I did not mention the fact that Dorothy Peterson, Harold Jackman, Walter White, and Langston Hughes seem to be at one with me in their willingness to make the forming of the collection a lifework. Hardly a day passes in which I do not hear from several of them, now with letters or information, and again with packages bulging with valuable material. A great many others, headed by such names as those of Countée Cullen, Zora Neale Hurston, who only this week presented the collection with the complete manuscripts of four of her books, including her new autobiography, *Dust Tracks on a Road*, William Grant Still, J. Rosamond Johnson, W. C. Handy, and many, many more, have turned over to the collection all of their personal material they are able to lay their hands on.

This dinner then is to commemorate the birth of a great responsibility, the responsibility of preserving the Negro present and the Negro past, historically and artistically, for the future when the united races will seek to learn what each has contributed towards the building of the nation.

PHOTOGRAPHS OF CELEBRATED NEGROES

On two occasions Van Vechten supplied brief notes for exhibitions of his photographs of black artists and writers: the first at Syracuse University in December 1945, the second for the Jerome Bowers Peterson Memorial Collection of Photographs of Celebrated Negroes at Wadleigh High School in Harlem in February 1949. The notes are combined here into a single paper to avoid repetition.

This particular collection was later exhibited at the Brooklyn Public Library by the Catholic Interracial Council, and similar collections—nearly a hundred photographs in each—were given to Howard University as the Rose McClendon Memorial Collection, named for the black actress; to the Detroit Public Library as the E. Azalia Hackley Memorial Collection, named for the pioneer black music teacher; to Atlanta University as the Countée Cullen Memorial Collection. The James Weldon Johnson Memorial Collection at Yale has more than five hundred photographs of black people of distinction, and blacks are well represented in Van Vechten's photographic collections in the New York Public Library, the Museum of the City of New York, the Museum of Modern Art, the Hammond Museum in New York, the Philadelphia Museum of Art, Princeton University, Brandeis University, the University of Iowa, and the University of New Mexico. To several of these collections Van Vechten continued to contribute new photographs, from the time he established them during the Forties until his death twenty years later.

Van Vechten gave up extended writing for photography in 1932. He had been interested in photography as a boy— at the age of sixteen, for example, he had photographed two black children smiling under an enormous umbrella on the front steps of the home of Harriet Beecher Stowe in Cincinnati, Ohio—and he returned to the hobby during the last thirty years of his life. Carl Van Vechten's photographic

catalog is impressive, beginning with Eugene O'Neill and
concluding with Lincoln Kirstein. In between, Matisse,
Gershwin, Pirandello, Faulkner, hundreds of dancers and
actors, and certainly hundreds of black artists and writers,
sat before his lens.

I am certain that my first interest in making photographs was documentary
and probably my latest interest in making them is documentary too. Nevertheless, even documents have an artistic value and I saw no reason to make
bad photographs merely because they were intended to be documentary. I
wanted to show young people of all races how many distinguished Negroes
there are in the world. However, the ratio in which Negroes become celebrated far outpaces my ability to photograph them. Indeed, if I were physically able to invite twenty such to sit in front of my lens every day, I do not
think I could catch up with the supply. Every ambition has its boundaries.
Nevertheless, I have been able to document a few of the more prominent
members of the race, and I have tried to make the photographs as honest
and as personal as possible. The subjects are representative, I think, although
several fields of endeavor are scarcely covered at all. They are certainly
more representative of the artistic fields than of the others. This is probably
due to the fact that my own interests lie more in this direction. . . . To
many, I suppose, this collection will come as a revelation of the great number
of Negroes who have achieved fame in America. If this be the case, it is
sufficient justification for making the photographs and exhibiting them.

A NOTE FOR *THE OWL* OF
WADLEIGH HIGH SCHOOL

When the Wadleigh High School yearbook, *The Owl*, was
dedicated to Carl Van Vechten in 1944, he wrote a brief
note of acknowledgment for inclusion. This particular
honor had been arranged, doubtless, through his old friend,
Dorothy Peterson — the model for Mary Love in *Nigger
Heaven* — who taught at the school.

On the opening day of the James Bowers Peterson Memorial Collection
of Photographs of Celebrated Negroes at Wadleigh High School, I learned
that one of the subjects of the photographs, Miss Elisabeth Welch, now a
famous star on the London stage, had graduated from this institution of
learning. I was not surprised. I would be surprised, indeed, if investigation
would not show that other figures in this series of pictures have attended
this school.

Any Wadleigh girl, any girl who lives in Harlem, somewhere within herself may have the seeds of creative ability and it is distinctly possible, even probable, that another Pearl Primus or another Zora Neale Hurston may graduate from Wadleigh this coming year. What has been done can be done again and whenever it is done again it is usually bigger and better than the last time it was done!

INCHIN' ALONG

The material in two similar papers is combined here in "Inchin' Along." Titled after a favorite Spiritual, "Keep A' Inchin' Along" appeared as a program note for the NAACP Benefit Ball in 1929; "Carl Van Vechten Comments," so titled by the editors, was published in *Challenge* in September 1934. Even though the kind of Harlem he refers to has ceased to exist, his "symbols of better days" have proven true. Carl Van Vechten did not live to witness the full flowering of black arts and letters during the years since his death, but this second Black Renaissance would not have surprised him. He always knew.

Occasionally, someone is heard to croak hoarsely that the Negro "renaissance" that was launched so bravely in 1926-1927 has not continued its voyage on the seas of art as triumphantly as might have been wished. Personally I feel no sympathy with these complaints, no disappointment in the results. On the contrary, I believe the Negro of today to be on a much more solid basis as an artist and as a social individual than he was then.

When, thirty years ago, I first began to attend the Negro theatre, it was possible to enjoy the entertainments of Williams and Walker, or Sissieretta Jones, the "Black Patti," or Cole and Johnson, or Ernest Hogan, no mean entertainments, to be sure. At the present day, however, the famous Negro stars on the concert, music hall, burlesque, motion picture, and "legitimate" stages of two continents are so numerous that merely to list them in small type would require a page or two of this program. Recently, we have been offered many Negro plays and revues, including *Africana, Blackbirds, Hot Chocolates, Black Boy, Porgy,* and *Harlem*, to mention a few of the most successful, and several Negro films, notably *Hearts in Dixie* and *Hallelujah*. It is likewise significant that nearly every third play now produced has one or more Negro characters and that these are now played by Negroes and not by white actors in blackface as was the ludicrous custom three decades ago.

Mixed casts like those of *Show Boat, Golden Dawn, Kongo, Deep River,* and *Goin' Home* are no longer uncommon, although it was but a short time back that Paul Robeson's appearance in *All God's Chillun [Got Wings]* raised a storm of protest.

It will readily be admitted that while Paul Laurence Dunbar was celebrated in his own day, he existed alone, a solitary luminary in the sable sky of poetry, while Charles Waddell Chesnutt was the only Negro prose writer of distinction in that epoch. Today there is scarcely a publishing house of any standing which does not advertise the name of at least one Negro author; certain houses have six or seven Negro names on their lists. Certainly James Weldon Johnson's *Along This Way* is an autobiography to rank with the very best books in that department and presently will appear two other volumes, each of which, fine in its particular way, should do a great deal to lift the excellent average of Negro fiction to a higher level: Langston Hughes's *The Ways of White Folks* (Knopf) and Zora Neale Hurston's *Jonah's Gourd Vine* (Lippincott). If you are as old as I am and were accustomed to reading the newspapers and periodicals of thirty years ago you will recall that the principal items concerning Negroes referred to lynchings and race riots. Nowadays you can scarcely pick up any Sunday supplement without reading about Negro dancing or the Blues. Negro politics are discussed in print, the Dunbar apartments in Harlem are described, Ethel Waters or Langston Hughes is interviewed, we learn that Mrs. Oscar de Priest was invited to tea at the White House, and Duke Ellington writes of the Negro influence in modern music. As for the magazines they contain dozens of short stories, essays, and poems, by and about Negroes. The articles by Negroes in the collected files of *The American Mercury* alone would make a respectable volume.

Miss Ethel Waters, who is very probably the greatest living singer of popular ballads, has paved the way for future Negro stars (if they are good enough) to climb into white revues, while the production of *Four Saints in Three Acts,* the Gertrude Stein-Virgil Thomson opera, utilizes Negroes in a new field, as singing actors in alien Spanish roles. Miss Caterina Jarboro, too, has exhibited her talents in the congenial character of Aïda.

These are all symbols of better days. If standards are higher, the talent or genius expressed is greater too. In fact, nowadays there is no inclination on the part of the great public to say "pretty good for a Negro." If it cannot say "extraordinary from any point of view," it is not likely to show much interest.

When I first came to New York in 1906, the Negro lived modestly around Fifty-third and Fifty-ninth streets (well and pleasantly do a few of us re-member the delightful old Marshall's on Fifty-third Street). Now the Negro is installed in Harlem, the largest Negro city in the world, with its banks, its churches, its theatres, its nightclubs, its private and apartment houses, its shops, its libraries, and its YMCA, its singers, its dancers, its actors, its poets, its novelists, its orators, and its preachers. So many celebrated persons of the alien race attended last year's NAACP Ball at Renaissance Casino that some wag facetiously suggested that, for the sake of convenience, the next dance of this organization should be held in lower Manhattan. These are a few of the bald facts. What they may signify you may determine for yourself.

7

Correspondence

When Carl Van Vechten died in December 1964, his correspondence filled twelve filing cabinets in the American Literature Collection of Yale University's Beinecke Rare Book and Manuscript Library. Except for those letters dealing specifically with his own books, his letters from English authors, and those from his wife, all of which are in the New York Public Library's Manuscript and Archives Division as part of the Carl Van Vechten Collection, virtually every letter he ever received is at Yale.

Correspondence is largely dead today, but Van Vechten never allowed the telephone to take over a pleasurable pastime at which he was particularly adept. His letters in return—from H. L. Mencken, Theodore Dreiser, Sinclair Lewis, Gertrude Stein and Alice Toklas, F. Scott Fitzgerald, James Purdy, Ellen Glasgow, and without exaggeration dozens of other American writers—offer a fascinating and intimate examination of much of the twentieth century's literary history. Fortunately, many of his own letters have also been preserved in various libraries across the country, including, in the James Weldon Johnson Memorial Collection of Negro Arts and Letters at Yale, including many from black writers.

This brief selection offers a more personal view of Carl Van Vechten in his role as friend and mentor. Certainly, he matched in number the letters addressed to him: nearly six hundred from Langston Hughes, the most prolific of the writers; nearly two hundred each from James Weldon Johnson and Walter White; one hundred from Chester Himes; briefer correspondences with Arna Bontemps, Countée Cullen, Zora Neale Hurston, Nella Larsen Imes, Claude McKay, Willard Motley, Ann Petry, Richard Wright; and some few letters from Charles W. Chesnutt, W.E.B. Du Bois, Rudolph Fisher, Wallace Thurman, Eric Walrond, and, toward the end of Van Vechten's long life, from the young novelist, Henry Van Dyke.

With few exceptions, I have chosen letters Van Vechten wrote to intimate friends. In chronological sequence, they cover the forty-year period between 1924, when he first fell under the spell of the Black Renaissance, and 1964, when he died. Again, I have silently corrected obvious errors in typing, spelling, and punctuation; I have bracketed my appended words and phrases of explanation; I have used elipses to indicate deletions. It was Van Vechten's habit to use his salutation as the beginning of the first line of his letter and then to type everything—salutation, block paragraphs, his often fanciful closing quip, and the date—flush with a single margin. He frequently underlined or capitalized for emphasis; he rarely underlined or used quotation marks for titles. In editing these letters, I have attempted to bring some conventional order and consistency to their appearance while, at the same time, retaining their essential flavor. Van

Vechten typed almost all of his letters on stationery engraved with his successive addresses: 55 West 55th Street, 1924-1937; 101 Central Park West, 1937-1953; 146 Central Park West, 1953-1964. I have not recorded this information for each letter.

      Carl Van Vechten met Walter White through their mutual publisher, Alfred A. Knopf, in the summer of 1924 and discovered "an entirely new kind of Negro," he wrote to the novelist Edna Kenton. Within two weeks, he later said, he "knew every educated person in Harlem" and he "knew practically every famous Negro in New York because Walter was a hustler." In this first letter, following their meeting, Van Vechten forwarded a copy of *The Reviewer* with his article about the black male chorus in which he and another novelist friend, Joseph Hergesheimer, had taken an interest. The pioneering black firm, Black Swan, issued the first recordings of Ethel Waters and other popular singers of the period. Eva Gauthier, the concert singer, was the first serious artist to offer — at Van Vechten's sugges- tion — a selection of George Gershwin's songs in a serious recital. Roland Hayes was the black tenor equally well known for Schubert lieder and Negro Spirituals.

Dear Mr. White,

    Yesterday I ran across an extra copy of the magazine in which I wrote about the Sabbath Glee Club of Richmond, and I am sending it to you herewith. Shortly after I wrote this, Hergesheimer offered the Club $500 to pay the rent of a hall for a year. Since then, I understand, the members of the club have been quarrelling among themselves as to where and what the hall shall be! If they don't make up their minds pretty soon Hergesheimer will probably withdraw his offer. I wish it could be arranged for the Sabbath Glee Club to make some phonograph records.

    By the way, can you tell me what shop on 135th Street or thereabouts sells Black Swan records?

    Eva Gauthier, whom I saw yesterday, spoke of Roland Hayes as one of the great singers of the world.

       with best wishes for your works,

Carl Van Vechten

SEPTEMBER 22, 1924

Carl Van Vechten once said that one met one's friends through one's acquaintances; he met James Weldon Johnson through Walter White. Johnson had published *The Autobiography of an Ex-Coloured Man* anonymously in 1912; the copy he loaned to Van Vechten and his wife, Fania Marinoff, belonged to his brother-in-law, Jack Nail. Johnson's and Van Vechten's common interests in black music and literature formed an immediate bond between them, but shortly they were to become each other's most intimate friend.

Dear Mr. Johnson,

I read through *The Autobiography of an Ex-Coloured Man* at one sitting, and Marinoff is engaged in reading it now. I shall, of course, return Mr. Nail's copy to you, but remember that I am looking for a copy for myself and that if you run into one you can do no better than present it to me! It is a remarkable book in more ways than one, but in no way more so than in the gentle irony which informs the pages from beginning to end. You have said everything there was to say and said it without passion. The book lacks, I think, sufficient narrative interest; the hero might have had more personal experiences, but after all you were chiefly concerned with presenting facts about Negro life in an agreeable form, through the eyes of a witness who had no reason personally to be particularly disturbed.

I was particularly interested to discover that you were apparently the first to sense the musical possibilities of ragtime and to predict for it a future as an art form. In reviewing [Alexander] Woollcott's book about Irving Berlin for the *New York Tribune* I have found the opportunity to give you credit for this.

I have not been the same person since you told me about Hayti. I have discovered a passage about Christophe in H. G. Wells's *The Research Magnificent*. He refers to a book called *Where Black Rules White*, by Hesketh Pritchard. Have you seen this? I have ordered it, but it seems to be out of print. You have not yet sent me the magazine article you referred to. I hope you won't forget this.

We shall see you Friday evening. In the meantime, will you and Mrs. Johnson, in the Victorian manner, please accept our compliments!

Carl Van Vechten

MARCH 23, 1925

Gladys and Walter White were regularly included — or perhaps, by the middle of 1925, Van Vechten and his wife were regularly included—in the all-night rambles to Harlem nightclubs and other entertainments of the period.

Dear Walter,

May I ask a favor? I want to secure the following books. They may be out of print, but still obtainable when influence is brought to bear. At least you will know to whom to write at Fisk, Calhoun, and Hampton. If you will do this, merely ask that the books be forwarded to me with a bill, and I will send a cheque at once.

Here is the list:

Calhoun Plantation Songs, collected and edited by Emily Hallowell; C. W. Thompson, Boston.

Folk Songs of the American Negro (subtitle, *New Jubilee Songs*), edited by Frederick J. Work, Nashville, Tenn. This is a Fisk publication.

Religious Folk Songs of the Negro as Sung on the Plantations, arranged by the musical directors of the Hampton Normal and Agricultural Institute from the original edition of Thomas P. Fenner; The Institute Press; Hampton, Va. 1918.

and I will be grateful,

Carl Van Vechten

MAY 3, 1925

Everybody missed you and Gladys the other night. We started at the *Opportunity* dinner, went on to A'Lelia Walker's, the YMCA dance, Bamville, and the Comedy Club, which we left at 8:30 [A.M.], driving home through the sunlit, flowery park. I got home just in time to let a man in to tune the piano.

Shortly after they met through White and Johnson, Carl Van Vechten and Langston Hughes began to correspond on a regular basis, a habit they maintained during their forty-year friendship. Van Vechten had offered Hughes some suggestions about the arrangement of a group of poems which he subsequently offered to his publisher, Alfred A. Knopf. It was published as *The Weary Blues* in January 1926.

Your letters are so very charming, dear Langston, that I look forward every morning to finding one under the door. I have been lucky during the past week! The poems came this morning and I looked them over again. Your work has such a subtle sensitiveness that it improves with every reading. The poems are very beautiful and I think the book gains greatly by the new arrangement and title. Knopf is lunching with me today and I shall ask him to puiblish them and if he doesn't someone else will. Would you permit me to do an introduction? I want to. . . .

I've never even heard of the Little Savoy; I wish I had been with you that night. I have never, in my experience of twenty-five years, seen a fight in a Negro cabaret; on the other hand I've never been in a white place when there wasn't one. The difference, I suppose, is that white people almost invariably become quarrelsome when they are drunk, while Negroes usually become gay and are not inclined to fight unless they want to kill someone. I'm going on a Harlem party tonight; if you were here we'd take you with us. . . .

You will find your name, by the way, in the note I have written about Countée Cullen in the June *Vanity Fair*, not yet out.

Will you do something for me? I want you, if you will, to write me out the story of your life—detailing as many of your peregrinations and jobs as you can remember. Is this too much to ask?

I'll let you know about your book as soon as possible. In the meantime, please don't forget

Carl Van Vechten

[*circa* MAY 1925]

O═O

Hughes, apparently, responded almost immediately to Van Vechten's suggestion about an autobiography by sending him some early version of what later must have become the first part of *The Big Sea*, published by Alfred A. Knopf in 1945. The "Negro novel" to which Van Vechten refers is, of course, *Nigger Heaven*. Six months earlier, James Weldon Johnson had encouraged him to begin: "I am quite anxious to have you write on the subject now out of your larger and more intimate experience. Besides, as I once said to you, no acknowledged American novelist has yet made use of this material."[1] Johnson was not only referring to fiction, but he and Van Vechten had already discussed such possibilities by that time. In January 1923, Van Vechten had jotted down in a notebook: "Idea for a novel, to be called 1950, in which negroes circulate in society, have their own theatres, operas, etc., negro mayor."[2]

1. Carl Van Vechten Collection, Manuscript and Archives Division, New York Public Library.
2. Ibid.

Dear Langston,

The histoire de ta vie was so remarkable both as regards manner and matter that I hesitated for some time before deciding what should be done with it. It seemed absurd for me to write a preface about you when you had written such a beautiful one yourself, but another idea has dawned which seems even better. I have discussed the matter with Mrs. [Blanche] Knopf and she agrees with me fully. As I wrote you before, I think you are a top-notch writer of prose: in this biography you have an amazing subject. Treat it romantically if you will, be as formless as you please, disregard chronology if you desire, weaving your story backwards and forwards, but however you do it I am certain not only that you can write a beautiful book, but also one that will *sell.* There will be in it not only exciting incident, vivid description of character and people and places, but something more besides: the soul of a young Negro with a nostalgia for beauty and color and warmth: that is what I see in all your work. Now this is why the book will have an enormous appeal, because hundreds of young people, nay thousands, have this same nostalgia but they do not know how to express it, but they react to it emotionally when it is expressed. What I want you to do, therefore, is to *write this book.* It may be as long or as short as you please. I know it is hard to write a book with all the other things you have to do, but *I am sure you can do it.* What I am going to suggest to you is that you *make yourself* write a little every day: say 300 words. You will find this method hard at first and very easy after a week or two. In fact, some days you will want to write 2,000 words, but however many words you have produced on a certain day make yourself write the stipulated 300 on the next. You might read a few personal biographies, Sherwood Anderson's *A Story Teller's Story* (which is all fiction), for example, or Edwin Bjorkman's *The Soul of a Child* (which is all fact). This may serve to give you more confidence to go ahead, but after you have learned *their way,* disregard it to any extent and do *your* book *in your way.* I shall be very happy when you write me that you have begun this book. Be as digressive as you please—when anything reminds you of something else, another experience, another episode, put it down. Try to be as frank as possible, but when your material runs a little thin, don't be afraid to imagine better material or to put down someone else's experience as your own.

I am infinitely obliged to you for your assistance in regard to the Blues. Zora Neale Hurston and W. C. Handy have given me further material; in fact, I feel soon that I could write a book on the subject. Bessie Smith is promised me for an evening soon. By the way, I think her rendering of the "Weepin' Willow Blues" on the Columbia [label] is almost the best of all.

I hope *Vanity Fair* will like your poems as much as I did; but if they don't, remember that that will not destroy their beauty. I can recall the time, not so very long ago, when a paper of mine would come wandering back refused by eight or ten magazines. Off I would shoot it to another and eventually it would usually be accepted. You have caught the jazz spirit and the jazz rhythm amazingly; some of them ought to be recited in stop-time!

Firecrackers is my new novel. In it appear characters from all the old ones. I hope soon to start work on my Negro novel, but I feel rather alarmed. It would have been comparatively easy for me to write it before I knew as much as I know now, enough to know that I am thoroughly ignorant!

There are so many things that one can't talk about in a letter—I think a long conversation would be advantageous to both of us. Perhaps, a little later, you can run over for a couple of days and talk and look at my books and make yourself as comfortable as you can chez moi.

pansies and marguerites to you!

Carl

THURSDAY [AUGUST 1925]. . . .

By the end of 1925, Fania Marinoff and Carl Van Vechten had become the closest of friends with Grace Nail and James Weldon Johnson.

Dear Grace and James,
Thank you—and bless you. Perhaps the most important thing to me of the past year has been the growth of our intimacy.

We both send our love to you both.

Carl Van Vechten

CHRISTMAS MORNING, 1925

Van Vechten sent a number of the reviews of *Nigger Heaven* to James Weldon Johnson. Johnson replied, "amused" by Hubert Harrison's diatribe in the *New* [York] *Amsterdam News*. He wasn't reviewing the book, Johnson said, but unconsciously reviewing the people in Harlem he did not like.[1] Meanwhile, the *Pittsburgh Courier*, which originally refused to carry advertisements for *Nigger Heaven*, had printed Charles Johnson's enthusiastic letter to Van Vechten about the novel.

1. Carl Van Vechten Collection, Manuscript and Archives Division, New York Public Library.

Dear James,

I thought you might like to see a few more. You will particularly enjoy, I should think, *Time* and Dr. Hubert Harrison's vivid report. The *Baltimore Sun* review is typical of the Southern reviews. Curiously enough, they have all been wonderful so far, and I've had them from Texas, Kentucky, West Virginia, California, and other states. Burton Rascoe writes for a syndicate and his review appeared in at least a hundred newspapers: I've had one of his clippings from Knoxville, Tenn[essee]. I thought Grace might like to read Charles Johnson's letter which the *Pittsburgh Courier* printed. I'm sorry I haven't a copy at hand of the editorial in the *Age*. A lot of rotten characters who come to a bad end, is Fred Moore's report: hence, a fine book. The *N.Y. News* (colored) says that anyone who would call a book *Nigger Heaven* would call a Negro Nigger. Harlem, it appears, is seething in controversy. Langston, the other night in Craig's [Restaurant], suggested to a few of the knockers that they might read the book before expressing their opinion, but this advice seems to be regarded as superrogatory. Will you please return to me (as soon as possible)* the *Transcript, Courier*, Rascoe, *Baltimore Sun*, and *Tattler*. The others you may keep, if you like.

Painters are all around and over us, but we shall be through by the end of this week. We send our love to you and Grace.

affectionately,

Carlo V.V.

SEPTEMBER 7, 1926
*I really would like them this week.

Langston Hughes continued to send Van Vechten copies of his poems and to supply him with issues of black periodicals. His poems for *Nigger Heaven*, written line for line to supplant the copyrighted lyrics of some Blues Van Vechten had inadvertently quoted (and accounted for at length earlier in this anthology), appeared with an acknowledgment in the seventh printing of the novel. Hughes had spent the weekend, prior to this letter, at the Van Vechten apartment on West Fifty-fifth Street, composing some of his most winning verses.

Dear Langston,

Thanks for the copy of the poem—and thanks for *The Oracle.* Your poems for *Nigger Heaven* have gone to the printer. As I assured you before, you are at liberty to use these poems in the future in any way you like. You know how grateful I am to you. Everything is settled, & I am *very* tired. Call me up when you come to town.

Bay crowns to you.

Carlo

FRIDAY, NOVEMBER 5, 1926

Langston Hughes wrote to commiserate about some of the negative criticism of *Nigger Heaven*, and to include — as was his wont at this period — a copy of a recent manuscript.

Dear Langston,

Thanks a lot for what you say about *me.* Thanks a lot for your paper which I think is *superb.* The situation is *easy* to explain: You and I are the only colored people who really love *niggers.*

Avocados & Navajo jewelry to you!

Carlo

MARCH 25 [1927]

Walter White's frightening study of lynching in America, *Rope and Faggot*, was published in the spring of 1929.

Dear Walter,

Thanks for *Rope & Faggot* which I read through in two breathless sittings. You have contrived, quite miraculously, to keep hysteria out of an hysterical subject, permitting the victims to do their own shrieking, & turning the limelight rather on their sadistic attackers. But for the fact that probably very few of these sadists can read I should say the book would have an immense effect. Even so, I think it will cause some commotion in that part of the South in which such crimes are winked at, if not actually approved. At any rate, *Rope & Faggot* is an historical contribution of no mean value & should be widely read by those who are interested in social, political, or religious questions. It may astonish some of these to learn that organized torture & murder are seldom punished.

My congratulations,

Carlo

MARCH 31—'29

Carl Van Vechten and Fania Marinoff spent the spring and summer of 1930 touring England and Europe. They returned with some upholstered stools, the pedestals of which were carved eighteenth-century blackamoors. These served as dining room chairs for several years and, later, as the bases for end tables. James Weldon Johnson's *Black Manhattan*, his study of Negro New York during the first quarter of the century, had occupied Van Vechten enroute, a book he equated in importance with Johnson's *Autobiography of an Ex-Coloured Man*. Of the figures Van Vechten singled out from Johnson's narrative, Marcus Garvey was the flamboyant founder of the Universal Negro Improvement Association, advocating that blacks return to Africa; Garland Anderson was the first black to have a production on Broadway, *Appearances*, which opened in 1925 following Anderson's cross-country publicity campaign on its behalf.

Dear Jim!
Yesterday was the roughest day I have ever spent at sea. The boat leapt in the air & came down with a bang. So I stayed in bed and reread *Black Manhattan*—all the way through with a great deal of pleasure & also *looking for errors*. Now, usually books of this sort are really *full* of errors. It is almost impossible, when you are stating so many facts, to keep them out. I can't find any, however—not *one*. Besides, I must say that I enjoyed the second reading even more than the first. There are depths to your irony that do not always pierce the ears at the first jab of the needle! I love the parts about the churches & Marcus Garvey & the classes in Harlem & I adored the Garland

Anderson story . . . ; of course, it will be a great source book for a long time to come as was the autobiography & no one—absolutely no one, except Defoe, can write prose like you.

I shall mail this from New York so you will know we are back & I hope that we shall see you & Grace soon. If you are in town please call up at once. For a couple of weeks we shall be mortared & painted & polished but after that we expect to be right pretty. Wait till you see our new dining room chairs! I have some new photographs for you which I think you will like. It is surprising how many Negroes there are in famous paintings. Some day I think it would be lovely to collect them all in a large volume.

> Much love!

> *Carlo*
> *& Fania*

[*circa* AUGUST 1930, AT SEA]

O■O

James Weldon Johnson's *Book of American Negro Poetry* was first published in 1921; Van Vechten's prediction about the longevity of its 1931 revision proved true. At about the same time, his sister, Emma Van Vechten Shaffer, and Duane Van Vechten, the daughter of his brother Ralph, had just met the Johnsons.

Dear Jim,

It must give you a great deal of satisfaction to feel that you are rounding up all your work so neatly. With the present edition of *The Book of American Negro Poetry*, it seems to me that you have polished up the last of your past work that needed it. For certainly so much has happened since this was published that a new edition was cried for of this particular opus. And here it is, fresh and clean as new & twice as interesting. This is the last word in Negro anthologies & will probably remain so for some time, as I fancy. The next comers will be likely to go in for prose. Really, everything considered, you have done a remarkable amount of work besides your own what with this book and the Spirituals. And I think it is quite likely that the auto-biography will be the summit of your *own* work. Well, I don't know what my life would have been like—had I never known you & Grace—but for-tunately it is not necessary to indulge in such idle speculation.

> My compliments!

> *Carlo*

MARCH 29, 1931

The critical biographies in the new edition are immensely valuable.

My sister & niece seem to have fallen in love with you both. I hope they haven't taken you away from US!

In 1931, nine black boys were accused of rape in the infamous Scottsboro Case. Carl Van Vechten offered to help Langston Hughes in his efforts to raise money for their defense.

Dear Langston,

With this I am sending you registered 9 photographs of Ethel Waters in 2 of her favorite songs, signed by *her* & by *me* for you to sell for the Scottsboro Boys. . . .

476 white lily petals to you!

Carlo

JAN[UARY] 6 [1934]

With the visiting English novelist, Hugh Walpole, Van Vechten had seen *They Shall Not Die*, a play by John Wexley about the Scottsboro Case. Several other theatrical entertainments and literary works seemed preferable to him: the Gertrude Stein-Virgil Thomson opera, *Four Saints in Three Acts*, featuring an all-black cast; Marc Connelly's *The Green Pastures*, a play based on Negro biblical folklore; Johnson's own autobiography, *Along This Way*; Ethel Waters's singing of Irving Berlin's "Suppertime," a woman's lament for her husband who has been lynched.

Dear Jim,

I was prepared to thoroughly agree with *They Shall Not Die* and to be much moved by it. I came away completely unmoved and disliking the play very much. I think it will react against the purpose for which it was written. It is a bad play, the point of view is often false, and the interpretation of the facts is so obviously inspired by hate that often you are forced to admit to yourself you just don't believe the author. The attack on the NAACP is childish and Lucy Wells's (Ruby Bates) love affair with the travelling salesman is enough to turn a strong stomach. The Southerners against whom the play is directed will, of course, never see it. Other Southerners will not find it important enough to answer. I should add, by the way, that the Negro boys are quite beautiful and the face of the one in the courtroom scene very haunting. But no play in which all the dice are loaded can be very convincing. Even in *Uncle Tom's Cabin* there were some good Southerners, some Negroes who escape the lash. But not in this opus. Hugh Walpole, who was with me, agreed with my judgment and so did that eminent radical, Emma Goldman, a member of the same audience.

I should say that the performance of *Four Saints [in Three Acts]* by a Negro cast was much more important to the Scottsboro cause and to the history of the Negro stage in general (in which it is one of the big milestones). I should say the success of Ethel Waters in *As Thousands Cheer* and the grand tour of *The Green Pastures* are adding to the respect and recognition which is being given to the Negro. Add to these *Along This Way*, Langston's new book, *The Ways of White Folks*, and Zora Neale Hurston's *Jonah's Gourd Vine* (which Lippincott's in Philadelphia will presently publish with Fannie Hurst and C.V.V. leading the cheering) and there is very much more REAL SOLID evidence of a "Negro Renaissance" than there was in 1926-27. I think, for instance, that Miss Waters does more in "Suppertime" to awaken the torpid imagination to a realization of what may happen to those boys in Scottsboro than any number of silly, unbelievable dramas like *They Shall Not Die*.

By the way, I think it is highly important you should see *Four Saints* and *They Shall Not Die*, even at some expense and the risk of a few other broken engagements.

Love to you both from us and a special kiss to Grace on Tuesday the 27th when she will be sixteen!

Carlo!

SUNDAY, FEBRUARY 25, 1934

Langston Hughes had been working on a new collection
of poems which he sent to Van Vechten for an opinion.
Some of these were published, four years later, by the
International Workers' Organization, as *A New Song*; others
awaited posthumous publication, in 1973, in *Good Morning,
Revolution*, by Hill and Company. Van Vechten much
preferred Hughes's earlier work, for example, "A Good
Job Gone," one of the stories in *The Ways of White Folks*.

Dear Langston,

In looking over your volume of poems again I find I like them even less than I did last year. In fact, I find them lacking in any of the elementary requisites of a work of art.* This opinion has nothing to do with the opinions expressed therein. I find myself violently at variance with the opinions expressed by Diego Rivera's flaming frescoes in the Workers' School on Fourteenth Street, but I am drawn back to them repeatedly by his vital and superbly imaginative painting. I think "A Good Job Gone" is 100 percent propaganda for the Negro (here an artist is working who exhibits a Negro character arrogant with a white character) than the whole book of poems which I find, as art, as propaganda, as anything you may care to mention, Very Very Weak. Doubtless I am wrong. At least you can rely on my being frank with you. If you are interested at all, I could say a lot more (would that you were here so we could talk), but doubtless you are fed up with the subject already.

*This is a little too sweeping, I am speaking "generally." There are certain poems in the book that are very good indeed, only less good than your best work in this form.—But nothing sufficiently novel or strong to rate as "first class." I think your public has a right to demand only the "first class" of you after *Not Without Laughter* & *The Ways of White Folks.*

768 white penguin feathers for 76 black swans to you! (and an owl)

[*unsigned*]

MARCH 20, 1934

When W.E.B. Du Bois openly advocated segregation of the races, James Weldon Johnson retaliated by writing *Negro Americans, What Now?* His editor sent a set of galley proofs to Van Vechten. At the conclusion of his evaluation, Van Vechten told Johnson he was "probably a Woo Jums!" This name—originally a Twenties cocktail made of gin, rum, and absinthe—became a term of endearment for Van Vechten, Gertrude Stein, and Alice Toklas, who called each other Papa Woojums, Baby Woojums, and Mama Woojums, respectively, for thirty years, but he never assigned it permanently to anyone else.

Dear Jim,

Robert Hatch of the Viking [Press] has sent me the sheets of your new book yesterday, and it had not been in the house many minutes before I had read it through. That is a fine line you've got in the foreword about the ofays! They'll eat it up. Anybody faintly interested in the Negro "question" is bound to read it and I think it should do more to convince those who do not believe there is any Negro "question" than anything that has yet been published. In the first place, you have never written in so superbly simple a style: as English it is a little masterpiece. Then you are so temperate, so reasonable, so logical that it would be difficult for any reader to resist your line of argument, certainly any white reader. It is more difficult to predict the effect of this book on the colored man. Will he read it at all? There is a passage that seems to fear that he won't. If he does read it will he support the NAACP or will the church and press work hand and glove with that organization? It hardly seems likely. And yet if the Negro put up a united front he could have what he wanted probably within the month because the forces against him for the most part are nourished only by an ignorant prejudice. Like you, however, I feel hopeful that *something* is bound to happen soon because so much already has happened. A little bit more here and a little bit more there and the dam will break and the waters no longer be segregated.

My congratulations!
Love to you both,

Carlo

I have written Hatch!
It is significant, I think, that the time has come when you can address *the race* rather than the other race!

You are probably a Woo Jums!

TUESDAY NIGHT
[1934]

For one of his Alba Books, Alfred A. Knopf proposed to reissue James Weldon Johnson's *The Autobiography of an Ex-Coloured Man.* Joe Louis and Jack Johnson were the most recent and the first black heavyweight boxing champions in America; Marian Anderson and Sissieretta Jones, the "Black Patti," were celebrated singers. *Slave Ship* was a motion picture and *Babes in Arms* a musical comedy of the period. From 1934 to 1937, Van Vechten and Johnson saw each other continually when Johnson was appointed on a year-to-year basis as Visiting Professor

of Literature at New York University, offering courses in
black culture.

Dear Jim,

Congratulations to Alfred for republishing this very important book. I
think it would be a mistake to change one word of the original text. This
was written for a certain period and time and to change it would give it an
air of falsity. I think the publisher's preface should be kept intact too. I have
been rereading my introduction and think that should be allowed to stand
as it is too, with perhaps a change of title: "Introduction to Mr. Knopf's
1927 edition." I would suggest, however, that you yourself add a further
introduction (or appendix) to this new edition, a chapter in which you can
relate how much further the Negro has progressed, how his presence at the
opera, concert, and art gallery is now very generally expected, how he is no
longer a Republican, how Joe Louis compares with the earlier Jack Johnson,
and Marian Anderson with the Black Patti; you know.* But this is not
necessary, only it would be nice.

I foresee a long career for this little book which has already had so many
adventures. You might peer a little into the future and predict a few of the
things that may happen by the time another edition is required.

much affection to you,

Carlo

JUNE 26, 1937

*There could be literally hundreds of items.

Have you seen *Slave Ship*? This goes a little further in the direction of
realism than most movies on this subject & you get a glimpse at heart of
how the Africans were packed in the holes of ships & treated, tho' you must
use your imagination to realize what the voyage was like. And don't forget,
if you haven't already done so, to look at *Babes in Arms*. This is Historical.

I forgot to ask you if you will be at New York University again this year.

James Weldon Johnson was killed in an automobile
accident shortly after he and Van Vechten had celebrated
their joint birthday together, on June 17. Alfred Knopf's son
shared this date with them, too, and they had customarily
observed it with a mutual party. From the Ritz-Carlton
Hotel in Boston, where he had gone following the funeral,

Van Vechten wrote to Johnson's widow. Gene Buck delivered the eulogy; he was president of ASCAP, with which Johnson had been closely associated, and had been active in the NAACP as well. Van Vechten served as one of six pallbearers; the others included Rabbi Samuel Stephen Wise, cofounder of the NAACP, and Arthur Spingarn, chairman of the organization's legal committee.

Dear Grace,

What can I write? You know how I feel. Above all else I am grateful we had that June 17th together. Pat [Alfred Knopf, Jr.] who is more upset than I could have imagined said he was glad of this too. I sent you a telegram as soon as you were awake and I have been with Mildred & Rosamond [Johnson] on the phone or at the house a good deal.

I can't tell you how many people wrote or called me that didn't even know Jim. They just loved what he was!

Fania sailed on June 25—the day before—so she missed the first shock & I thought it better not to radio her.

The funeral was beautiful. The day was fine. The church looked lovely with the banks of flowers, and the music was exceptionally good.

"Go Down Death" was always my favorite of the sermons [from *God's Trombones*]. Do you remember how often I would ask Jim to read this? And Juanita Hall's choir gave an extraordinary rendering of this. Have you heard them do it? When they sang "Since You Went Away," I cried & so did everybody else.

Gene Buck was marvelous in his eulogy. I hope somebody made a copy of this for preservation. With the pallbearers I sat between Arthur Spingarn & Rabbi Wise. Theodore Roosevelt [Jr.] & W. C. Handy were adjacent. Could anyone else bring out such a strange combination of people in united love?

I hope, dear Grace, you are much better. Is there anything you want or want done? If so . . . let me know. When you come to New York and want to see me, let me know. Phone and I will come at once.

Lots of love and Fania would send hers too if she were here.

Carlo

JULY 2, 1938

I shall be in Boston for a few days longer possibly but I'll be back in New York next week and 101 [Central Park West] is still the safest address for me.

On occasion, during the Harlem Renaissance and after,
Van Vechten loaned or gave money to several aspiring
black artists and writers, as canceled checks among his
papers attest. In acknowledging Langston Hughes's repayment, Van Vechten addressed several matters. Hughes had
just read the first chapter of Van Vechten's *Peter Whiffle*,
reprinted as "First Day in Paris" in *Modern American Prose*,
edited by Carl Van Doren in 1934. The Daughters of the
American Revolution refused to allow the black contralto,
Marian Anderson, to sing in Constitution Hall, leading
Eleanor Roosevelt to invite her to sing at the White House,
and leading Van Vechten to an attendant suggestion.
A'Lelia Walker and Nora Holt were friends from the Twenties, referred to earlier in this anthology; William Grant
Still, the black American composer; Robert Earl Jones,
the black actor; Morris Ernst, the theatrical producer;
Edward Wasserman, another friend.

Dear Langston,

To get a cheque for $100 just before the income tax is due is something
that doesn't happen to this baby often. Thank you very much. I was even
more pleased to hear about all your good luck. The piece of prose you read
about my first night in Paris is an early chapter of *Peter Whiffle* which I
certainly thought you had read. A Negro *Diamond Lil* sounds swell and I
hope it comes off that way. A'Lelia Walker could have played that part! I
think the greatest break the Negro race has had in a long time is this BAD
PUBLICITY for the DAR and isn't Mrs. Roosevelt a honey? Edward [G.]
Robinson in Hollywood has a painting by Grant Wood called *Daughters
of American Revolution* depicting four hatchetfaced old crones looking
mean over the teacups. There are postcards of this (I used to have some) but
I don't know where they could be found. Why don't you write E[dward] G.
Robinson? ANYWAY I think it would be delightful if all the Negroes in the
USA, including CVV, would begin to use this postcard extensively. By the
way, I wrote *Who's Who*. I was surprised NOT to find the names of Marian
Anderson and Ethel Waters and it seems (the editor wrote me back at once)
they have been bombarding Miss A with questionnaires since 1936 and
never had ONE reply. They asked me if I could help. So I am using the
influence of the NAACP . . . to see if I can get her to send in the required
information. The editor also told me [he] had just sent a questionnaire to
Miss Waters. So I asked about that and she had already thrown it away. So
I got her another one and I am working on that myself! Miguel [Covar-
rubias] is doing a mural for the Mexican Building in the San Francisco Fair.

It is probably finished but I think he is still out there. His address in SF is the Plaza Hotel. Do you see Nora Holt? If you do, please give her my love. I miss her very much and please tell William Grant Still to call me when he comes East as I MUST photograph him. Earl Jones at last accounts was doing Joe Louis in the movies. Tonight the Negro Actors Guild Ball. I have a box and Morris Ernst and his wife and Eddie Wasserman, among others, are going with me. Fania is well and sends love and so do I,

with 131 silver (housebroken) dachshunds to you!

Carlo!

MARCH 1, 1939

Carl Van Vechten wrote "The Proposed James Weldon Johnson Memorial" for *Opportunity*, which the editors accompanied with a misidentified photograph. Richetta Randolph suggested that the NAACP publicly endorse the project; she had been with the organization for several years as "the best confidential secretary I have known or known of," according to James Weldon Johnson.[1] The "articles" Van Vechten referred to included a second one on the same subject in *Crisis*.

1. Carl Van Vechten Collection, Manuscript and Archives Division, New York Public Library.

Dear Walter,

Opportunity has committed the gaff of all time, tho' Life and God have occasionally made whoppers, in printing a photograph of Augusta Savage's UNFINISHED (at the time) head of Jim [James Weldon Johnson] with a caption attributing it to [Richmond] Barthé. This accompanies my article. But this may even do some good in an odd way!

Miss Randolph's suggestion, as usual with her, is a good one. I mean about the NAACP Board.

And shouldn't publicity to the newspapers occur about NOW. It has to be hooked up with something timely: "the board will meet tomorrow" or something, you know. I have asked you about this several times and you don't reply. But I know how busy you are and where your heart is: so okay.

Only now that these articles of mine are coming out is the time the newspapers should carry some mention of this.

Four* wonderful Dreams to you!

Carlo

FEBRUARY 4, 1940

*Five, if you prefer!

To compensate for the error in identifying the illustration, *Opportunity* ran off a number of reprints of Van Vechten's article that could be used for publicity purposes. *Trouble in July* was a current novel with black subject matter by white novelist Erskine Caldwell.

Dear Walter,

Your letter explains everything. Not that anything needed EXPLAINING. I enclose my cheque for $50 towards the James Weldon Johnson Memorial Fund. If more is needed I'll be glad to send more later.

I have packed up three hundred copies of the Memorial reprint from *Opportunity* for Miss Randolph to send for tomorrow. If more are needed let me know before they are all gone. I am sending them out, with notes, to people as far away as Bali, China, and Australia.

The reaction to the error in *Opportunity* does not surprise me and may prove actually helpful. Certainly these reprints, which we couldn't have expected otherwise, are a Godsend.

My prayers are with you constantly and I must say that Chapter XIV of *Trouble in July* is certainly as good writing as I know about.

141 buckets of rubies to you!

Carlo!

MONDAY, FEBRUARY 19, 1940

Don't you think the NAACP should send you away on a warship for a rest, too?! . . .

Van Vechten sent a number of copies of the *Opportunity* reprint to his friend from the Twenties, Harold Jackman.

Dear Harold,

I hope you will help us collect funds for the James Weldon Johnson Memorial. If you can use some of the enclosed reprints, let me know how many and I will send them to you.

Have you read Erskine Caldwell's *Trouble in July*? A magnificent book which touches on the race question in the South from the most subtle angles.

On April 8 the Booker T. Washington 10 cent stamp makes its appearance. He was no great admiration of mine, but he is the first Negro to have his portrait on a USA stamp and so I am laying in a supply to use on special delivery letters, etc.

mes compliments, mon cher,

Carlo

MONDAY [*circa* MARCH 1941]

Richmond Barthé's early sketches for the Johnson memorial included nude bodies, which gave Walter White some consternation. Van Vechten hastened to assure him of their appropriateness. At the same time, he had been making photographic prints of Jane White, Walter White's actress-daughter.

Dear Walter,

One of the points about a nude which I didn't bring out very clearly is that it is novel, classical, and modern, whereas this same statue in pants would be "picturesque darky folklore," unobjectionable, and unnoticed. Here are the leaflets I promised you.

The main monument in Columbus Circle includes two nudes. They are sitting, but you can get the whole idea from any bus or taxi passing. Take a look next time you go by. They have never created a revolution. *Civic Virtue*, which stood in front of the City Hall for years, was to all intents and purposes nude and quite sexy. A discus thrower stood back of the Metropolitan Museum for years. Mr. Moses has moved this to Randall Island, I think. At the World's Fair practically everything was nude and practically everything was 30 feet high. No fig leaves. Other cities have more nudes. Are we more provincial than St. Louis? Carl Milles's new fountain in front of the railway station has twenty or thirty nudes, male and female. The Garden of the Museum of Modern Art (which can be seen by the public from 54th Street) has dozens of nudes of both sexes. Lachaise's *Man of Heroic Size* with a terrific penis brazened it out there for months.

He has returned to Walter Chrysler's country garden!

I have been told confidentially that NO statue, work of art or dub, ever got by without a fight!

I am printing pictures of Jane, way out of turn.

oak leaves and dahlias to you!

Carlo

TUESDAY

If you want me to meet you or talk to anybody or help in any way, command me. I think psychologically it would be helpful to get this thing done before the election!

[24 SEPTEMBER 1941]

When Van Vechten requested manuscripts for the Yale Collection, Claude McKay replied that he had only one — *Home to Harlem* — which he wanted to hold on to for his daughter in case it might have some monetary value in time. He suggested that Van Vechten could write to the publishers of his other novels who had kept the original manuscripts. When Van Vechten was able to procure two of these, McKay changed his mind and decided he wanted one of them back. Eventually, however, he gave the manuscript for *Home to Harlem* to the collection as well as other materials.

McKay and Van Vechten had not met until 1929, when they were both in Paris, although McKay was familiar with *Nigger Heaven* and Van Vechten was familiar with *Home to Harlem* since the novels were frequently compared. In his autobiography, *A Long Way Home*, McKay recounts having been warned against Van Vechten by "a white non-admirer" who claimed McKay "would like him because he patronized Negroes in a subtle way, to which the Harlem elite were blind because they were just learning sophistication! I thought it would be a new experience," McKay continued, "to meet a white who was subtly patronizing to a black; the majority of them were so naïvely crude about it. But I found Mr. Van Vechten not a bit patronizing, and quite all right."[1]

1. Quoted in Carl Van Vechten, *Nigger Heaven* (New York: Harper and Row, reprint edition, 1971), p. xii.

Dear Claude McKay,

Even though you did write that [we] could have "one or two" of your manuscripts for the James Weldon Johnson Collection at Yale, and even though Yale wants as many manuscripts as you will give them badly, Mr. Bernhard Knollenberg, the librarian, thinks, and I agree with him, that you have a perfect right to change your mind, and he wants you to be satisfied. If then, you have definitely decided that you would like to have the manuscript of *Banana Bottom* returned to you, write to him . . . or to me to that effect and it will be returned to you at once. Or, if you prefer that it be retained in the collection, please let us know that. We want you to be happy in the matter!

    sincerely,

                    Carl Van Vechten

OCTOBER 25, 1941

Harold Jackman sent Van Vechten René Maran's black French novel for the James Weldon Johnson Memorial Collection of Negro Arts and Letters. Joel Spingarn had been chairman of the board of the NAACP at its inception. Wallace Thurman, a black novelist from the Twenties, had favorably reviewed *Nigger Heaven* a month following its publication, in the September issue of *Messenger*, a black publication, titling it "A Stranger at the Gates."

Dear Harold,

Coeur Serre is here in an association copy and you are a honey kid and my favorite Harlem beauty! Thanks for everything and God and Yale will reward you and maybe the RACE! Anyway this collection is going to be a killer diller. Walter [White] has just supplied the two missing copies of *Crisis* in my collection! As for letters, of course, many of them are too personal for immediate examination by strange eyes. You get around that by presenting them SEALED until a certain date. ALL of Edith Wharton's private papers and letters were presented to Yale sealed with the proviso that they can be opened in 1960. The Gertrude Stein correspondence (364 letters) which I presented Yale last year is sealed and can only be examined after *both* of *us* die. She is giving them my letters with the same proviso. On the other hand, Amy Spingarn has given Yale James Weldon Johnson's letters to Joel with no proviso whatsoever and I imagine none is needed on ANY JWJ letters. We'd be tickled to death for the Wallace Thurman letters, as material on this young genius is rare. I recently ran across the enthusiastic review he gave *Nigger Heaven* in *The Messenger*.

So, thanks for everything and my pontifical blessings on you!

Carlo

DECEMBER 5, 1941

Roy Wilkins printed Carl Van Vechten's "The James Weldon Johnson Collection at Yale" in the July 1942 issue of *Crisis* and reprinted it as a broadside at the same time.

Dear Mr. Wilkins,

Here is the piece about the James Weldon Johnson Memorial Collection at Yale you asked me to do for *Crisis*. Altho' I have tried to keep it within the bounds you set, it has gone on a little longer, and it would be easy to make it longer still. If you possibly can, I hope you will print it as it stands, as I have already been obliged to omit mention of some important material. If, however, you find it too long to use in its present form I hope you will do me the favor of letting me cut it myself, as there are certain things I should hate to leave out.

Have you an idea how soon you can use this?

sincerely,

Carl Van Vechten

MAY 10, 1942

I am enclosing the bookplate of the collection which you may wish to reproduce.

Langston Hughes and Zora Neale Hurston had once collaborated on a play entitled *Mulebone*. Lawrence Langner and Theresa Helburn, directors of the Theatre

Guild, had considered producing it. At this time Van
Vechten was regularly working at the Stage Door Canteen,
but he paused to reminisce about a celebrated brothel he
had visited in his youth where, on occasion, he would spell
the piano player.

Dear Langston,

I've been away for a few days and when I come back, I find your letter.
. . . I've also been reading many Negro letters for Yale, including the correspondence re *Mulebone* which includes letters from YOU and Zora and
Barrett H. Clark and Lawrence Langner and Theresa Helburn. It's a pretty
complete tale and your letter regarding Zora's tantrum in your mother's
room in Cleveland is wonderful. She had a tantrum in my library at 150
West 55th Street, too, and threw herself on the floor and screamed and
yelled! Bit the dust in fact. You woulda loved it, had it not concerned you. . . .

The Everleigh Club in Chicago also had a fountain in the living room.
Some of the best families used to fall in. Affection to you and FM [Fania
Marinoff] even sends a kiss, after your "Tell Fania I love her!"

Carlo

Monday (I'm off to the Canteen SOON)

AUGUST 17 [1942]

O▭O

The Harlem race riots of 1943 led to several letters
between Van Vechten and Langston Hughes. Pearl Showers
and Mildred Perkins were the Van Vechtens's servants for
many years. Meanwhile, Hughes continued to contribute
to the Yale Collection.

Langston!

. . . I know *why* the riots and so I can understand and they MAY have
done some good locally, but the effect on the general public is extremely
bad and has given the other side unexpected comfort and ammunition. If
such riots are organized the people who organize them should do so publicly
and then others would know what they are doing and WHY they are doing
it. Ferinstance, the suffragettes broke windows, then waited till they were
arrested, then went on a food strike till they were released, then broke more
windows and went through the whole program again. Eventually they got
the vote. The trouble is in the present case too many people are saying,
"Negroes are hoodlums and DANGEROUS. Keep them DOWN." If they

had a good reason to break these windows they should have announced it.[1]
Propaganda, as you know, is often more effective than action. Thank you
for the use of the hall! Anyway, if the riots were organized[2] and intended as
a lesson to extortionists and exploiters, WHY did they attack pawnshops
which hit hard at Harlem? Pearl [Showers] and Mildred [Perkins Thornton]
tell me many of their friends lost their dearest possessions. . . . Mildred . . .
being in very bad health is leaving us which leaves a hole in our lives which
nothing or nobody else can quite fill. Fortunately Pearl . . . is still here. The
boxes for your manuscripts (seven or eight of them) are here and will probably be here till you get back as I still hadn't enough *Defender* pieces for a
box yet. *The Sun Do Move* is not yet boxed because you said I hadn't the
final draft yet. But gradually you are piling up in grand style in this collection
and may be studied at leisure by some future historian of American writers
in general and the Race in particular. Excuse me for being long-winded and
allow me to remain affectionately yours,

Carlo!

AUGUST 12, 1943

[1]and of course the effect would have been doubled without the looting.
[2]I have been told just by people who should know.

It was Van Vechten's habit to have all contributions to
the Johnson Collection boxed in sturdy, blue cloth-covered
cases, with dark red leather labels stamped in gold. Roi
Ottley, a young black writer, agreed to contribute his
papers, at Langston Hughes's instigation, and Hughes
himself continued to contribute. Bricktop was the nick-
name of Ada Smith, whose Paris bistro was well known
during the Twenties and Thirties. Dorothy Peterson and
Sidney Peterson were friends from the Twenties, the former
the model for the heroine of *Nigger Heaven*. Sugar Hill
refers to the elegant Edgecomb Avenue in Harlem.

Dear Langston,
    What letters *you* write! Maybe I do too. Sometimes I wonder if OUR let-
ters won't be the pride of the collection. I haven't got around to sending
yours to me yet, but will this winter! My remarks on the riot were based on
the sworn statements of certain Harlemites that they had been organized for
weeks (everybody had his orders). Yours are based on the belief that it was

a casual turnout. I have an idea that both of these theories were true. A FEW had planned something, probably, and the mob trailed after. You are right that Harlem is much more indignant about (and much more aware of) these riots than downtown and I don't know anyone more indignant than Pearl Showers and Mildred [Perkins] Thornton. So it isn't all Sugar Hill indignation. Roi Ottley came to be photographed Saturday and definitely we are getting the manuscript. When he saw your new beautiful boxes, he almost swooned and exclaimed, "The Schomburg Collection doesn't keep things like this." Of course, nobody else does and even Yale wouldn't, if I didn't do it myself. The material turned into this collecton is in a condition, thanks to my energy and foresight, which not many other collections can boast. It is hard work and endless, but I think it is worth it. I have a DEFI-NITE FEELING that in LESS than five years Yale will have a chair of Negro life and culture and whoever sits in that chair will have the best source material in the country to guide him. Anyway, Ottley promises all letters, manuscripts, what not, in the future. Of course I have the IWO Educational Alliance edition of *The Sun Do Move*, but I had noted something on the other mss. about waiting for the "final draft" and got confused. I'll have a box made for *The Sun Do Move* soon. Florence B. Price of Chicago sent me her *Symphony in C Minor* (manuscript of the full score). This is Harold [Jackman]'s work. . . . I expect to be deluged with manuscripts and letters when you return. The boxes will still be here, as certain things have to be signed. Besides, I have to catalogue the contents of these boxes before they go and am up to my ears in other matters for the moment. . . . Even if you don't reply to other letters, answer MINE. Our correspondence will be historical. . . . Bricktop had a birthday last Saturday. Was she up your way?

Dorothy P[eterson] is moving again. So is Dr. Sidney [Peterson]. Have you read a book called *Race*, by Ruth Benedict? When are you coming back?

> fondly,

> > > > > > > > *Carlo*

AUGUST 16, 1943

A loan repayment from Langston Hughes added to the George Gershwin Memorial Collection which Van Vechten had founded at Fisk University. (Shortly thereafter, he founded the Florine Stettheimer Memorial Collection of Books about the Fine Arts there as well.) If the Johnson Collection at Yale would draw black scholars to a white

university, Van Vechten reasoned, a white collection at a
black university would attract white scholars.

Dear Langston,

Your very sweet letter and the cheque arrived this minute and touched me
very deeply. I kept no record of any transaction like this and it was a complete surprise to learn that you owed me money. However, I know someone
at the moment who needs help very badly and I will apply part of it to that
cause; the rest will go towards buying more expensive books for the George
Gershwin Memorial Collection at Fisk University. . . .

Hearts and Flowers to you and after the war maybe I'll be coming to
YOU for crutches,

Carlo

JUNE 27, 1945

Of course, I am very happy you are making money.

Following Van Vechten's lead, James Weldon Johnson's
widow began turning over her husband's papers to the Yale
Collection, even though she seems to have been reluctant
to do so in the beginning. In acknowledging the gift, Van
Vechten apprised her of his latest activity involving black
performers.

Dear Grace,

In the first place, thanks for your beautiful official letter in which you
turn over Jim's manuscripts and other material for the James Weldon Johnson Memorial Collection of Negro Arts and Letters at Yale University. You
have done it very charmingly indeed. In the second place, I am sending you
three balls of strong cord, the kind Pearl [Showers] and I use to fasten
packages for Yale. I'll send you more when you need it.

Arthur [Spingarn] gave me a later version of the manuscript of *Negro
Americans, What Now?*, but NOT "Go Down, Death." If he has this I shall
try to persuade him to do so later, together with whatever else he has in
Jim's hand. He will, I am sure, see the advisability of keeping everything
together. Do you know if you have the manuscript of "The Creation"? Do
you know if anyone else, besides Arthur, possesses manuscripts of Jim's?

Thanks for bringing up the matter of the secretaries. Doubtless I'll have
many questions to ask them later. Miss Randolph, as you know, has given
the collection Jim's letters already.

I hope to receive more material from you soon. *But take your time in this bad weather.*

I attended the [Adam Clayton] Powell-Hazel Scott wedding reception at Cafe Society and it was very badly planned and managed. I was forced to wait an hour and fifteen minutes in the street before I could get in at all. Once inside, the crowd was so dense it was impossible to find the refreshment table. I didn't even get near the bride and groom. Every fifteen minutes a loud speaker invited you to return to the street to let others in.

Did I tell you that I am in charge of entertainment at the American Theatre Wing Tea Dance for service women, given every Sunday afternoon at the Grill Room of the Hotel Roosevelt? Ethel Waters will sing for us next Sunday. Others I have had recently are Laurette Taylor, Celeste Holm, Alicia Markova, Mia Slavenska, Katharine Cornell, Tallulah Bankhead, Paul Robeson, Norma Terriss, and Bill Robinson.

Our love to you,

Carlo

AUGUST 3, 1945

Walter White contributed the manuscript for the best-known sermon from James Weldon Johnson's *God's Trombones* to the collection at Yale. As Van Vechten indicates, he was only interested in adding original manuscripts and corrected proofs to the collection, and other original material. The papers connected with the dinner given in his honor by the James Weldon Johnson Literary Guild at the Port Arthur Restaurant in Chinatown—drafts of Van Vechten's speech, guest lists, Langston Hughes's poem written for the occasion, notes for speeches by some of the guests—also had their own protective, matching box in the Johnson Collection. Walter White's profile in the *New Yorker*, which he asked Van Vechten to write, was written by Ely Kahn; Van Vechten's alternative suggestion, Margaret Case Harriman, was the daughter of Frank Case whose Algonquin Hotel had been a meeting place for literary celebrities during the Twenties. The work on which Van Vechten was concurrently embarked was published as *Selected Writings of Gertrude Stein* several months later. Meanwhile, plans for James Weldon Johnson's memorial statue had bogged down because, during the war years,

there was no bronze available. Eventually, the funds
already collected — minus Richmond Barthé's commission
for his design — were donated to the James Weldon Johnson
Memorial Collection of Negro Arts and Letters.

Dear Walter,

Thanks a terrific lot for the manuscript of "The Creation" which will be
one of the gems of the James Weldon Johnson Collection when it is filed in
its proper box. It is one of the few manuscripts of Jim's that Grace didn't
have and as it is one of Jim's most important works you may judge how
happy I am to get it from you. You will receive thanks from the Yale Library
when it is eventually deposited there.

As for your own "manuscript" I think you have sent me back material I
returned to you when you originally sent me some of your source material
in 1942. At any rate I can find no manuscript of *Rope and Faggot* in your
packages. That was sent to me and deposited at Yale in December 1942.
The manuscripts of *Flight* and *The Fire in the Flint* that you send me today
are carbon copies without corrections and of course valueless. The proofs
for the most part are proofs without corrections, but I'll give the whole
business a more extensive once-over before I ship it back to you. I note that
the manuscript of *Flight* with proofs also went to Yale in December 1942
and so did the proofs of *Rope and Faggot*. I note that you are sending the
original manuscript of *A Rising Wind* and we shall be only too happy to
receive these.

The dinner for me was given at the Port Arthur Restaurant on November 20, 1942. I have been holding the box of this material all this time, hoping
you could be induced to supply something. As I wrote you originally it is
certainly impossible at this late date to reconstruct your speech, but what
you can do is to write a short flowery speech of introduction and then write
in longhand above it that you spoke extemporaneously on this occasion and
that this is the gist of your remarks as well as you can remember. The
reason for all this is that the shorthand reporter that Roberta Bosley said
she was supplying fell down completely. Don't take this too seriously. You
could dash off something in ten minutes that would do very nicely, as Fannie
Hurst, Lin Yutang, and the others have already done.

About the *New Yorker*, it is impossible for me to take on any more work
at this time. I have just sent off 22 files of Jim's letters to Yale, having read
and listed them, but the apartment is a shambles with so much more material
that walking about is difficult. Not only material of Jim's but that of lots of
other people. Further, I have committed myself to edit and introduce a
Gertrude Stein omnibus which is a terrific job. Besides, *New Yorker* Profiles
require a very special technique with which I am not equipped. I am sure
that Margaret Case Harriman would fill your bill very nicely. As you know,

she is probably the most brilliant of the Profile writers and Knopf published a volume of her profiles some months ago. You can find her in the telephone book or, latterly, she is a good deal with her father at the Algonquin since his wife died.

I hate to remind you, but I think it is important that you and Arthur and I get together soon about Jim's memorial statue. Some matters have come up which should be discussed before it is too late. Further, I think inactive committees are a menace to progress. If we can do nothing we should turn this matter over to others who can and will.

Four magnums and champagne to you and a squirrel pie!

Carlo!

FEBRUARY 27, 1946

A. C. Sterling had interviewed Harold Jackman for an article about the Harlem Renaissance called "Those Were Fabulous Days." It appeared in the *Pittsburgh Courier* whose editor, Van Vechten's warm friend, George Schuyler, had not liked Richard Wright's *Native Son.* Eric Walrond and Nella Larsen Imes were black novelists of the Twenties; Donald Angus had been Van Vechten's frequent companion at the time.

Caro Harold,

As you remind me this is the sixteenth anniversary of the day Eric Walrond took Donald [Angus] and me to Dorothy P[eterson]'s and we met you and Dorothy and Nella [Larsen Imes]. All I can say is every year I like you better and you have never been sweeter or more efficient than in getting me the *P[ittsburgh Courier]* so promptly. I wouldn't have missed it. Seldom have I had a greater compliment paid me and from somebody whose opinion I respect very much. [George] Schuyler and I also agree about *Native Son,* an overrated book if there ever was one, and one which has done the Negro an inconscionable amount of harm in the minds of many an ofay who has read it.

Rubies, orchids, and everything nice to you!

Carlo

SATURDAY, FEBRUARY 8[1951]

Arna Bontemps, another member of the Harlem Renaissance, described by his friend, Langston Hughes, as "a
young edition of Dr. Du Bois," later became librarian at
Fisk University, to which Van Vechten gave his collections
of musical compositions and correspondence and a
number of books about fine arts. Having moved from West
Fifty-fifth Street to 101 Central Park West in 1937, he
moved again in 1953 when the building went cooperative.
New friends, singers William Warfield and Leontyne Price,
had recently married and taken a house in Greenwich
Village.

Dear Arna,

Tomorrow, BY RAILWAY EXPRESS, I am sending you a carton and a
smaller package, for the Gershwin and Stettheimer Collections. This time
the material for the two collections is mingled. The lists are enclosed.

Moving day is approaching rapidly and it won't be long now when we are
(un)settled at 146 Central Park West. You will get a card notifying you of
the change of address when the event occurs. The telephone remains the
same number.

Langston came down recently, the first time I had seen him since 1492. I
was happy to renew our acquaintance. O yes, I had encountered him the
Sunday before at Bill Warfield's housewarming in his new house.

This moving business is getting us down, but otherwise we are in pretty
good shape.

Yours, with faith, charity, and certainly HOPE,

Carlo

OCTOBER 11, 1953

Fisk suffered a drop in enrollment during the Korean
War, leading Bontemps to try to recruit students through
Van Vechten.

Dear Arna,

Material for the Gershwin Collection went to you today in two packages.
By Railway Express. The list is enclosed.

Every youth I know has gone to Korea or environs and cannot go to college yet, but I am keeping my eyes peeled.

Caviar and Crackers to you,

Carlo

JUNE 3, 1953

Van Vechten met Chester Himes in 1945 and after reading some of his work persuaded his own publisher, Alfred
A. Knopf, to buy Himes's contract from Doubleday. Himes,
in turn, began to contribute his work to the Johnson Collection, and he and Van Vechten became warm friends. In his
Columbia Oral History, Van Vechten said, "Chester is
intransigent and I'm about the only person, black or white,
that he's ever got along with more or less permanently. . . ."

Dear Chester,
   . . . For an old gentleman on the way out I do seem to be quite lively. As
for the race, it seems to be doing even better than usual. Someday we will
all wake up to the fact that EVERYTHING has been changed. This agreeable
ending will come with a rush, like the spring flowers and leaves after a
fallow winter. The most extraordinary things will happen with nobody
paying any attention (paying any mind would be a more harmless way of
saying this). Your PS reads, "I'm asking World to send the scrapbook and
French clippings for inclusion in the collection." I don't know exactly what
you mean, but I am grateful to you for keeping the Collection in mind.
When there is no distinction between the races, it will be pleasant to have
a repository like this where one can examine what the race did single-
handed. . . .

Easter Eggs to you, Shish Kebab, broiled kid, and Raumschnittle,

Carlo

APRIL 23, 1954

In 1955, Van Vechten's seventy-fifth birthday was widely
acknowledged. The New York Public Library offered an
extensive exhibit of his work, the first such show ever given
a living author; Alfred A. Knopf issued a Van Vechten
bibliography by Klaus Jonas of the University of Pittsburgh;

the Yale Library published a series of memoirs Van Vechten
had written over the years for the *Yale Library Gazette*,
boxed in two small volumes; *Carl Van Vechten and the
Twenties*, by Edward Lueders, was published by the University of New Mexico Press; Fisk University awarded him
an honorary doctorate; hundreds of congratulatory letters
reached him.

Dear Mr. Wilkins,
    I have had a wonderful 75th birthday, but your letter, representing the
NAACP, was the climax. Thank you!

        sincerely,

                                                                    Carl Van Vechten

JUNE 28, 1955

    Chester Himes had decided to live in Paris. He proposed
leaving a number of copies of his most recent novel, *The
Primitive,* with Van Vechten for distribution among
sympathetic readers. Van Vechten had sent him, in turn, a
copy of *Fragments*, the collection of memoirs Yale had
published for his seventy-fifth birthday.

Dear Chester,
    Your letter upset me very much and also pleased me because I realized
that you will be happier in Paris, even with very little to live on. You must
not imagine, however, that ALL people who write books attempt to live on
their royalties. Unless the books are best sellers this is not very practical and
hardly anyone attempts it. Wallace Stevens, for instance, one of the best of
the modern poets, who has just died, supported himself at a desk in a Hartford insurance company office. Charles Ives, the composer who is just
coming into his own after a lifetime of composition which never sold but
which piled up into an enormous list of works, founded his own insurance
company and eventually became a millionaire. Now he is considered the
most important American composer. These are two examples. I could give
you dozens more. Anyway, I was about to call you to meet Peter Abrahams,
the South African Negro writer (who makes a living lecturing). He has just
been here and I wanted to introduce you. Most dreadful of all, I had sent
my new book to you. I hope this will either be forwarded to you or returned
to me because it is a limited edition and I MAY not be able to get another

one. All the copies I had at my disposal have gone out. It seems that it would be almost impossible for you to be reduced to Horn and Hardart, but, on the other hand, I realize that nothing whatever is impossible. I am sorry you didn't confide in ME. You write that you are sending me 50 copies of [The] Primitive, or rather that the publisher is. Are these to be held for your instructions or what? You do NOT explain. May I hope that things will be better from now on? I daresay they could never be much worse.

> affection to you always and much admiration, to you as a writer and to you as a man,

> I hasten to get this off.

Carlo

DECEMBER 28, 1955

Van Vechten wrote to Chester Himes in Paris about the paperback version of *The Primitive*. Another Paris-based black acquaintance, James Baldwin, had come to Van Vechten's attention through his *Notes from a Native Son*. Pearl Bailey and Dizzy Gillespie, both popular entertainers, were also part of the Van Vechten photographic archive. A few years later, when Van Vechten repeated the story of his having encountered a black person he disliked, in his Columbia Oral History, his interviewer suggested that Van Vechten had become prejudiced at that point. "It had nothing to do with prejudice," Van Vechten replied. "I didn't dislike him because he was a Negro. I disliked him for other reasons — I forget what they were now. Perhaps he was unkind to his mother or kicked his dog or something. I don't know."

Dear Chester,

I've read *The Primitive* with great excitement and have sent copies around with great success where I thought they would do the most good. But I had an awful time getting them. They first sent me the Henry Miller as I wrote you and they sent them to an address on East 41 Street. Where they got this address I'll never know, as I have NEVER lived on East 41 Street. Then when they [were] apprised of this fact they sent *The Primitive* to East 41 Street. Well, anyway, it took a long time, but finally I got the book and presently read it. In some ways it is an improvement, this abridged edition, because it moves so fast that you can't lay the book down (in other words the lays prevent you from laying) but I missed some scenes and characters from the original, missed them very much indeed. . . . Your new book about Harlem socialites sounds most promising and I burn to see it finished and published. You should have known A'Lelia Walker. Nothing in this age is quite as good as THAT. Her satellites were shocked and offended by her appearance in *Nigger Heaven*, but she was nicer to me after that, even than before. I miss her. She always treated me to champagne when we had locked our-selves in her boudoir and locked the toadies and sycophants out with a bottle of beer apiece. What a woman! What you write about people who under-stand that Negroes are human is very marvellously put and thanks for the compliment to me. You see, like everybody else who goes into this new world, at first I had a Messiannic complex (My God, how DO you spell it). But one day I came home shouting, "I HATE a Negro! I HATE a Negro!" It was my salvation and since then I've had no trouble at all. From that point on I understood that they were like everybody else that is, they were thieves and cut-throats, generous and pious, witty and wise, dumb and foolish, etc., etc. But you put all this very nicely. How understanding you are! Most Negroes wouldn't understand this about their own people, let alone US. Write me when you have time. Do you know Jimmy Baldwin? He lives in Paris. He is somebody that I admire. I know him slightly, but I admire his writing, not so much his fiction, but his ESSAYS: he lays about with a stout bludgeon and smacks 'em down in every direction. How scornful he is of pretension.

It is a great pleasure to know people like you and him. Two wonderful things have happened to me recently. Pearl Bailey introduced me to the Apollo Theatre audience one afternoon when she was playing there last week, and I recently met Dizzy Gillespie.

Chitlings to you, pigs knuckles and sauerkraut, and hominy grits,

I am in favor of seceding from the SOUTH.

Hands across the seas,

Carlo

FEBRUARY 4, 1956

At the age of seventy-seven, Van Vechten had not slowed down. In addition to writing an introductory essay for a book by Gertrude Stein and another about George Gershwin, and photographing novelists James Purdy and Coleman

Dowell, dancers Geoffrey Holder and Carmen de Lavallade,
and most of the cast of Langston Hughes's musical comedy,
Simply Heavenly, he found time to write to old friends.

Dear Langston,
    . . . I am up to my neck working on my collections, photographs, and
two prefaces, but expect to emerge in time to go to heaven.
    With the warmest possible greetings (I wish to GOD you would stop
signing yourself "sincerely." One is sincere with the butcher. It is taken for
granted one is sincere with one's friends. Certainly I get letters from no one
else in the world with such a conventional signing off),

Carlo

NOVEMBER 19, 1957

As music critic for the *Amsterdam News*, Nora Holt
took a group of young black musicians up to Yale to go
through the James Weldon Johnson Memorial Collection
of Negro Arts and Letters. It distressed Van Vechten when
blacks misunderstood his intentions or otherwise refused
to become involved with the collection.

Dear Langston,
    . . . Perhaps I did not make myself clear to you last night about the way
I feel about the JWJ Collection of Negro Arts and Letters. For the past ten
years I have devoted at least fifty percent of my waking hours to this perpetuation of the fame of the Negro and it saddens me to realize how few
Negroes realize this and how still fewer make any attempt to assist the
collection. That was why I was so enchanted with Nora [Holt]'s effort. I
know it is not easy to organize such a group, but she carried it off like a
general. And with glorious results.
    One of the most brilliant episodes in the collection is my mounted photo-
graphs of Negroes prominent in the arts and sciences. It would seem a simple
matter to permit oneself to be photographed for so good a cause and that is
why it makes me very sad when someone like Sidney Poitier (who SHOULD
know better) acts like a spoiled child when he is asked to pose. In the end of
course it is his own loss. Also he is one Negro who has rebuffed me personally
with exceptional rudeness. That has not been my experience with Marian
Anderson or Joe Louis for that matter!
    I am not running this show as a benefit for myself. It is even named for

someone else. It is conducted solely to glorify the Negro and I hope that someday at least a majority of the race will begin to realize this fact.

yrs, with too much impatience and some faint hope!

Carlo, the Patriarch!

OCTOBER 11, 1959

From Paris, Chester Himes had been sending copies of his enormously successful *Cotton* detective stories to Van Vechten.

Dear Chester,
 . . . It is a great relief to know someone who can write about other things occasionally besides the Negro "problem." . . . Long ago (perhaps nearly 40 years) I said, to James Weldon Johnson, the Negro "problem" will be settled by the artists. It is coming nearer to be every year; the writers, the painters, the actors, and singers have done the most. The writers the least, because most of them "harp" on the problem. . . . This sort of thing MUST eventually bring about changes with those dumb creatures who constantly reiterate the Negro is inferior. . . .

[unsigned]

[30 JANUARY 1961]

The National Institute of Arts and Letters initiated Carl Van Vechten and Langston Hughes in 1961, along with Leonard Bernstein, Jacques Lipschitz, Norman Dello Joio, and others. At that time, W.E.B. Du Bois was the only other black member.

Dear Chester,
 . . . I am now 81. Just the same I feel as I did when I was 18, except that I have more sense. Also my health is better. I never felt better and I never seem to have serious illnesses. I stopped smoking thirty years ago, but I believe I drink more than ever. . . .
At this advanced age I have been voted into the Institute of Arts and Letters. I was too daring for the sober set that governed the Institute when I was writing books, but now that Henry Miller is a member there is little

reason to keep me out. . . . Langston Hughes was initiated with me. Dr. Du Bois already belongs and I can probably get you in when you write another serious book. . . .

James Baldwin's new book, *Nobody Knows My Name*, is fine. He had an award from the Institute years ago. I had lunch with him recently. He told me he likes you and your books very much and he speaks of [*If*] *He Hollers* enthusiastically in *Nobody Knows My Name*.

Yesterday FOUR BOOKS came from you which will go presently to the James Weldon Johnson Memorial Collection of Negro Arts and Letters in the Yale University Library. You have always been fine to me and the collection and I shall never forget it. . . .

Carlo

JUNE 24, 1961

Carl Van Vechten always hoped Chester Himes would return to serious writing, despite the success of his detective fiction. He did not live to read Himes's moving autobiography, *The Quality of Hurt*, published eight years after his death, but his photograph of Himes adorned its dust jacket.

Dear Chester,

If my letters touch you, it is nothing to what your letters do to me. This last one is a masterpiece and it makes sense. You are at last, I believe, growing and beginning to understand what one has to face sooner or later, the mysteries, the agonies, and wonders of life. There is seemingly no solution for any of this. We actually have to learn how to grin and bear it. Some people prefer to be angry and scowl and to grind their teeth, but the other method is the better one and when you say you have decided to pursue pleasure you seem to have perceived this. I have always wanted you to write a book to top *Lonely Crusade* and I think you can, a book about loneliness and sorrow and every kind of torture that the flesh is heir to. You can write about Negroes or white people, but no race problems this time, please. When you have written this book you will be able to return to America, but I think it would be a mistake to come back before. You actually have many admirers here, some people actually love you, but no one more than

Carlo. . . .

AUGUST 8, 1961

Henry Van Dyke was recipient of the Avery Hopwood
Memorial Award at the University of Michigan, named for
and endowed by one of Van Vechten's oldest friends. Van
Vechten read Van Dyke's early work and, of course, added
his photograph to the growing collection at Yale.

Dear Henry Van Dyke,

At last I got around to reading "Miss Desdemona" which I did at one
sitting. I was very pleasantly surprised. I was expecting something rather
arty and this story turned out to be by a man who knows the vernacular of
very ordinary Negroes. I was amused and delighted by the story and predict
you should go far as an author. I have yet to read the story in the magazine,
but will do so shortly.

Your color pictures are not back yet.

Warm greetings from

Carl Van Vechten

OCTOBER 15, 1961

I hope you received the black & white pictures.

At eighty-two Van Vechten began to take occasional
spills while walking along, though never of serious consequence. Later, Van Dyke made affectionate use of this
frailty — as well as of Van Vechten's physical appearance
and whole personality — in the character of Max in his
second novel, *Blood of Strawberries.* His first novel, *Ladies
of the Rachmaninoff Eyes,* was dedicated to Carl Van
Vechten who had continued to read his work.

Dear, dear Henry,

This time I really LOVED your letter. It shows you can write. The im-
personal literary epistle DIDn't. If you would make your commercial stuff
more personal, more like your talk, you would have no difficulty selling it.
The episode with the priest is terrific. It could be published as is with very
little added. But if you prefer not to, transform yourself into a girl and
write it that way.

My wrist is fine and has been since the second day. My only difficulty is
getting out of a bathtub. But that is probably due more to fear than lack of
strength. . . .

I am most interested in your plans for a series of radio scripts. I think you can do it if you try. Become freer and more daring, breathe deeply and easily, let your hair down and take off your pants. You are much too congested, inhibited, and tied to a TREE.

WHEN is your birthday? What is your age? These questions are NOT rhetorical. . . .

The priest story is interesting, but not entirely novel. I have heard of one behind the high altar in the choir in a church in Florence who permitted pleasant indignities during a service, but it seems it is only in foreign churches where there are often strangers there to view the murals that one is allowed to visit such an intimate place during a service.

My life is quite proper but I continue to receive vast numbers of joyously indecent letters. . . . I work in the darkroom, I write, I go to the theatre or a concert. . . .

> Anyway, I send you my love, and suggest you write me some more.

Carlo

OCTOBER 24, 1962

Following a party given by Rita Romilly, a mutual acquaintance from the Twenties, Carl Van Vechten wrote to thank his old friend Langston Hughes for *New Negro Poets*, a volume edited for the Indiana University Press. He thanked Hughes, too, for what may have struck him as a new Black Renaissance.

Carl Van Vechten died six months later, on 21 December 1964, in his sleep. In *Proceedings of the American Academy of Arts and Letters and the National Institute of Arts and Letters 15*, Langston Hughes paid him this tribute; it appeared in April 1965:

A sure sign of old age is when a man begins to disapprove of the young. At the age of 84, Carl Van Vechten had not yet grown old. His enthusiasm for youth in the arts, and his quest for new talent, remained until the end unabated. . . . Almost always Carl Van Vechten was ahead of his times insofar as public taste and the canons of publicity went. The times had to catch up with him. . . . Deftness and charm were so much a part of Carl Van Vechten's articles and critiques hailing his various enthusiasms, that some,

accustomed to more ponderous academic criticism, felt that the
Van Vechten personality consisted mostly of fanfare and fun. It
did possess these attributes. But behind the fanfare lay genuine
critical acumen, often of a highly prophetic nature. And humor,
wit, and sophistication in the best sense gave yeast to all the fun
Van Vechten found in writing and living. He might be called both
a hedonist and a humanist. . . . He had a wide circle of lively,
intelligent and decorative friends, particularly in the arts. There
were no ethnic or religious barriers to his friendships. . . . And, of
his long and happy sojourn among us, his friends possess a
rainbow of memories (504-06).

Dear Langston,

 You and I have been through so many new Negroes that we are a little
tired of it all. BUT I am really excited about the group you have brought
together. LeRoi Jones, who appears to be somebody, I photographed long
since. I wonder when he & [James] Baldwin will have a fight! It will be a
big one. I am very happy to receive your book with its beautiful inscription.

 Much affection to you. . . .

Carlo

It was certainly old home week at Rita's. I had a really wonderful time.

JUNE 2, 1964

Index

ABOUT THE EDITOR

Bruce Kellner is Associate Professor of English at Millersville State College in Millersville, Pennsylvania. He is the author of *Carl Van Vechten and the Irreverent Decades* and a forthcoming bibliography of Van Vechten's work.